MAKING

THE WISEGUYS

WEEP

MAKING

THE WISEGUYS

WEEP

THE *Jimmy*

Roselli

STORY

DAVID EVANIER

FARRAR, STRAUS AND GIROUX / NEW YORK

Farrar, Straus and Giroux
19 Union Square West, New York 10003

Copyright © 1998 by David Evanier
All rights reserved
Distributed in Canada by Douglas & McIntyre Ltd.
Printed in the United States of America
Designed by Abby Kagan
First edition, 1998

Library of Congress Cataloging-in-Publication Data
Evanier, David.
Making the wiseguys weep : the Jimmy Roselli story / David Evanier.
    p. cm.
ISBN 0-374-19927-2 (alk. paper)
1. Roselli, Jimmy. 2. Singers—United States—Biography.
3. Italian Americans. 4. Mafia—United States. 5. Sinatra, Frank,
1915- . I. Title.
ML420.R8758E93   1999
782.42164'092—dc21   98-11739

To

Dini Evanier, Theodore Mitrani, Eva Fogelman, Pete Cavallo,

Stephen Gregg, Carl Capotorto, Leon Axelrod, and Joan Suall

There is no word for "home" in Italian. There is casa *(house),* fucolaro *(hearth), but no word for home (as if they had no need for it) as in English. . . .*

Yet there is . . . a yearning for the home left behind—and more so for the second generation, whether it be the home of childhood, or the land their parents left.

All immigrants, from the first English Puritans to the latest arrivals, have felt this yearning—a sense of loss (even guilt) and of anxiety at tearing up home roots. For this reason, the word "home" has a special meaning in America.

Italian-Americans as individuals bound together by the commonalities of language, environment and heredity have found their American home, with all the conflicts inherent in most families.

La Storia:
Five Centuries of the
Italian American Experience
by Jerre Mangione and
Ben Morreale

MAKING

THE WISEGUYS

WEEP

1

RAGING BULL

JIMMY ROSELLI IS HOBOKEN'S OTHER GREAT SINGER. And to a greater degree than Frank Sinatra, who quickly entered the American mainstream, Roselli has maintained his ties to his old neighborhood and its people—indeed, made a career of those ties. He's a link to their cultural heritage and to Italy, since he continues to sing a good half of his repertoire in Italian.

Roselli comes out of the tradition of the wandering Italian balladeer, via the street singers and the troubadours he saw at the Italian vaudeville houses of his youth in Hoboken. The tradition did not begin in America. "It was the same thing in Sicily and Italy," noted historian Ben Morreale. "Men working would always be singing, singing in the fields. I remember as a kid in Sicily singing: 'I'm a lost chicken; I go crow, crowing all day long, but nobody calls . . .' My father used to sing a lot of opera; he loved it. And then on the railroads in America the Italian workers would sing: 'Where do you worka, John?' 'On the Delaware Lack-a-wan.' Jimmy Roselli is a beneficiary and a proud representative of that tradition."[1]

I first heard Roselli's voice in 1985 on the jukeboxes of the Limehouse, the last Italian bar in New York's Chinatown, and at Lanza's on First Avenue—the Limehouse has now vanished—as well as at Arturo's bistro on Thompson Street. The elderly waiter at Lanza's came over to my table at dinner when I played Roselli's "Just Say I Love Her" ("Dicitencello Vuie") on the jukebox to let me know I was listening to both the most beautiful Italian love song and the greatest Italian singer of all time. Then I started noticing Roselli's picture everywhere in Little Italy. (According to an unascribed survey cited in a 1991 profile of Roselli in *The Wall Street Journal*, his photograph was the most commonly displayed celebrity head shot on the walls of Little Italy restaurants.)

I could not get Roselli out of my head, so I started buying his albums, thirty-two of which are in print. His voice captivated me: its reach, passion, power, and warmth make it one of the great experiences in American popular music. Wildly theatrical, it was also heartfelt, with unabashed feeling and raw torrents of emotion. It was the most intimate sound I'd ever heard from a singer. Roselli sang with unparalleled versatility: Neapolitan songs, American ballads, saloon songs, and standards. He had an entire palette of colors in front of him, and he chose them artfully. But like the troubadours or the great Hebraic cantors who preceded him, he also wasn't afraid to lay it on really thick. And it worked. This was a man baring his soul.

In his Neapolitan songs, Roselli had the quality of a street singer, coupled with a very legitimate, proper, and formal background in classical singing. Yet there was a second, equally potent side of Roselli: that of the American saloon and ballad singer. And here he utilized an entirely different mode of singing: sometimes very off-the-cuff and reminiscent of the music hall balladeer. There was something for everyone in that style.

Referring to Roselli's Neapolitan songs, vocal coach Scott Harlan commented: "There's no other pop singer I can think of that can sing that legitimately in such a pure, romantic style—certainly not Sinatra or Tony Bennett—and also have the capability of doing the pop stuff too. It's just not something they [Bennett and Sinatra] cultivated doing. This guy could sing bel canto at Carnegie Hall as well as at a little corner bistro.

"He has incredible control. Because he knows how and when to let it go. When he does, it's so focused and legitimately placed that you could be listening to a Metropolitan Opera singer. There's an authority and masculinity in Roselli's sound that's not put on. It's authentic and it has great appeal. There's no posing, pretension. You get the feeling you wouldn't want to meet this guy in an alley. I wouldn't want to be around him when he loses his temper."

After falling in love with Roselli's sound, I encountered him in person at the Westbury Music Fair in 1987: a simple, plain-looking, unsophisticated man whose performance was one of the most moving experiences I had ever had since seeing Judy Garland at the Palace, or Sinatra or Ray Charles in concert. When Roselli appears onstage, the audience responds with an onrush of cheers and sighs. He has a powerful, authentic, commanding presence, a profound simplicity. From the moment of his appearance onstage, with his huge orchestra of forty to fifty musicians almost spilling off the wings, the effect is thrilling. The bigness of it, the dramatic orchestrations, are overwhelming. The Neapolitan songs require it: in "Senza Mamma e Innamorata" ("Without a Mother, Without a Lover"), the narrator sees himself in the rear of a church while the woman he loves comes marching down the aisle to be married to an-

other man. Just hours before, in the same church, he had buried
his mother and he'd been kneeling in the same pew, mourning
for her. Then they wound up the funeral mass and moved into
the wedding. Hokey, but even great opera librettos sound that
way when you analyze them. Roselli told it passionately, and
the audience wept.

But Roselli likes to balance maudlin or romantic songs with
playful ones. At Westbury, he moved on to "Guaglione," a
lighthearted song in which a mature woman sings to a boy that
he's just a little sprite: "Get out of here." She tells him he
doesn't know what love is. "Go home to your mommy." He
then turned to the American saloon songs he sings hauntingly,
the "3 a.m. songs" ("For All We Know," "But Not for Me,"
"Maybe," "You'll Never Know," "I Should Care"); the ballads,
a host of little-known or long-forgotten songs to which he's
given his own indelible stamp ("When Your Old Wedding
Ring Was New," "I Lost All My Love for You," "A Million
Dreams Ago," "The Greatest Mistake of My Life"); and finally
the torchy, tragic Italian songs, most of which are considered
by his Italian fans to be his sacred property: "Mala Femmena,"
"Innamorata," "Anema e Core," and "Passione." Roselli will
sing for an hour and a half; he never shorts an audience. He
once told me: "I'll fall down to give all that's in my body. Because they came, they paid for that and they deserve it. They
should get the best that's in me."

There is no way of exaggerating Roselli's importance to the
Italian-American community. Essentially an orphan himself,
Roselli symbolizes family and home to several generations of
Italians. Again and again I encountered Italian men and
women whose memories of childhood, of their grandparents
and parents, of landmark occasions like births and deaths, were
linked to Roselli's music. The young playwright and actor Carl
Capotorto told me: "When he sang 'Guaglione' ['Little Boy'],

my grandmother would get very excited, actually stop what she was doing in the kitchen, sing along and do a little dance, her little 'Guaglione dance' . . . I start to get vivid images of the apartment I grew up in, and both my grandmothers, and just what childhood life was like. It starts to bring back everything, very personal, very specific."

For Philip Capotorto, Carl's father and a contractor in the Bronx who died in March 1998, Roselli was the embodiment of an entire culture: "He sings Neapolitan the way it should be sung," Capotorto said. "The way he does it in his recording of 'Mala Femmena' ['A Bad Woman']. The word is passion. Extreme passion. Exaggerated passion. I mean, passionate passion. Killing: a passion that drives you to kill."

What Capotorto feared was the loss of the Neapolitan dialect that only Roselli retains in his music, "because there's no such thing in Italy anymore. The dialect was given up and replaced by Italian. That became the spoken language," he said. "The dialect was shunned, although some people retain it somehow. When you speak that dialect, there's a passion involved. Even a little word they say, *Ey!*—there's so much that's said by that. Just a little nothing, the sound, but it speaks volumes. That doesn't exist any longer, anyplace. Even here."

Like Philip Capotorto, many of the Italian-American children of his generation knew no English. They had to learn the hard way, at school and by going to work. In the Italian enclaves where they lived, dialect was all they heard when they came home from school or work and on the weekends. Consequently, Capotorto said, "comes a guy like Roselli and he makes all the noises these people heard when they were kids. And there's a blood association, a consciousness of their whole past. To lose the dialect is to surrender the culture, down deep inside, the cultural memory. It's home.

"Pavarotti is the best, I love that voice. It moves me and it's

the best there is. However, Roselli is where my heart is. Pavarotti sings about it, but Roselli, this guy *is* it. There's a whole
history and culture that will close when he does. I don't know
if he himself understands this."

"There are people who can get up and act out a song and
break your heart, but it's not about singing," said Carol Lees,
a composer, songwriter, and vocal coach. "It's not about singing, and it's not about the song. It's about their act. A person
without a great voice can get up and perform a song and never
hit a note right but put it over. There are people who can do
that, and it's a lot of what actors have to do. There's Walter
Huston's 'September Song'; Durante's 'I'll See You in My
Dreams.' Sinatra did it in the later years. That's all about style
and interpretation and how they play with the song. Roselli
doesn't do any of that. He honors the music as it was written
and the meaning of the words as they were written, and he
allows it to come through his beautiful voice in a really pure
way. And you can't learn that: it's just totally biological and
natural. That takes a great deal of self-restraint, confidence,
and intelligence: to know the power of what is real in music.
His art is one of communication, pure and simple.

"You're taking a sound that exists in nature and running it
through muscle and your brain and out comes this beauty,"
Lees explained. "It's different than being a great violinist,
where if you don't have the great instrument, or the instrument's out of whack that day, you're in trouble. This is self-
contained. Put him on an island and he can sing like that. He
doesn't need anything. He's an artist, but not because he took
his talent and worked at it, went to school and studied with
Leonard Bernstein. He's not that kind of artist, but a kind of
inborn artist of the people. It's not an academic, intellectual
thing. He's an artist of the Italian people, of the culture."

Roselli's audience is large—and diverse. The wheelchairs

that line the back of the hall tell part of the story: elderly men and women from Italian enclaves around the country who would go to see no other singer. The buses that have brought them from New York, New Jersey, South Philadelphia, St. Louis, New Orleans, Chicago, and San Francisco wait outside the hall. Roselli is their voice. And their man. Ask them about him, and you're apt to hear the same phrases: he's a stand-up guy, he's defied the wiseguys (but he won't rat against them either), he does things his way.

In its front-page profile of Roselli in 1991, *The Wall Street Journal*'s Timothy K. Smith wrote:

Maybe if his ears had been bigger, Jimmy Roselli's singing career would have been different, and it would have been he, not Frank Sinatra, who ascended to the show-business pantheon. . . . Or maybe if their nicknames had been reversed, and Mr. Roselli had been billed as "The Swooner" while Mr. Sinatra labored as "The Dynamic Belter of Song," things would have turned out differently. . . .

As it happened, though, Mr. Sinatra became the most famous Italian-American balladeer born the only son of a prizefighter on Monroe Street in Hoboken, N.J., and Mr. Roselli the least famous. Not too surprisingly, Mr. Roselli has little use for Mr. Sinatra. "He looks like a cab coming down the street with the doors open," Mr. Roselli says, alluding to Mr. Sinatra's ears.

Readers involved in loan-sharking may have heard Mr. Roselli's music (his rendition of "Little Pal," not Mr. Sinatra's "My Way," is the authentic wise-guy anthem, according to law enforcement officials) but many more may not have. Mr. Roselli, a 65-year-old whose high tenor voice is still intact, has for the past 22 years been packing aficionados into sold-out dates while being completely ignored by the public at large. . . .

They say Mr. Sinatra is the mob's entertainer of choice. But it was Mr. Roselli who sang last year at the Helmsley Palace wedding reception of John A. Gotti, son of the reputed crime boss. Mr. Roselli says he has never done any business with organized criminals, but he is resigned to the association between the Mafia and his music. "Every time they write a book, by the time you get to the fourth page there's a dead guy in a car with my tapes beside him on the front seat," he sighs. . . .

By now Mr. Roselli is trailed by myths of his own, spun by fans to explain how a man can fill the Trump Plaza in Atlantic City with screaming, stomping fans one week and retreat into perfect obscurity the next. Some say he is afraid of flying (he isn't). Others say he got into a tangle over a mob-financed Carnegie Hall concert (never happened, he says). And they all say there is a sinister Sinatra influence at work. Mr. Sinatra declined to be interviewed. . . .

In the late 1960s, just as he was beginning to achieve stardom, Roselli really did something that antagonized the mob. He stopped playing footsie with it and declared his independence of Mafia control. (He would vacillate back and forth on this issue for many years to come.) His problems with the wiseguys came about because they saw Roselli as a meal ticket and kept trying to skim their cut off of the top of his earnings. Roselli, naturally, resented this, and rebelled against it again and again. At the same time he was drawn to the mob as the

family he never had. Finally, his feuds with Frank Sinatra and
Sinatra's mother, Dolly, and also with Joe Colombo, head of
the Profaci crime family, got Roselli blacklisted from many
nightspots and even radio stations, forcing him to start again
almost from scratch. In fact, the long-standing rift with Sinatra
continued through the 1990s. Roselli says that before John
Gotti, Sr., went to jail, he offered to broker a truce between
the two singers. Roselli would have none of it. "I didn't want
anything settled," he told a reporter. "I don't like the guy personally, and I don't need to sit down with him."

Does Roselli regret any of this to this day? Not a bit. "I'm a
defiant guy," he says. "If you let these guys conquer you, they
want to own you. They want to stick a flag in your navel, like
'I conquer you for Queen Isabella of Spain.' But I wasn't looking to be conquered. You say to me, 'I can't take this, I gotta
shoot you'—I say, 'Go ahead: you can only kill me once.'"

But this is not the whole story. Roselli's career has had a
powerful current of self-destructiveness. His ambivalence toward the wiseguys involved him in cyclical, roller-coaster al-
ternations between acts of independence and reentanglements
that ended in Roselli being betrayed and feeling increasingly
bitter about it. Tempting the fates with the company he kept,
Roselli continued taking chances with his life. Frank Gauna,
art director at United Artists Records when Roselli was under
contract there, told me, "The interesting thing about Roselli
was that he used to hang out with people who killed people,
but he never killed anybody. Never even carried a piece."

Roselli was just beginning to achieve stardom in the mid-
and late 1960s. He had been considered the sweetheart of the
Mafia. But with the mob blacklisting him, his career spiraled
downward. The love-hate relationship with the Mafia and with
Mafia wannabes continued nevertheless. The mob couldn't live
with Roselli, and it couldn't live without him. As *The Wall*

Street Journal reported, one of Roselli's best-loved songs, "Little Pal," is a favorite of the wiseguys. And there were many godfathers who continued to love him. According to Roselli, mobster Larry Gallo was buried with a Roselli record in his hands. "He was a sweetheart," Roselli says of Gallo. "Nice, warm individual. Hell of a guy."

"We followed Jimmy pretty good in the old days," says Lefty Jimmy Geritano, an acquaintance of Larry Gallo's. "We slept in cars just to see him sing. A lot of guys don't like him. All these years, guys were trying to put a stranglehold on him. He pushed them all away. He's been threatened more times—guys saying, 'I'm gonna kill him.' " Lefty Jimmy knocks wood. "It never happened. Because of the women. Even though the guy don't wanna go, his wife, his mother, will say, 'We're going to see Jimmy tonight.' The next night, his girlfriend tells him, 'You're goin', you're goin'.' "

One passionate fan is John Gotti. The New York *Daily News* recently reported that Gotti was paying a fellow inmate of the penitentiary where he is incarcerated five dollars a day to "sing Jimmy Roselli songs."

Despite the threats against him, Roselli has done more than survive. Today, when most of the Italian-American singers of his generation are lucky to make a living at all, Roselli takes in well over a million dollars a year.

Roselli commands a staggering nightly fee of up to $100,000 a performance, when Julie Andrews draws weekly earnings on Broadway of $50,000 for a total of seven performances. The obvious question is why is Roselli so unknown?

"Jimmy is an enigma in our business," said composer Herb Bernstein, Roselli's son-in-law. "You go west of the Hudson. A lot of places I'll say, 'Jimmy Roselli's my father-in-law.' The response is 'Oh, it sounds familiar; what does he do?' And I say, 'Are you kidding?' Then you come back East and you go to the Garden State Arts Center or Caesars [in Atlantic City]. They pay him $100,000 for one show and the audience stands up and screams before he even comes out. And you say: What's the incongruity here? Why is he a superstar here and unheard of there? In this business, out of every thousand performers, nine hundred and ninety-nine fail miserably. One person out of a thousand survives. Out of maybe fifty thousand, four or five survive and perhaps one becomes a major star. There are very few gray areas. You're starving or making a quarter of a million a night. But Jimmy, it's weird. I was at a party for [composer] Julie Styne and sat next to Donald Trump. Trump leaned over to me and said, 'You know, I'm paying your father-in-law more than I pay Sinatra.'

"As a singer," Bernstein continued, "Jimmy's got a tremendous range and clarity; his articulation is unbelievable and his power is incredible. He hits a high B flat, which is way up there. A lot of the women singers who would hit a high D, when they pass forty they bring it down so their top note's a C. Their top notes are not there. With people like Tony Bennett and Mel Tormé, they start to lose in their low range. Bennett's low notes warble. What amazes me is that Roselli has his whole voice. To have that vocal power and clarity at his age, and with all he's been through, is astonishing. And since his quadruple by-pass operation in January 1992, he's been better than ever.

"In my opinion Jimmy should be right up there with Sinatra, Tony Bennett . . . he should be one of them. But there was his own hardheadedness, his defense mechanism ('Oh, you're not gonna interview me? See ya around, pal'), his desire to do things the way he wanted to do them. He would never let anyone manage him, he was unmanageable, defying the mob, doing everything his way. Look, why should a segment of the population, maybe twenty-five million Italian people, worship the ground he walks on and the other two hundred million never have heard of him?"

A man without pretension or affectation, Roselli conjures up a disappearing breed, those artists who unerringly cling to their own vision and love of their art without compromise. Although he is seventy-three, he doesn't remotely resemble a senior citizen. He talks like a wiseguy, in rapid-fire staccato, spiced with profanity. He's quick to laugh, quick to take offense. Once, I asked Roselli about his Damon Runyon persona. "I was around Runyon characters all my life," he said. "What the fuck was going to rub off on me, a lawyer's personality?"

Roselli has never left his roots. In fact, he still lives near the Hoboken community of his boyhood, hangs out there at a grimy storefront clubhouse, the Monroe Street Buddies, with his childhood friends, and if you see him at a card table, he is indistinguishable from the Hoboken pals seated beside him.

He is the authentic guy, a man's man. And he is full of rage. His strengths and his weaknesses stem directly from his refusal to accommodate the world, his determination not to bend, compromise, or equivocate. Jimmy Roselli may be the real "raging bull" of show business.

Despite all of the acclaim, Roselli is embittered. In many ways he is still locked into the isolated, impoverished years of his childhood, still believes that "every time I let down my guard, I got plowed in the ass."

As genuine as he is, in one sense Roselli has lived behind a façade his entire life, hiding the emotions he expresses in his music. Initially the façade enabled him to survive on the mean streets, and he had to keep it up. In time it became a reflex, and at times Roselli can seem like a one-man barricade.

The authenticity and integrity of his music, his refusal to dilute its passion or sanitize it, are inseparable from his rage and isolation, his rawness. His suspicion of the outside world keeps him "pure." He continues to bridge the generations because he himself refuses to cross that bridge.

When I came to know him better, Roselli, who has felt a rivalry with Sinatra his whole life, told me with a certain dispassion that he was puzzled that Sinatra continued to perform when most of his voice was gone. He said with certainty that the moment he lost his voice, he would pack it in and retire.

I came to understand that for Jimmy singing was only about the music, the lyrics, and the voice—nothing else. Mesmerizing as he is onstage, he doesn't dance, joke much, or move around beyond a couple of steps. His act, so to speak, is only about the music. The rest: the smoking, "how cool I am," the patter, forgetting the words, having a drink on stage—it's all folderol and he refuses to have any part of it. He's a serious fellow. This is not about a hobby or a rat pack game. This is about what music can be.

2

HOME

THE MASS ITALIAN IMMIGRATION TO THE UNITED States that occurred between 1880 and 1924 represented a culture leaving its ancient roots for the unknown pitfalls of America. Eighty percent of that immigration came from southern Italy—the Mezzogiorno. This region encompassed the provinces of Abruzzi, Molise, Campania, Lucania, Apulia, Calabria, and the island of Sicily. The immigrants made the decision in the face of despair and near-starvation.

The establishment of Italy as a modern, unified nation dates back to 1871 and the leadership of a charismatic general, Giuseppe Garibaldi. After Garibaldi's ascension to power, there was a surge of economic and social progress, increased agricultural production, rising wages, and higher employment. But this forward movement did not include the south of Italy. From the start, the south was reduced to near-colonial status.

Northern interests dominated the new Italian parliament's

concerns. New tariff systems that benefited the industrialization of the north destroyed southern industries that had been
functioning at the time of unification. Public works programs
were concentrated in northern and central regions. As the nation was reaching a new level of industrialization and improv-
ing the situation of the peasants, the south was still ignored.
High taxes, increasing unemployment, widespread usury, poor
wages, continued deforestation, and soil erosion made life for
southern Italians unbearable.

Woven into this unequal state of affairs was a deeply in-
grained belief on the part of the ruling elite that held that the
south was *Italia bassa* (low Italy)—a region of lazy, shiftless,
criminal elements who were to blame for the conditions in
which they found themselves. The north, on the other hand,
was *alta Italia* (high Italy), where the enlightened and the hard-
working lived. Southern Italy, it was held, was only good
enough to contribute cheap labor for the industrialization of
the north and cannon fodder for the Army.

Due to an absence of waterways, drinking water was scarce.
Many southern villages had no water at all, except rainwater—
this in a country that elsewhere had broad, flowing rivers and
deep natural lakes.

A poor quality of undrinkable water was sold in southern
Italy for washing purposes. In desperation some people drank
it, which led to the spread of trachoma among the poor. Chol-
era and malaria epidemics were rampant. In the first years of
the century, 20,000 southern Italians died of malaria annually.
Between 1884 and 1887, 55,000 men and women died of chol-
era.

In 1887 a severe economic depression further demoralized
the south. In the following years, intermittent volcanic erup-
tions of Vesuvius and Etna completely destroyed many villages.

In 1908 the worst disaster of all took place: 100,000 died in an earthquake and tidal wave that engulfed the provinces of Messina, in Sicily, and Calabria.

These conditions, combined with the fact that there was virtually no industry or prospects of development, contributed to a huge surge in emigration. Between 1900 and 1910, more than two million Italian men, women, and children immigrated to the United States, mostly from the south. By 1925, the year of Jimmy Roselli's birth, there were more than five million Italians in America.

Leaving Italy for an unknown land was a traumatic experience for many of the immigrants, as well as for the women who were left behind while their husbands got settled in America. In his book *Vita moderna degli Italiani*, Angelo Mosso described the scene at a railroad station in Castrofilippo, Sicily, in 1905:

> The stationmaster told me that thirty emigrants were departing. . . . They had been waiting two months for a ship, and last week they received word to go to Palermo for embarkation. When the train began to move, a piercing cry arose from the crowd along the platform. Each person had an arm upraised clutching a handkerchief. One woman broke away from the crowd and began to run alongside the train as it pulled out of the station, yelling out: "Say hello to him [her husband]; remind him that I am still waiting for him to send me the money for the steamship ticket. Tell him I am waiting, and tell him . . . tell him . . . that if I have to stay here any longer I will die." As the train chugged into the next station, Racalmuto, the anxious platform crowd broke out into a long, confused roar that sounded like a clap of

thunder. Six or seven emigrants boarded, and the same tearful goodbyes were repeated.

The passage by steerage across the Atlantic was punishing. The emigrants were crowded together. Many were seasick, lying among piles of blankets and rags. To relieve their misery, they sang to the accompaniment of tambourines, accordions, mandolins, mouth organs, and guitars. They danced and presented Punch and Judy marionette shows; magicians performed tricks. A hurdy-gurdy played Italian arias.

The immigrants arrived at Ellis Island exhausted, drained, but not bereft of hope. Angelo Mosso watched them leave the Ellis Island ferry in 1906:

> The ferryboat was full of migrants, all of them with a look of apprehension. I had read many terrible things about the Italians. Here in America they are called "those dirty Italians" and "undesirable people," so I was expecting the worst. They were workers . . . some dressed in festive clothes, others in everyday wear. They did not look dirty at all. While disembarking, many smiled and laughed as if happy to be on solid earth again. Each carried a sack or a battered suitcase held together with cord. Others carried large bundles containing blankets and mattresses. All of them wore a yellow numbered card attached to a jacket button.[2]

They feared that their families would be separated, and many of them were. While awaiting their fates, seventeen hundred women and children were crowded into a vermin-infested room with a capacity of six hundred. They were fed only rye bread and prunes for breakfast, lunch, and dinner.

In Italy, they had been treated as pariahs; in America, they were viewed, as were Negroes, as an inferior dark-skinned people. "The Americans," wrote Napoleone Colajanni in 1909 in his book *Gli Italiani negli Stati Uniti*, "consider the Italians as unclean, small foreigners who play the accordion, operate fruit stands, sweep the streets, work in the mines or tunnels, on the railroad or as bricklayers." The U.S. Immigration Commission published a study in 1910 revealing that the average annual earnings of Italian families were $688, $112 below the $800 considered necessary to support a man, woman, and three children. Negroes had the lowest income; Italians had the second lowest.

They were often victims of the *padrone* system of work control, a method that could be likened to feudal serfdom. *Padroni* were Italians in Italy and America who were supposed to act as friends, smoothing the path for illiterate or confused emigrants in unfamiliar circumstances. In actuality they were often exploitative brokers of immigrant labor. In the nineteenth century, they were found wherever Italians lived abroad. Promising economic security, they persuaded Italians to come to America to work under their protection and supervision.

The immigrants, eager to gain steamship passage to America, often signed contracts in Italy. The *padroni* negotiated these for immigrants seeking work as miners, railroad workers, and field hands. The *padroni* often later repudiated their employment contracts and pocketed fees after leading workers to far-off places where jobs did not exist and their clients were left abandoned. If jobs did exist, they consisted of pick-and-shovel work or other unskilled labor. Boys were sent out on the streets as newsboys, bootblacks, thieves, and beggars; women were often sent to brothels. At the end of each day the money earned was consigned to the *padrone*, and he, in turn, provided his workers with minimum necessities.

By the late 1880s in New York City, Italians controlled the macaroni market, sold plaster figurines of religious and secular leaders, ran candy stores, and manufactured and sold artificial flowers. Michael La Sorte writes in *La Merica* that "apparently every village or city on the east coast had an Italian fruit peddler or an Italian fruit stand. In winter the fruit merchants sold roasted chestnuts and peanuts, and in summer dispersed slices of watermelon and soda water to the children."[3]

The older Italian men, many of whom were physically incapacitated and unable to find other jobs, worked as organ grinders, walking the streets day and night. Most of the shoeshine boys in the larger cities were Italian. In New Haven, Connecticut, the shoemaking and repairing businesses were run by Italians. Italians took over trash and garbage removal in Philadelphia and San Francisco. Much of the import commerce between Italy and the United States was controlled by New York Italians. Italians also moved into the factories, including the cotton and woolen mills of Lawrence, Massachusetts, and the silk mills of Paterson, New Jersey.

Many of the immigrants worked in sweatshop factories. The women often toiled at home doing "piecework": making pins, cheap jewelry, and notions. Italian men did most of the dirty work in Manhattan: sewer laying, tunneling, subway construction, street grading, general construction, and street cleaning. Twelve hundred Italians swept the streets of New York in 1904; four thousand labored to construct the Lexington Avenue subway.

Overall, Italian-Americans were confined to a very low rung of the economic ladder. Even Italian professionals and tradesmen were largely restricted to functioning within Italian colonies.

The most common occupation for the able-bodied immigrant working outdoors was that of laborer, using a pick, shovel, sledge, ax, or wheelbarrow. Italians were first hired by the railroads in the 1870s, and they soon monopolized the labor forces on most lines throughout the United States and Canada, brutal work that wore them out rapidly. The poet Emanuel Carnevali wrote in his autobiography:

> *You gave me sorrow for my daily bread.*
> *You threw cheap words at me.*
> *And I found what scant nourishment was in them,*
> *and bit into them like a rabid dog.*[4]

Perhaps the worst nightmare for Italian immigrants was the work camps. The 1900 census reported that three thousand unskilled Italian laborers toiled in these camps in New York State alone, most of them on mining, quarrying, railroad, and lumbering crews.

According to La Sorte: "The work camp immigrants came close to becoming the new American slaves of the post–Civil War era."[5] In some camps workers were held as prisoners; if they wanted to leave, they had to escape. These men did not fall under the protection of any national jurisdiction—only the laws of the camp applied. Living and working conditions were among the most primitive and oppressive that any immigrant group endured in America during those years.

Of all immigrant groups, Italians often did the most dangerous work. There were frequent injuries and deaths on the job without compensation—daily accidents that were forgotten by the employers, who were more upset by a broken shovel than a dead laborer. Amy Bernardy, in her book on Italian immigrants, estimated that at least one-fifth of the Italians who emigrated to the United States to work were victims of work accidents, and that up to 25 percent of the industrial casualties befell Italians.[6] Coroners, undertakers, police, and lawyers colluded to cover up accidents. The immigrants, ignorant of their rights but keenly aware of their second-class status, did not know how to seek justice.

The area around Mulberry Street in New York City was the first and largest of the nation's Italian enclaves. Jacob Riis, a Danish-born reporter, described the Italian section of Mulberry Street called "the Bend" in his classic study, *How the Other Half Lives* (1890). By day, he wrote, "it was a purgatory of unrelieved squalor," and at night "an inferno tenanted by the very dregs of humanity where the new arrivals lived in damp basements, leaky garrets, clammy cellars, outhouses and stables converted into dwellings." The Italian, he continued, "comes in at the bottom and . . . he stays there." The windowless railroad tenements were cold, dirty, and dark. Most had no hot water. None had bathtubs or electricity.[7]

Outside the Italian neighborhoods, the experiences of the immigrants were often equally embittering. "A day did not pass that the Italian was not vilified in one manner or another," commented Michael La Sorte. "The Americans laughed at his speech, his clothes, his customs, and where and how he lived. Such treatment caused Italians to be wary of all Americans." And to Americans, Italians were guineas, wops, dukes, dagos, tallies, macaronis, or spaghetti benders.

Americans also began to ascribe a kind of innate criminality to Italian-Americans. The historian Richard Gambino, writing in *Blood of My Blood*, noted that Americans in the late 1800s were debating "whether Italian Americans were somehow all disposed to criminality by their genetic endowment or cultural inheritance." In pursuit of the "Black Hand," a supposed secret society of Italian criminals in which somehow all Italian-Americans were implicated, mass police raids against Italians broke out all across America. A riot took place in Hoboken in May 1909 when police entered the Italian section. *The New York*

Times reported on May 6 that Italian residents exchanged gun-shots with police from tenement windows. In New York City, a special squad had been established in December 1906 to investigate crime among Italian-Americans, and in 1909 a typical raid took place in Chicago in which 194 Italian-Americans were arrested. According to Gambino: "The police charged en masse into Little Italy and collared anyone who appeared to be suspicious. . . . When the authorities were unable to produce any link whatsoever between the prisoners and crimes, the police reluctantly released all 194 men. . . . In many cities these tactics designed to keep the Italian immigrants in line created a state of open hostility between police and Italian-Americans."[8]

But no one has captured the scalding, racking pain, humiliation, and isolation—and the nobility—of the Italian-American immigrant experience as vividly as Pietro Di Donato in his 1937 novel, *Christ in Concrete*.

The story of a young boy whose father, a bricklayer, suffocates to death when he is caught under a falling structure and is impaled on iron rods by a torrent of wet cement, *Christ in Concrete*, while sometimes raw and awkwardly written, is nevertheless heartbreakingly, uncompromisingly realistic.

A bricklayer himself from West Hoboken, Di Donato knew his subject. In an early scene, he captures the brutal racist attitudes to which Italian immigrants were subjected when a young boy goes to the police station, desperately seeking news of the fate of his father, Geremio:

> The sergeant thought for a moment, and called to the next room: "Hey, Alden, anything come in on a guy named—Geremio?"
>
> A second later, a live voice from the next room loudly answered: "What?—oh yeah—the wop is under the wrappin' paper out in the courtyard!"

Despite the debilitating conditions in which they lived, the Italian immigrants in *Christ in Concrete* resort again and again to music to raise their spirits and express their stalwart souls. When summer comes, the bricklayers "played pranks and sang."

> Alfredo the Neapolitan would pause at [the] wheelbarrow, put hand to mouth and joyously lift [his] rough voice. . . .
> And the men . . . midst ring of brick and steel, and glow of sun and dust of building, sing from their hearts about "white breasts like hills of sand on shore of sea."[9]

Among the cities the Italian immigrants flocked to was Hoboken. Once a backwater tidal swamp, Hoboken flourished in the nineteenth century, fueled by the cheap labor of Dutch, German, Irish, and, later, Italian immigrants. By 1910, a population of 70,000 lived in the mile-square municipality in sturdy brick and stone dwellings.

A busy port across the Hudson River from Manhattan, Hoboken received the world's grandest boats at its piers. Shipping magnates and robber barons built turreted mansions on the hill overlooking the waterfront.

The city, like neighboring Paterson, was a center of the silk industry that had attracted weavers from northern and southern Italy. It was a stronghold of the anarchist movement in the first decade of the century. At Tivola and Zucca's Saloon in West Hoboken, two itinerant Italian anarchists, Enrico Malatesta and Giuseppe Ciancabilla, had frequent debates before large audiences in a back hall lined with red-and-black banners. Between debates, musicians played arias from Verdi's operas, for example, while large pitchers of beer were passed around.

With more than 240 saloons on the River Street waterfront, Hoboken was a vibrant, raw, and swinging town in the '20s and '30s. Sailors, soldiers, hookers, and tradespeople gambled and drank. Smokestacks punctuated the industrial skyline and railroad tracks cut through the city. The streets were filled with peddlers and bootleggers.

There were at least fifteen theaters, including the famous Old Rialto and the Hudson burlesque house. Soon after World War II, the city's economy would start to wane. The major manufacturers deserted Hoboken for sprawling industrial parks in southern and western New Jersey. Formerly the cornerstone of Hoboken's commerce, the factory buildings, now empty, became hollow, crumbling relics.

To those who remember the grimy smokestacks and decaying storefronts of the 1950s, it would be hard to believe that in the nineteenth century Hoboken had been a pleasure resort for affluent New Yorkers. Thousands came on weekends for its flowing esplanades, groomed Riverwalk, and views of the Manhattan skyline. A glimpse of the old Hoboken can be found in Christopher Morley's book *Seacoast of Bohemia* (1929), about resurrecting the Old Rialto theater on Hoboken's Hudson Street. The theater, built in 1863, had fallen into disrepute as a burlesque house. Perhaps wishfully, Morley romantically described Hoboken as "this last unspoiled Bohemian coast, unpolluted by sophistication."

Of Hoboken's vanished past, Morley wrote:

> The old joke about Hoboken being foreign territory had some truth in it. You stepped off at the other end of the ferry and found yourself in a delightfully different world. There were ships, and quiet streets sunning themselves in a noonday doze, and comfortable German hotels where men sat lingeringly at

their meals. . . . On warm days, then, as now, the
firemen on Hudson Street would turn on the hydrant
. . . and not only children but grown-ups too bathed
happily in the misty shower.

    . . . In the palmy days of the Elysian Fields, when
all the Hoboken river front was a rustic picnic
ground, a little classic temple was built round the
spring; it became a place of almost pious pilgrimage.
Isn't it in one of Poe's stories . . . that the arcadian
charms of the Elysian Fields are described? Then the
region became a favorite center of athletic pastime.
There were boating clubs, and fishing clubs, and
clubs for the preparation and consumption of turtle
soup. International cricket matches were played there
. . . and I have met young college men who are
amazed to hear that the first Yale-Princeton football
game took place in Hoboken.[10]

    By Jimmy Roselli's day, that pristine Hoboken was long
gone. Steamships had arrived at the docks. The population was
divided among the Irish, Italians, and Germans. For forty-two
years Barney McFeeley was mayor. The Irish operated the
mile-square town, from 1st to 16th Street, just as Mayor Frank
("I am the law") Hague ruled Jersey City for half a century.

    At the bottom of the social scale in Hoboken as elsewhere,
the Italians lived on the west side of town, packed into five-
story wooden tenements. The Roselli family lived on Monroe
Street, which was the heart of Little Italy. The Italian colony
was situated west of Willow. Italians couldn't cross Clinton
Street or go beyond 9th Street, the borderline, without being
beaten or ridiculed, and were barred from uptown Irish and
German clubs and churches. The Irish would shout: "Get
downtown, you guinea bastards, and stay with the nanny

goats," which were common in yards, streets, and the open fields of the Italian section of town. Italian families would milk them to feed their children.

Michael Roselli, Jimmy's paternal grandfather, came first to Chicago and then to Hoboken in 1902 from Nole, a province of Naples. Anna Bernadette Lavella, Jimmy's mother, hailed from Solofia, a province of Avelina, and arrived in the United States in 1908, when she was a year and a half old. She was a seamstress, and met Michael's son Phil in 1922. They married in 1924, formed a home together, and Jimmy was born a year later. But there was no home when Jimmy was born.

It was home that Jimmy Roselli would sing about with such longing in his music, and it was home that he started life without. Home would have meant the mother and father he did not have, home would have meant Naples. He sang in the language of his Neapolitan grandfather: the songs were redolent of unrequited love and of the flowers, orange groves, lemon and olive trees, and fields of Italy. And throughout his life he has come close to breaking down when he sings about mothers.

He was born on December 26, 1925, in West New York and at first he was called Mickey. Two days later, his mother died, and his father, a professional boxer named "Fighting Phil" Roselli, took off for good. Jimmy was baptized Michael John Roselli in St. Ann's Church in Hoboken after his grandfather Michael. He would be known as Mickey until his mid-twenties, when his first agent, Bob Gans, decided it sounded "like a four-round fighter," and renamed him Jimmy.

Jimmy was raised in Hoboken by his grandfather, a long-shoreman who spoke no English, and four aunts, Frieda, Anne, Antonetta (Etts), and Filomina. It was a lonely childhood: "When I was crawling on the floor," Jimmy recalled, "nobody took me by the hand: 'Make a left here, don't go near the stairs.' I had to make all my own decisions. That's embedded in me from birth."

As Jimmy tells it, his father, Phil, initially had hired a woman to take care of him in January 1926, when Jimmy was two weeks old. Then he refused to pay her. The woman took Jimmy in his baby carriage to his grandfather's apartment house and waited for the old man in front of the house. She explained to him that she had to return the baby to him. Jimmy imagined his grandfather peering down at him and touching his face. In Jimmy's version, his grandfather picked him up, handed him to his daughter Frieda, and said, "The way seven of us eat, eight of us will eat. Take him upstairs and put him in my bed." "From that day on," Jimmy said, "I was with the old man." The family of four daughters and two sons lived in a crowded cold-water flat with a tub in the kitchen.

Jimmy's Aunt Etts recalled that when she first saw Jimmy, "it was rainy, cold, and we were all young girls, we didn't know nothing about babies. The lady brought him in a stroller. Jimmy was sick; he had whooping cough. We were all frightened, because we didn't know what to do. We asked people for help. We took him to the park. The Italian people said take him around the gas tanks; that will help with the whooping cough."

From the Sunday he arrived, Jimmy slept with his grandfather. Their relationship was warm but testy. Already in his mid-fifties and widowed, with a full-time longshoreman's job on the waterfront, Michael Roselli still tried hard to fill the role of father for Jimmy. "He used to tell me stories in Italian at bedtime," Jimmy remembered fondly. "We would argue back and forth. He would tell me a story about the wolf. All of a sudden he'd fall asleep. I'd wake him up. 'Papa, what happened with the wolf? What happened?' "

But it was not easy to be without a real father—especially since Phil Roselli was nearby, working in a local bar, his rejection of his son a constant source of pain. From his early years, Mickey Roselli tried to puzzle out his father's desertion. "I often ask myself how could he leave a kid," he wondered. "I tried to figure out what kind of fucking man he was. Because my family was very warm. All of them. I asked him myself many times. He answered, 'I left you in good hands. I left you with my father.' I said, 'But I wasn't your father's responsibility. I was your responsibility. You think that made everything okay? You left me with a guy who had nothing to begin with.' But whatever my grandfather had, he gave me, which was nothing. My father was a selfish man. All he cared about was himself. Never bought me a pair of shoelaces, a pair of shoes. Nothing." Jimmy and his friends would see Phil Roselli on the street. Vito Pedesta, a childhood friend, recalled Jimmy pointing out his father and saying, "There's the old man over there."

Michael Roselli never condemned Jimmy's father for abandoning his child. "My grandfather might refer to him as 'that rat' on occasion, but that was all. He rarely mentioned him. My father was just the black sheep of the family." But in addition to his grandfather, Jimmy found emotional support in his four aunts. "My aunts were all hard workers. They made nine dollars a week in the General Foods factory. Everybody used to chip in. My Aunt Frieda was like my mother. She had no kids. She'd lost all three of them. She spent all her money on me. She worked in a shop making twelve dollars a week: Franklin Bakers, right here in Hoboken. She took me to a shop to buy me clothes, bathed me." As Pete Cavallo, Jimmy's close friend and road manager, explained the relationship between Jimmy and his aunt, "Frieda went out of her way, took money out of her salary to clothe him. Not just clothe him with bargains, but clothe him to look nice."

Husky and tall, Michael Roselli spoke only Italian, and insisted that others speak only Italian in his house. "He was a typical godfather," recalled one of Jimmy's childhood pals, but "a gentleman, a working stiff." Without a wife himself, "he moved pretty quick with the women; went through the neighborhood pretty good," and he commanded—if not demanded—the respect of his family.

Because of his grandfather's fierce love, Jimmy was accorded a special status in the poverty-stricken household. "We had to go on the avenue to get a certain kind of milk for him," said Aunt Etts. "And my father—oh boy, if we ever touched Jimmy we would get killed. He loved him so much. In the house, my father gave us all chores to do. We didn't have an easy life, but we survived. If we had an apple, my father would cut it in seven pieces. I shaved coconuts in the factory. The men would throw them down and take the shell off; we shaved the brown skin and put them on conveyors. I worked there eleven years. You were always wet and sweating. To steam the coconuts, the temperature had to be almost three hundred degrees. We had to do it. Jimmy used to bring me food at the factory. He always helped.

"But Jimmy was the apple of my father's eye. I used to fight with my father. Sometimes Jimmy would come in late because he was shoe-shining. My father said, 'Don't holler when he comes; if you holler he'll go away on us.' I said, 'No, he won't go away. Where's he gonna go?' But he was a good boy."

Despite the constricted space in the small apartment, Jimmy's aunts brought their husbands there to live. "At the table," Jimmy remembered, "my grandfather used to comment about them: 'You only see the top of their heads; everybody's eatin'.' I got my straightforwardness from him. The husbands knew he had no great love for them because they weren't his type guys."

While Jimmy was critical of his aunts' marital choices, he loved two of his father's brothers, Frankie and Scoop. His Uncle Frankie was the youngest in the family, and when Jimmy was four, he contracted pneumonia. "They took him on a stretcher to the hospital on Saturday. I was crying. On the way out he said to me, 'Don't cry. Bring me the papers tomorrow.' Next day he died. I remember like it was yesterday when they put him on that stretcher."

His Uncle Scoop was also good to him. Scoop used to work nights in the Washington Meat Market in New York. He'd come home at eight o'clock in the morning, and before going to bed, he'd bathe his feet, because he had been on them all night. Jimmy would bathe them too, "and I had to sing to him. I was only a little kid. Then he would cut the calluses on his feet. 'Come here, hurry up, pull my hair while I cut.' He was teasing me. 'Pull hard, pull hard.' He had no hair to begin with; he was all bald."

When Jimmy was older, he visited his maternal relatives. "Some Saturday mornings I would take two buses to visit my grandmother, my mother's mother," he said. "I was seven or eight. She'd open the door and the first thing she'd say was 'How's that rotten bastard, your father?' She blamed my father for my mother's death. For half an hour I had to listen to her rave and rant; then she'd calm down."

He didn't see his mother's parents for years after that. They sent no gifts, nothing. They'd visit only every five years, "so we had to put on a show like royalty was coming. No matter how broke my grandfather was, he always had to do the right thing."

Jimmy's grandfather was his bedrock of security. Whatever the tensions between them, Michael Roselli earned Jimmy's respect and affection. The young boy loved and admired him, and his lifetime code of morality would be based on his grandfather's character. "My grandfather wasn't a bullshitter, he didn't try to impress people," said Jimmy. "He was an honest, down-to-earth man. He knew he was a poor man, and he didn't try to act like a fucking wealthy man. This is what I am: you accept me for what I am."

Once when Jimmy went into his grandfather's candy store, he saw his Aunt Etts refuse to give her own daughter a Popsicle because she wanted her to eat "balanced meals." But a minute before, when he had asked her for one himself, she thrust it into his hand without a word. "I noticed the difference," he said.

For many years Jimmy hated holidays because they reminded him of his mother's death. He would never forget the Christmas he turned five. When he visited his friends, Jimmy could see the other children with their mothers putting up the Christmas tree. His aunts didn't want to put up a tree in the apartment; they had their own families by that time. Jimmy found a small abandoned tree on the street and put the tree in the one empty room in their railroad flat to make his own holiday, but one of his aunts shouted at him to take it down. Afterward he lay under his bed, crying about not having his own tree.

As much as he loved his grandfather and his grandfather loved him, there was a fifty-year age difference between them, which created inevitable distance in their relationship. Michael Roselli's habits were established—as well as his parsimony. As Jimmy remembered it: "One time my grandfather took me to buy a pair of shoes at Grant's five-and-ten-cent store. At the first rainfall the shoes melted. They were made of cardboard. He was like a crazy man: 'I just bought you these shoes.' I said, 'From now on, you don't buy me anything no more. I'm gonna go out and buy my own clothes. Because you buy me cardboard shoes. You mean well, but cardboard shoes gotta melt.' From that day on I bought my own clothes. I went shining shoes, selling papers, I did everything."

But it wasn't simply his grandfather's stinginess that was painful. The hurt was compounded by his playing on the sympathy of others as he replayed his own hard-luck story. "Like a salesgirl should do something about giving him a bargain," remarked Donna Roselli, Jimmy's wife, because "Jimmy's mother had died. That was the typical thing years ago. Jim would be embarrassed and say to his grandfather, 'Please don't do this to me when you go into a store.' It was humiliating. But he would do it."

Michael sought his grandson's company to assuage his own loneliness, but the old man had a possessive, hermetic streak. As Jimmy described it: "When it snowed, he'd want to stay indoors and play cards. After an hour I'd fall asleep. He'd get mad. 'When you're outside with those bums you hang around with, you stay awake,' he said. We were like two old men. And it was cold in that cold-water flat. I'd get in bed at night and my grandfather would say, 'Get up close to me because it's cold.' So I got up close. I threw nine fucking blankets on top of the bed. You couldn't turn over there were so many blankets."

But the tough memories are interlaced with warm, loving ones. His grandfather would make his own bread and wine, and he'd let Jimmy stay home from school to help him. He'd send him for liver, which they would wrap in bay leaves and cook over charcoal, seasoning it with lemon, salt, and pepper. They'd eat it with the wine, as at a banquet. His grandfather didn't eat lunch, but would have a big meal at night, for three, four hours, during which time he'd consume a gallon of wine. "A gallon!" Jimmy exclaimed, adding, "If he was in good shape, a gallon and a half. And you never knew he had a drink."

Like many of the Italian men, Jimmy's grandfather was anti-clerical and had little use for the church—unless Jimmy was singing there. "I sang in the church choir when I was eight. My grandfather would enter the church backward, looking upward, shielding his eyes, searching for me among the choirboys in the loft overhead.

"I had a priest work with me, teach me the Latin, and the 'Ave Maria.' Nothing came easy. Nothing. One day he said we have to go next door to his house to have confession. I was only a little kid, but I was on the streets quite a bit, so I wasn't the average naïve little boy. Next thing I know he's got his arms around me. I'm saying to myself, 'What kind of a confession is this?' So I pushed him away. I says, I'm leaving. I left. Left. Never went back to church again."

Not knowing how to explain it, Jimmy kept silent about his reasons for staying away. "My grandfather couldn't understand why," he said. "I never said anything to him about this incident. So he abused me: 'You became a professor. You learned one song and you're a big shot.' I didn't know how to even begin to tell him. All I said was I don't want to sing in church no more because they don't pay me. But I knew it wasn't good; it wasn't right. So I just left it alone. And the old man was very, very angry because he was very proud of me, you know. I gave him every reason to be proud of me because I never did anything I was ashamed of. But that was the end of my career in church."

For three years Jimmy worked in a drugstore, six days a week, after school and all day Saturday. He washed windows with the squeegee and worked at the fountain. His salary was three dollars a week, and his grandfather gave him only a quarter from that sum.

"And then I started getting smarter," Jimmy said. "I got the shine box and used to sneak into the saloons at night. I did a good job with the shines. Used to get a nickel a shine in them days. When I got done work at the drugstore, I'd go in three or four saloons. I sang in the Three Deuces saloon and made ten dollars. I sang 'Danny Boy,' 'My Gal Sal,' 'Oh! You Million Dollar Doll,' 'That Old Gang of Mine.' Then I thought, What am I doing with the drugstore? What do I need with this bullshit here? I started singing regular in saloons. I'd make fifteen, twenty, twenty-five dollars. Me and my pal Clarkie would kneel in the sawdust, shining the thigh-high boots of German sailors. Then I thought, What am I doing with the shine box? I gave my grandfather eight, ten dollars: 'You must be a good shiner,' he said. I took the money and put it in a handkerchief on the roof. Because he used to go in my kit. If you gave him ten, he wanted thirty."

By the age of ten Jimmy sometimes sang professionally at the Gay Nineties room at the Meyers Hotel in Hoboken. The manager dressed him in a bellhop's uniform because he was legally too young to perform.

But his precocious talent and resourcefulness sometimes had unforeseen consequences. "I came home late from singing in a bar; it was two in the morning. I slept near the wall. So I had to climb over my grandfather. I'm trying not to wake him up. I figure I made it. Then: boom with the arm. 'You vagabond,' he shouts, 'this is the time you come home?' He put the light on. It was a whole scene. He asked me where I'd gone, and what they paid me. I said nothing. 'Are you a charity?' he said. I started getting mad. 'Will you leave me the fuck alone?' I shouted at him. 'What are you breaking my balls?'

"My grandfather smiled. He said in Italian, 'Ah! Your head it came out of the sack. You got to be a big man.'"

Music held a central place in the hearts of Italian immigrants. The fondest dream of Italian parents was that a child become a concert artist. In Italy, opera, not theater, had been the reigning art form, and the theatrical tradition took second place to the musical one of popular songs and operas. In America, opera singers aroused the immigrants' visceral attachment to Italy, but live Italian opera was for the wealthy. Others worshipped Enrico Caruso from afar, and listened to opera singer Carlo Butto every Sunday on the *Italian Radio Hour* on radio station WHOM. The program, sponsored by Pastene foods, was broadcast through the 1930s and 1940s.

But the earliest Italian immigrants forgot their troubles through vaudeville, religious festivals, theater, puppet shows, family games, wedding parties, and picnics. Family celebrations were held on Sundays to honor engagements, christenings, baptisms, graduations, and birthdays. Italian arias were played on the gramophone or guitar and mandolin players would perform solos. Theater clubs in the New York–New Jersey metropolitan area included the Ria Rosa Company (which played at the Brooklyn Academy of Music), the Fil-drammatico Spartico of Greenpoint, Brooklyn, the People's Theater on the Bowery run by Alberto Camboeasso, a writer, director, and impresario, and the Vincenzo Martinelli and Family Company. These groups presented farces in Neapolitan or Sicilian dialect followed by solo dancers, guitar and mandolin soloists, comedians, magicians, and vocalists.

The novelist Carl Van Vechten described the atmosphere of an Italian-American vaudeville theater in the 1920s:

> Audiences became as talkative and gregarious as they might at a wedding feast or picnic. Whether the curtain was up or down, they conversed with one an-

other, shouted greetings upon spotting acquaintances and, when the curtain was up, addressed themselves directly to one of the actors on stage. Depending on what was unfolding, the audiences sang, wept or laughed . . . [they] hissed the villain with the same intensity they cheered the hero. The management seldom objected. Theatre managers were known to keep the house lights on during performances so as not to inhibit conversations in the audience, which at times were louder than the lines being delivered on stage. For the audience often would call a warning to the actor playing the role of the husband that his wife was being unfaithful, or that the villain was about to kill the hero.[11]

Michael Roselli took his grandson to the Italian opera and vaudeville shows every week at Hoboken's Rialto and Jefferson Hall Theater. It was here that Jimmy first became acquainted with the Italian classics he would eventually claim as his own. Among the major Neapolitan performers in the 1930s were Gilda Mignonette, Gennaro Gardenia (father of the actor Vincent Gardenia), Ria Rosa, Clemente Giglio, Giuseppe Milano, and Rosina de Stefano; the actresses Mimi Cecchini and Olga Barbato; the comedians Giuseppe de Laurentis, Gennaro Amato, Giovanni De Rosalia, and Angelo Gloria; and the songwriter and monologuist Pasquale Vittori. It was Gilda Mignonette who influenced him most. "She was what you would call a real belter," he told the *Philadelphia Inquirer.* "When I was a kid I kind of took my style from her."

Dramatic skits were based on favorite Italian and Neapolitan songs like "Senza Mamma," a song popularized by Giuseppe Milano, about a man who's been away and has lost his mother. (The song and skit were used in the Italian theater scene in

Francis Ford Coppola's movie *The Godfather, Part II.*) In the same vein, a story was concocted from the song "Senza Mamma e Innamorata." The title is similar, the story only partly different—about what it's like to be both without a mother and abandoned by a lover. Rosina de Stefano, a singer and great beauty of the period, helped make it a hit.

Many of the routines were based on double entendres. Mimi Cecchini did routines with Matteo Cannizzaro, a *capo-comico* ("top banana"), a singer and actor who came to America from Sicily in 1930 when he was seventeen and was active in Italian theater and film until he died in May 1998.

In one routine, Cannizzaro clutched the microphone stand, looking impishly at the audience before saying, "This thing goes up and down. It gets better if I hold it for a while." In another, Matteo asked directions to the rest room in a department store: "The man responded, 'Escalator.' 'Ask-a-later?' I have to go now." And a favorite joke on marriage was this one: "A man's wife is killed by his dog. 'Can I borrow that dog?' asks a bystander at the funeral. 'Sure, get in line behind those seventy-five guys,' replies the grieving husband."

At the Stanley Theater and Patsy Demenza's Italian theater, Jimmy witnessed the extraordinary bond between vaudevillians and their audience. He discovered the power of song, and after each performer, his grandfather would say, "You can sing better than this guy."

"You could hear my voice ten blocks away," boasted Jimmy. "I used to sing on the top floor of my house, and the people on the next block would look out their windows and holler requests: 'Mickey, sing this.'" Aunt Etts has a story about the impact of Jimmy's voice: "I knew he was a singer when he sang in the school auditorium one time. He was so young. He sang 'Stout Hearted Men.' The curtain fell down with his voice, that's how powerful it was."

Jimmy got very emotional when he sang Italian songs. "I would cry," he admitted. "I looked at my grandfather and at my aunts. They had broken down and they were crying too."

But since he wasn't allowed to go into a bar as a minor, "we continued to use the gimmick with the shine box," recalled Clarkie, one of Jimmy's boyhood friends, known for his large chin, proud paunch, and, unfortunately, for never taking a bath. "When we got in, Jimmy sang, then I sang, and he passed the hat. In one place, there was this Irish guy who always wanted to hear Jimmy sing 'Danny Boy.' As soon as Jimmy began, this guy pulled out his handkerchief. As soon as he started crying, I grabbed his money off the bar and threw it in the hat. Then you'd stand there when Jimmy finished the song, and the guy would give you another nickel or dime. It was a big score in them days."

Once, with Jimmy as the singer and Clarkie as collector, Jimmy noticed some paper going into Clarkie's pocket. At the end of his performance Jimmy asked, "Clarkie, where's the paper?" Clarkie replied, "What do ya mean?" Jimmy continued, "I saw some paper go into this hat." "I only got change," Clarkie claimed.

"Jimmy made Clarkie get stark naked," said his cousin Dennis Della Fave. "He took off all his clothes to look for the money. The only thing he forgot to look in was the hat. Clarkie's standing there naked with the hat on. Jimmy says, 'Take off the hat.' And in the hat were the dollar bills and five-dollar bills. Jimmy says, 'You tryin' to rob from *me* while I'm singin' my ass off?' "

Money would always be an issue for Jimmy, who was the first to be convinced he wasn't getting his fair share—and in many cases, he was right.

When he was thirteen, Jimmy won first prize on the famed

Major Bowes' Original Amateur Hour radio show contest. "The Major put me on his knee," Jimmy recalled. "He had a new quarter, a new dime, and a new nickel. He whispered in my ear, 'Take 'em and put them in your pocket. Don't show them to anybody.' Like I was stealin' something. Forty cents this fucking bum bought me for. He says, 'I want to hear you sing like you never sang before.' I went on that fucking stage and I sang like a canary. I sang 'Pocketful of Dreams.' "

Al Certo, a childhood buddy of Jimmy's, who was both a fighter's manager (handling Buddy McGurt) and a tailor, remembered "a shit-ass kid talking in Italian and arguing like a bastard. He and his grandfather argued like hell. They were comical, really. The grandfather would say at the feast: 'Go up and sing and I'll give you a hot dog.' Jimmy would say: 'Give me the hot dog now. Then I'll sing.' This son of a bitch had talent when he was eight years old. He had the voice of a great singer. The talent you see today is the talent he had as a young boy. He always had it. He was always a cocky son of a bitch. He was eleven going on twenty.

"On Thanksgiving we celebrated like Halloween today. We went around begging with costumes on and everything. Jimmy and Clarkie would go in the backyards, and people would throw pennies, or apples, whatever they had. Jimmy was a little embarrassed, but he done it for a while as a little boy. And he would shine shoes on River Street, and the piano players would call: C'mere, Jimmy, they said, sing this song. And that's how he learned a lot of those saloon songs."

"The only singing rival Jimmy had as a kid," recalled Skinny Skelly (Tony Petrazelli), "was Nunzio Pascalle, alias Clarkie Gable Big Ears. But he could never really compete with Roselli."

Jimmy's father continued to keep his distance from his son, but he was clearly ambivalent about it. Phil Roselli would telephone Al Certo from the bar where he worked and ask him to tell Jimmy to visit him. But whenever Jimmy did, he and his father would end up arguing, and according to Certo, they weren't on speaking terms when Phil passed away.

In spite of Michael Roselli's dalliances, Jimmy's neighborhood was the kind of place where angry husbands wouldn't hesitate to defend their wives' honor. Once Michael Roselli took Jimmy to visit Bach, the poormaster of Hoboken, to get him shoes. "Son of a bitch German bastard. Some woman with a family went to him for help while we were there. Bach said, 'You're a nice-looking woman. Go out swinging a bag. You should make some money easily.' She went home and told her husband. He stabbed Bach with a penknife right in his heart. He picked the penknife up from the guy's desk, he was so angry; he didn't even go there with a weapon."

But while it was a neighborhood of poverty and occasional outbursts of violence, it was also a community that understood the importance of family—if only by necessity. "We lived in a cold-water railroad flat," recalled Matty Rega, Jimmy's brother-in-law, who married the sister of Jimmy's first wife. "Four rooms going straightaway. My parents, four brothers, and three sisters. The bathroom was in the hallway. No refrigerator. The iceman used to bring the ice up for the icebox. We made our own heat with paper, wood, and coal. Eventually the stove with oil came out, but that only made heat in the kitchen. There was no other heat. My mother would cover us with many blankets, and if not blankets, coats."

Matty and Jimmy worked at the R. C. Bennett Box Company in the basement of the Lipton Tea building when they were sixteen. "Somebody would cut the wood and I would catch it, get the pieces. I fed it to Roselli and he stapled the two pieces together. After work we'd take the trolley and go. up this hill to get to the Stanley Theater in Journal Square." That was back when Hoboken's piers were thriving. Ships calling from Germany docked in Hoboken, and their passengers then stayed at the Grand, the Lincoln, and the Meyers hotels.

If Jimmy's family and friends had little financial security, they also had few concerns about their personal safety. "We used to go to bed with the doors open," Matty remembered. "As we walked up the flight of stairs, we could smell what gravy everybody was cooking. If you needed an egg, you knocked on the neighbor's door. And if she needed a potato, that's how it worked. If anybody ever burglarized the house, the whole block went after him. Most people couldn't pay the rent, which was ten to fifteen dollars a month. The landlord would never chase you out."

When the railroad trains passed through and hit bumps on the tracks, there would be mothers waiting to pick up the loose coal they spilled to use in the stoves that helped keep their families warm.

On Madison Street, where Matty lived at number 519, there was a constant stream of peddlers. Some would hawk greens; others, who came on Fridays, sold fish. "You would call out your window: 'Give me ten cents' worth of oranges,' and they would bring them to you. Or just go down and pick from the peddler's wagon." The old Jewish peddlers, they'd pay weekly. "If you spent seven dollars, you paid them maybe ten, fifteen cents a week. No interest or nothing."

"At night in the summertime everybody sat in front of the house and the lemon ice cart would come by. For a penny. Or we had Yum Yum ice cream. And they'd send out for pizza pies, half with mozzarella, half with anchovies. That was like thirty-five cents for a big pie. Or maybe a piece of provolone or salami with Italian bread and a little wine."

Sometimes the adults would ask the youngsters to take a can to the local tavern to purchase fifteen cents of beer. The old-timers played bocce in the alleys. Street singers would come by and serenade in the yard.

"Hard times, but happy times," Matty remembered fondly. "A good lesson to learn about life."

Still, harshness was not uncommon among these families, and Jimmy's grandfather could be punishing with him as well. Once, Jimmy arrived late for dinner and apologized to his grandfather. "That's okay," he replied. "No problem." Then when Jimmy took his fork and began to eat, Michael Roselli put his hand on the back of Jimmy's head and pushed it hard into the plate. Blood poured from Jimmy's nose. His grandfather said, *"Ccase mangia a e cingue. Nun e risturante cca. Si nunte trueve cca e cingue, nuns se mangia."* ("Here we eat at five. This isn't a restaurant. If you don't find yourself here at five, there will be no eating.") He took the plate of food and emptied it into the garbage can.

Michael Roselli could be tough, even mean, but he ardently supported Jimmy's singing career. On amateur night at Patsy Dimenza's Italian vaudeville theater, he'd push Jimmy toward the stage. *"Cante, guaglione, cante"* ("Sing, little one, sing"). Summoning up the spirit of home and family, at his concerts Jimmy still repeats the phrase into the wireless microphone backstage just before making his entrance.

Since Prohibition went into effect in the 1920s, New Jersey had served as a breeding ground for organized crime. A short truck haul from the speakeasies of Manhattan, Newark became the bootleg capital of the eastern seaboard. Arthur Flegenheimer, the Prohibition-era beer baron, who was better known as Dutch Schultz, had his saloon headquarters in Newark until he was gunned down in 1935 by a newly organized New York crime syndicate. After a period of bloody intramural warfare, mob chiefs Abner Zwillman—one of the most powerful bootleggers along the East Coast—and Ruggiero (Richie the Boot) Boiardo split up Newark between them.

Many other major Mafiosi became politically powerful in New Jersey. Albert Anastasia, chief executioner of Murder, Inc., lived in a lavish mansion in Fort Lee, where he entertained the elite of the New Jersey underworld, including Willie Moretti and gambling czar Joe Adonis, the partner of Frank Costello. In the late 1930s Adonis built a series of plush gambling casinos in New Jersey. He also set up a headquarters in a tavern where a working crime council met daily. Its members included Adonis, Anastasia, Willie Moretti and his brother Solly, and Anthony (Tony Bender) Stroller, a top associate of Vito Genovese. The council convened on a weekly basis with members of the national syndicate, Frank Costello and Meyer Lansky, until Anastasia was murdered in 1957 while getting a shave at a hotel barbershop.

One of New York's three highest-ranking Mafia bosses and the man who came close to consolidating all of organized crime in America, Vito Genovese was another luminary of the state. For eighteen years, he lived in a modest one-story clapboard house in Atlantic Highlands on the Jersey shore. An early cohort of Lucky Luciano, Genovese fled to Italy in 1934 to avoid a murder trial. He was brought back in 1945 and acquitted in 1946. He had taken his place alongside Frank Costello but eventually plotted against Costello, Luciano, Carlo Gambino, and Meyer Lansky, before being convicted and sentenced to an Atlanta penitentiary on a narcotics-smuggling charge in 1958.

Once, when Jimmy Roselli was still in his teens, some of the local mobsters came up to him with tears in their eyes after he sang, kissed him on both cheeks, and told him he made them cry with his beautiful voice. As one put it: "You made me bawl like a fag, you little prick." Jimmy thanked them.

"Guys like them," his grandfather said in Italian after one performance, referring to wiseguys, "they're not the Italian people. We work a lifetime for a few coins, and they steal them from us. I'm proud that I work hard for a living. Be a good man, Jimmy. From your singing you will make an honest living. You'll never have the taste of ashes in your throat. Never let me hear the police knock at our door. That would break my heart."

Jimmy nodded. "I promise, Papa," he said.

3

A FATHER,
A GRANDFATHER

JIMMY ROSELLI LIVED AT 514 MONROE STREET, FRANK
Sinatra at 415. Both Sinatra and Roselli have December birth
dates. Both of their fathers were ex-boxers. Sinatra's family was
middle-class; Roselli was a street kid. But despite the growing
economic gulf between them, Dolly Sinatra, Frank's mother,
her husband, Marty, and a neighbor, John the Florist, hung
out with Jimmy's grandfather. Aunt Etts recalls, "Dolly loved
my father. They wouldn't go no place without him."

"Dolly Sinatra was a go-getter, a midwife," explained Al
Certo. "The Italian women were knocking out babies like kit-
tens, so she would help them out. She didn't do it for money,
which was a great thing."

Jimmy encountered Sinatra for the first time when he was
around twelve. As he remembers it: "I was singing on a Hoboken corner with the shine box. Sinatra got out of the car.
He had ten years on me. He had one of those collars that stick
out, and a sleeveless sweater. He stops, stands there, and he's

listening. He hands me his card and says, 'I want you to come
to my house.' I went home, cleaned up, shined, put a clean
shirt on. When I got there, he sat down and played the piano
with one finger and had me sing the scales. He was amazed at
my two-octave range. He said, 'Christ, listen to this kid.' I
never heard from him no more after that."

Jimmy first heard Sinatra sing on the radio in 1936 when
Sinatra sang for free on WAAT, a New Jersey station, and
then in 1938 when he sang from the Rustic Cabin in the Jersey
Palisades on the *Saturday Dance Parade* broadcast on WNEW.
"This fucking guy couldn't even sing," he recalled. "Horrible.
I said this guy is singing bad, he can't even sing in tempo,
nothing, he's a fucking bum. But he developed into a *great*
singer."

Sinatra had gone on a tour with the Hoboken Four, four
young "singing and dancing fools" from Hoboken, as Major
Bowes introduced them, who won the amateur hour contest
and were hired by Bowes as part of his vaudeville touring unit
in 1935. The group consisted of Sinatra, Skinny Skelly, Pat
Principe (Patty Prince), and Tamby (Fred Tamburro). "But
Frank broke it up," Jimmy remembered. "He was in love with
his wife, Nancy, and he wanted to be with her. Besides, three
of the guys went to work on him. Tamby and Patty Prince
whacked him. Patty Prince was a little guy, but he hit him a
shin on the chin. Skelly punched him. Frank said, 'What the
fuck, I'm a punching bag for these guys,' and he left them.

"But Frank was determined to get somewhere. Determined.
He had so much determination. Unbelievable, for one man.
He sang anywhere and everywhere. Anyplace and anytime. Not
me. I sang when I felt like singing. He had to learn how to
sing, and he had the opportunity. He worked with one of the
best, Tommy Dorsey. Dorsey groomed him. When I got up to

sing, I was determined to do a good show. But I didn't plan on next month, next year."

For a time, Al Certo confessed, "Jimmy idolized Sinatra. He used to dress like him, and would walk down the street with that cocky strut, wearing a bow tie, white shoes, and a two-tone sports jacket with a square front.

"The thing is, Frank liked to act tough. But I remember he was always a sick kid, fragile. He had an operation for an abscess on the inner ear. In his younger years Frank didn't have the experience with the older guys that Jimmy did. Jimmy was hanging out with kids who were eighteen or twenty when he was twelve. He was always on the hustle, trying to make a buck. Frank liked to have that tough guy image. But Jimmy had the experience and was the real thing. He was always raised with tough guys, racket guys, wiseguys. He knew them all. We all had that kind of experience. Jimmy was never a follower, though. He was always his own person."

Instead of sticking to Hoboken pals, Sinatra surrounded himself with show business professionals. "That's where he got all the knowledge and everything else," Certo remarked. "Jimmy surrounded himself with friends, the people in his environment, with Hoboken. Frank knew how to bend and back off. Jimmy came on with boxing gloves. He was always on the defensive."

A loner from the beginning, Roselli was at once a part of the Hoboken scene and removed from it. And he and Sinatra would never be friends. With the ten years he had on Jimmy, Sinatra was on the rise when Jimmy was still shining shoes. Sinatra's fame, even in the early days, would shadow Jimmy wherever he went—and nowhere more than in Hoboken, because Sinatra was in a position to help Jimmy, though he never did. The similarities between them—their origins, volatile temperaments, and talent—were among the many factors that would keep them on edge with each other. When they finally shared the stage for the first and last time—at the dedication (presided over by Mayor Barney McFeeley) of the Christopher Columbus Statue in the Christopher Columbus Park in Hoboken on October 12, 1937—Sinatra was on his way. Roselli was twelve; Sinatra was twenty-two. Today Roselli's house looks down into the park.

The next year Jimmy had his first girlfriend, Mary Lou Vinalia, who lived next door to St. Ann's Church, where he was christened. Jimmy would sing in the street outside her window and she would look out. In the following years, he worked at "every joint and sewer and toilet," as he put it. "I worked in joints where they used to have intermission to take the wounded out." Club owners told him to "keep singing no matter what happens."

He worked the Red Robin, across the street from the Hudson burlesque in Union City, Stout Petie's Imbriago, the Fabian Theater on Wednesdays (vaudeville night), the Caddy Club, the Stagecoach, the Log Cabin (a strip joint on Staten Island), the 80 Club. His Hoboken childhood pal Johnny Marotta observed, "All those jobs—that's how he learned to fight for his rights."

Sinatra often talked about taking the three-cent ferry ride from Hoboken to New York and never going back. But there was unfinished business in Hoboken for Jimmy: a mother he mourned, a wastrel father he kept encountering in bars where he sang. The relationship deteriorated even further when his father remarried, completely excluded Jimmy from the marriage, and went on to have another child—a daughter, named Joan.

But despite his coldness, Phil Roselli still made occasional, halfhearted attempts at reconciliation. "In the early days,"

Jimmy recalled, "we'd get together and go out for a drink. After a few drinks he'd be fighting three guys at once. Three guys."

But there was another, wider gulf they couldn't bridge: Jimmy's own mother. "Even when I was a kid, talking to my aunts and uncles, nobody seemed to know anything about my mother," he said. "She was eighteen when she died. Nobody could elaborate and say oh yeah, this and that. Even my Aunt Felicia, her sister, was a young kid when my mother died. Nobody really knew her that well. I never, never remember my father talking about her."

Paradoxically, it was Jimmy's father, Phil, who initiated one of Jimmy's first professional jobs.

"My father said he was going to get me a job at the Rhumba Bar in Keansburg, New Jersey, when I was fourteen. I said no. But he came and grabbed me out of bed. So we went there and my father introduced me to Al Segal, the owner. They'd known each other from childhood. Segal said, 'Go ahead. Let me hear you sing. Get up there.' On one side was the boardwalk, the other side the street. As I sang, people started coming over from both sides. 'Very good. You can start tonight,' Segal said.

"I hemmed and hawed. Then I walked up to him. 'Mr. Segal, how much are you going to pay me?' "

" 'Hey, kid, I could blow my license. You're only a kid. You want to work or not?'

"Well, I said I would try it for a week. I gave the waiters fifty-cent pieces to throw on the floor when I started to sing, as an example. I would grab ten, fifteen dollars every show— three shows a night. Worked until five a.m. Sleep maybe an hour, sweep up the joint, then bang, start all over again.

"I used to stay at Al Segal's house because I had no money to go home. You never knew who was going to jump in the bed, a waitress or waiter, most of them alcoholics, a couple of gays. I didn't know if I was going to be a fag next day. Comes the end of the week, Al hands me an envelope. Five singles in it. I opened it and laughed and said this must be a joke. He says, what do you mean, a joke? You don't want it, don't work here no more."

Jimmy stayed, having nowhere else to go and wanting the professional experience. The following year, Jerry Shean, the owner of a competing club, heard about Jimmy and asked him if he wanted to work for him. Jimmy recalls, "I said to Shean, 'I get sixty a week down at the Rhumba Bar and I got my own room.' He says, 'I'll give you seventy and your own room.'

"'All right,' I said. I ran down the boardwalk. Ran. I didn't have a valise. Got a big empty Supersuds cardboard box. I put everything in it and ran back to Shean's place. I worked there that night. Afterward, Tiny, who worked for Segal, comes in and says Al is outside in the car; he wants to talk to me. I go outside. There's Segal, with big crocodile tears running down his face.

"'You could have at least let me make you an offer,' he said.

"'What kind of an offer? You gave me five dollars. I asked you forty times. If you gave me a hundred I wouldn't want to work for you. You're a miserable creep.'

"Much later, when I got my breaks and was becoming known, Segal calls me again and says everybody wants to hear Jimmy Roselli. He says, 'I'd like for you to work for me on Saturday night.' 'Sure,' I said. 'I'd love to work for you. You gotta give me twenty thousand.' 'Twenty thousand for the night?' 'Yeah. That's a favor,' I says. 'I don't even want to work there.'"

It was at Jerry Shean's that Jimmy got drunk and had sex for the first time. He was fourteen. "This broad used to come in with her husband and would make jokes that she was gonna tease me. She must have had seven or eight years on me. I never drank, I was only a kid. She gave me Coca-Cola with Carstairs rye in it.

"Now I go across the street to my room. She comes in there and takes all her clothes off. And I laid her. Her husband walks in. Grabs me by the hair, pulls me off her. And he gave her a beating. You have no idea what a fucking beating she got. She was a pretty girl, a blonde. She came back the next day all battered up, crying. 'See how much I love you. Look what happened to me.' "

But the bartender, Guy Bowen, also loved Jimmy, and told the husband: "I know what the whole setup was. You thought you were gonna be funny, but it backfired on you. Don't even touch this guy unless you want trouble with me." Jimmy added, "He left me alone, never touched me. She was a fool-around broad anyway, you know what I mean?"

Jimmy, in this case, might have had a friend in the right place, but there was a distinction between Jimmy's real "pals" and the wiseguys. As one childhood friend, Matty (Action) Jordan (formerly Giordano, and now proprietor of Matteo's restaurant in Los Angeles), explained: "Jimmy was always partial to a couple of dozen guys: all the guys from 4th Street, 5th Street, 4th and Monroe, 5th and Madison, 5th and Jefferson. . . . He never really hung out with a lot of other people." And it's true that the retired troupe of regulars who come in and out of Roselli's house are all from those Hoboken streets.

"If he'd given the wiseguys a piece of him," Matty asserted, "he'd be doing better than Sinatra. Frank got some good advice, he knew what to say, the right things. Otherwise they slap ya down."

Wiseguys often hung out at—and sometimes were in control of—the feasts, the annual religious festivals honoring the Madonna or a favorite patron saint. These events replicated in detail the way festivals had been staged for centuries in southern Italy, with music, dancing, eating, drinking, and fireworks. Thousands of worshippers would follow the holy statue through the streets to the accompaniment of marching bands. The saint with the largest constituency was San Gennaro, the patron saint of Naples, martyred by Romans during the reign of the emperor Diocletian.

It was at the San Gennaro feast in New York City's Little Italy that the wiseguys first heard Jimmy sing. Milly Dellecave, a veteran Italian-American singer, recalled a shy young Jimmy coming up to her and asking for permission to sing. When he did, the response was tumultuous. "They went crazy," Matty (Action) Jordan remembered. "There were speakers all over Mulberry Street. People at the windows on their elbows, all the old ladies listening. When Jimmy sang them songs, you fucking cried. He used to sing 'Little Pal' for me. I fucking bawled like a bastard.

"Today Jimmy's got his voice. Jimmy's got his memory. Jimmy'll have it all when he's eighty years old."

Why?

"Because he was gifted, and he didn't abuse. Frank used to drink. At seven or eight in the morning. Sleep most of the day, then go to work that night. Smoked only at night. Drank a fucking double Jack Daniel's. Jimmy drank wine. Stay with the grapes."

Jimmy was sixteen years old at the onset of World War II, and he wanted to fight for the United States. In the 1930s, according to Jerre Mangione and Ben Morreale in *La Storia*, thousands of Italian immigrants had been "swayed by nostalgia, pride and a newfound nationalism" to support Mussolini's Fascism. In 1935 Fascist sympathizers in the United States had requested immigrants to mail their wedding rings to Mussolini to provide financial assistance to the war in Ethiopia.

The Italian community in those years was split between the anti-Fascists, including the famed anarchist Carlo Tresca, labor poet Arturo Giovannitti, and ILGWU (International Ladies' Garment Workers' Union) leaders Luigi Antonini and Vanni Montana, and the pro-Fascists, who found support in the newspaper *Il Progresso* and dozens of other papers such as *L'Italia* and *Il Grido della Stripe* (The Cry of Our Race). (Generoso Pope, publisher of *Il Progresso*, traveled to Rome to be knighted by Mussolini as *Cavaliere* and *Commendatore*.) When the American Black Shirts held demonstrations, the anti-Fascists, often led by Carlo Tresca, were there to oppose them.

But as soon as Mussolini declared war on the United States, there was a mass defection of pro-Mussolini Italian-Americans from the Fascist cause. That defection was so significant that although the Italian immigrant population in 1941 included more than 600,000 Italians who were not yet American citizens, only 250 were interned by the Department of Justice at the start of the war as potentially dangerous aliens. Later, in October 1942, a presidential executive order of the Roosevelt administration exempted all of the noncitizen Italian population (except for the 250 who were interned) from the restrictions imposed on other aliens of enemy nationality.

Roselli joined the Army at age eighteen in 1944.* Soon after he enlisted, Jimmy received word at Camp Rucker, Alabama, where he was doing his basic training, that his grandfather was critically ill. He went to the chaplain, told him of his grandfather's condition, and said he was going back to be with him. The chaplain said that Roselli had just returned from leave, and besides, a grandfather was not a close enough familial relationship to justify another furlough.

*His old neighbor Frank Sinatra was declared 4-F until 1945, when he was reexamined and declared 2-AF, disqualified because of a punctured eardrum and because he was "necessary for the national health, safety and interest." In her biography of Sinatra, Kitty Kelley writes of a "national debate" over Sinatra's draft status, which resulted in his undertaking an overseas tour to sing to the troops.

Roselli said, "Look, I'm not asking you, I'm telling you. I'm going back no matter what. He was my father, my mother; he was everything to me."

The chaplain told him he could go.

Jimmy returned to Hoboken and rushed to his grandfather's house. "He was sitting on the stairs," Jimmy recalled. "I got out of the cab with my duffel bag full of clothes. At first he didn't even recognize me because he'd had a stroke. I walked up to him. He started crying. He grabbed me. We went inside, and I spent ten days with him. Then I went back to camp. When I got back, there was a telegram on my cot. He had passed away."

For the rest of his life Jimmy would search for a father figure to replace the old man, a search complicated by the icy indifference of his real father, Phil. Years later, when Jimmy was twenty-five, Johnny Marotta, Augie Delano, Jimmy's *gumba* (best friend), and some of the gang tried to patch things up between Jimmy and his dad. "We went with Jimmy down to the bar where Phil was working. Phil had a short temper, you know. But it was amazing to us how he just stood there as Jimmy talked. Jimmy had a few drinks in him. Jimmy said, 'You never showed up when I needed you. Where were you when—' And Phil just took it. Nothing came of it, but we did try. Jimmy cried. There was love expressed," Marotta recalled.

The search for a substitute father would take Jimmy down endless byways and sidetracks as he came closer and closer to the "mustaches"—the smiling, gleaming paternal types who would promise him the world and then reject him as heartlessly as his real father. That search was further complicated by his yearning for the mother he never knew, and perhaps it is just that which has endowed his singing voice with a quality of unrequited love and longing, a haunting loneliness and passion that would earn Roselli a unique niche in the heart of the Italian community and, most especially, the hearts of Italian women.

It was the voice of an orphaned child.

And it would ultimately save his life.

4

GYP THE COLLAR

ROSELLI SERVED IN COMPANY E, 266TH INFANTRY, 66th Division, and after seventeen weeks of basic training at Camp Rucker, the 66th left New York in November 1944, stayed in England briefly, and crossed the Channel on Christmas Eve. Two of the four platoons were on Jimmy's ship, the *Cheshire*, and two were on the other troopship, the *Leopoldville*.

During the crossing, the *Leopoldville* was torpedoed by a German submarine. Roselli was on the deck of the *Cheshire* and watched with horror as it happened. Eight hundred and two soldiers died that night. He and the other men thought they would be hit next, but they made it to shore. The unit served on the front lines of northern France from December 1944 until the German surrender on May 8, 1945.

When the combat was over, the unit participated in the occupation of Vienna in the Soviet zone. Though he had the duties of an infantryman, Roselli also sang with the swing band at the GIs' nightclub. A yellowed copy of the 209th Battalion's newsletter, *Bayonet*, reports: "Pfc. Mickey Roselli singing in his sweet lyric tenor 'The Sunshine of Your Smile' and 'Goodbye Sue.' Well received, he came back to sing a parody which had the crowd calling for more. . . . [Afterward] it was a jitterbug's delight as the crowd poured onto the stage and the band played number after number with numerous GIs pairing off for a little rug cutting." Jimmy remembered that "they'd take me out of the hole where I'd be digging for potatoes for the kitchen, put me in front of the band, then back in the hole when I was done." He also performed on the radio with the 42nd (Rainbow) Division band from Linz.

Jimmy returned from the service in 1945 and began courting his wife-to-be, Angeline Guiffra. Tony (Skinny Skelly) Petrazelli, a Hoboken childhood friend, had introduced Jimmy to her years before when he had sung at Jerry Shean's. He was fifteen; she was sixteen. "While Jimmy was rehearsing one day, Angie and her sister Kathy were on the boardwalk outside. These two kids, like bobby-soxers, were thrilled. 'Gee, I'd love to meet him.' He finished a break and he ran across the street to his apartment. I said to him, 'Roselli, there's two beautiful girls out there want to meet you. Especially the blonde. She's a knockout.' 'Tony,' he said, 'you never change. You're a snake in the grass.'

"Jimmy was a snake in the grass himself at the beginning. Anyway, when I told him about the sisters, he says, 'Where are they?' I tell him. So I brought them around. It looked like nothing to me. These two girls were raised, forget about it! Like nuns. Whenever Angie went to see Roselli, she was chaperoned. The aunt or the uncle—they always had somebody there. Nobody was gonna screw these girls. This went on and on and on."

As Matty (Action) Jordan put it: "Angie was his girlfriend for a hundred years. Personally I think she was a great lady."

Jimmy and Angie were married on September 28, 1946. He was twenty-one years old. He paid for the wedding with the $1,800 he had saved in the Army. The wedding, including a dollar-and-a-half-per-person chicken dinner, took place at the Hitching Post on Route 22 in Springfield, New Jersey. Jimmy's *gumba*, Augie Delano, served as best man.

After the wedding, Jimmy moved in with Angie's family in Hoboken, and found a job as a construction worker. One day Jimmy told Angie's father, Bill Guiffra, that the work was murder. "That's not your job," his father-in-law said. "That's my job. Your job is to sing."

"Yeah, but it's a long climb," Jimmy said.

His father-in-law handed him an envelope with money in it. "You do your job," he said. "We take care of you meanwhile. This is your home now." Tears came to Jimmy's eyes.

Yes, Jimmy wanted to be a singer more than anything. But there was a side of him that responded to the evidence all around him that the easier route was to be a bookmaker. The attraction of the wiseguys, the allure of easy money, was powerful—and it was interlaced with the brutal rejection by his father, the fear that he would never amount to anything.

Still, he kept trying. During those years, there was an open mike on Sunday nights at Leon and Eddie's, one of the legendary cabarets on 52nd Street in Manhattan. "Sunday nights, all night long, to seven a.m., everybody sang there," he said. "Dean Martin and Jerry Lewis . . . everybody got up and sang, and all the big agents were there. All the racket guys were there. They said I should go see Lew Perry, this big agent who handled Dean Martin. I go up there in 1947. He calls me in the office. He said, 'This is what you got to do.' He grabs a microphone and he's throwing it from this hand to that hand. I said, 'Listen to me. I came up here to sing. I'm not a juggler. That's for guys who have no talent. Throwing the mike this way, grabbing the wire that way. I get up and I sing. I can sing anything you want, from opera to rhythm tunes to ballads, whatever.'

"We got into a scuffle. I said goodbye and I left. And that was the end of my career with him. I wasn't a patient guy with people who were bullshitters. Tossing the mike up in the air, catching it in the back—what kind of bullshit is that? So I didn't see Lew for a while."

In 1951 Jimmy was working with just a pianist on 52nd Street in a small saloon, La Cava, where B. S. Pully, the comic in *Guys and Dolls*, had a separate after-hours act. Joe E. Lewis used to come in every night to hear Jimmy sing, still carrying the torch for his ex-wife, Martha Stewart. "I used to sing his favorite song: 'I got her off my hands, and now that she's off my hands, I can't get her off my mind . . .' He used to come in and say, 'Sing that song for me, Jimmy.' One night he gave me three hundred dollars; twenty every time I sang the song."

After his show, at 4 a.m., Jimmy would go across the street to Billy Hong's. "There was a guy, Fat Freddy, who used to come in there. He wore a bow tie and he wanted to be a singer. He wasn't too bright. Pully used to say, 'We have a big celebrity with us.' He used to bring him up onstage at La Cava. Then one night when we were at the restaurant, Pully felt sorry for the guy and called to him, 'Come on. Sit down and eat with us.' The guy picked up the menu, looked at it, and ordered the most expensive item on the menu: 'I'll have the filet mignon with the herbs.' Pully grabbed him: 'We eat grass and onions; you want to eat filet mignon with the herbs?' Pulled him right over the table. Then Fat Freddy went crazy. Threw the table upside down, like he went out of his mind. Pully got up and said to the other diners, 'Don't get excited, ladies and gentlemen. He's an actor; he's rehearsing for a play.' "

Soon after Jimmy ended the La Cava engagement in which he shared the spotlight with Pully, he received a long-distance call from him at the hotel where he was staying. "Jimmy, this is B.S. here," he said. "How ya doin'?"

"Everything's fine," Jimmy replied.

"Hey, pal," B.S. said, "I got a little bit of a problem. I need two thousand."

"What?" Jimmy said. "What?"

"I need two thousand," Pully repeated.

Jimmy clicked the receiver. "Operator! I got a bad connection on this line."

The hotel operator said, "I'm sorry, sir. You don't have a bad connection."

"You can hear the party?" Jimmy asked her.

"Yes," she said.

"Then you give him the two thousand," Jimmy said, and hung up.

Roselli got his first real break in 1954 when he appeared with an idol of his, Jimmy Durante, at the Latin Quarter in Boston. Durante was a mentor to many younger Italian entertainers who would learn from his lack of pretense, his warmth, and his powerful bond with his audience.

Unlike Roselli, Durante wore his heart on his sleeve. In the 1950s, his ability to mock himself and express deep emotion were qualities men did not display in public. (Durante was not only "funny-looking"; his personal life had an undercurrent of tragedy. His wife, Jeanne, the "Mrs. Calabash" of his sign-off song, "Goodnight, Goodnight," was an alcoholic who had to be tied into a straitjacket before going to sleep every night.) Durante was impressed by Roselli's talent, and when he learned of Jimmy's financial difficulties, he made sure that the young singer's salary was doubled, that he saved money by sharing a hotel room with Durante, and that he called home every day. Although they rarely saw each other after that, Durante remained a precious memory to Jimmy.

The Durante connection came about because of a wiseguy, and while in some instances Roselli was bitterly resentful of the mob's interference in his life, in this case he was grateful. "Trigger Mike Cappola was always good to me. He was one of the sweethearts. Beautiful man. He used to call me up every Sunday in Florida: 'Come on down and eat.' Used to cook for me. He loved me."

Trigger Mike of the Genovese crime family had been boss of the numbers racket in (Italian) East Harlem, where he met Roselli, who sometimes hung out there. According to Nicholas Gage, Cappola moved to Miami Beach "because New York had become a bit too hot for him." Roselli had gone to Florida with Angie in search of work. He went to see Trigger Mike and told him he needed a job. There was a big club in Miami Beach, the Patio. According to Roselli: "Mike said, 'Who's got the joint?' I said, 'The Blade' [Charlie (the Blade) Torine, a big 'mustache']. Mike said, 'Give me the phone.' Picked it up: boom boom boom. 'Hello, Charlie? Mike. I got my friend here, Jimmy Roselli. Give him five hundred a week.' Charlie said, 'He's got it.' All the wiseguys came there, Frankie the Knife from the pipefitters' union, all the high rollers, society people."

It was Trigger Mike who arranged for Roselli's engagement with Durante at the Latin Quarter. "Paid for the arrangements and everything," Roselli remembered. "Never said, 'I own you,' never, never gave me any problem. This guy put up his own money, and not only that, he went to George Woods [the booking agent] and said, 'I want this guy with Durante at the Latin Quarter.' It was a start for me. There were a couple of guys did me some good, never asked for a quarter. But for every Mikie Cappola, there were twenty shit-heels."

Not everyone shared Jimmy's high opinion of Trigger Mike. His nickname was not a matter of poetic license. Mike viciously

beat his wife, Ann, and "had a strong sadistic streak that included rather bizarre practices," as Nicholas Gage described
them in 1972:

> When Ann became pregnant, her husband insisted
> on calling in an underworld doctor, who performed
> an abortion on her while she lay on the kitchen table
> and Trigger Mike helped. She quickly realized that
> this was her husband's idea of a really good time. He
> assisted at four abortions in all, until, during the fifth
> pregnancy, she managed to fake a miscarriage, which
> was then treated at a hospital.[12]

Cappola's wife later committed suicide.

While Roselli was performing in Miami at the Beachcomber
lounge in April 1954, Frank Sinatra was appearing at the same
time in the Beachcomber's main room. Jimmy arranged to see
Sinatra rehearse, though he didn't want Sinatra to see him. "So
I went down, sat in the back, all by myself, brought nobody
with me. I watched this guy sing the whole rehearsal. He was
great at what he did. Ya know, he was great. It was a pleasure
to watch him."

There was an inevitability to Roselli's forming a relationship
with wiseguys like Trigger Mike. They were everywhere in show
business, and for a young, struggling Italian singer they could
open critical doors. And New Jersey, because the music scene
was so controlled by wiseguys, was their lucrative playground.

"A singer in that situation really did not have any choice at
all, if he wanted to play in the restaurants and the clubs," according to Robert Buccino, deputy chief investigator of the
New Jersey division of the Criminal Justice, Organized Crime,

and Racketeering Bureau since 1985, and before that a state trooper beginning in 1962. "All the Italian entertainers, in order to get ahead, had to deal with [the Mafia]. The restaurants, the bars, the clubs they would work in, all had some influence from the Cosa Nostra. So they buttered up to one another. It was both sides. For the Cosa Nostra, it was a badge of honor to be with entertainers and politicians. And the same with the entertainers: it was their moment of glory to be arm in arm with the Cosa Nostra—look at the old photographs of Sinatra with Carlo Gambino. That was a trophy kind of thing.

"Jimmy, like a lot of entertainers, was in awe of the style and glamour of the Cosa Nostra. They imitated it and tried to act like wiseguys. Jimmy was a frustrated bookmaker. He wanted to be a bookmaker probably more than he wanted to be a singer. But he broke [with the Mafia] because they took his money. As long as you're playing by their rules and they're earning off of you, you're okay. But once that doesn't happen— it's like a type of extortion scheme. What they do is find your weak spot. They prey on it; once you're on your knees and you're humble to them and need them, that's when everything goes according to their rules.

"Now, Sinatra was always there for them: if they asked him to do a charity, a casino, he did it. What really benefited him was that he showed loyalty to them. He never talked; he had opportunities to denounce them. Now, Jimmy would never talk, but he didn't play ball with them either. He wasn't totally loyal to them; he was more loyal to himself. I think [his attitude] was more greed than anything else . . ."

Buccino grew up in the same kind of environment as Roselli. Before he became a police officer, he hung out with the wiseguys and was involved in "small stuff" himself, not even realizing it was wrong. "Loan sharks were there. We used to borrow shylock money all the time like it was a muffin and shoot out to the Latin Quarter in Manhattan." The fathers in Buccino's neighborhood were either bookmakers, cops, or firemen. "When I was eighteen, I had a friend whose father was a bookmaker in the Ironbound section of Newark. He arranged for me and my pals to see Bobby Darin at the Copa. The Bruno family controlled the Ironbound section; the head of it was Tony Bananas.

"My friend said, 'All we have to do is go there and tell the maître d' that we're with Tony Bananas, and he'll take care of it.' Remember *Goodfellas* when the wiseguys were walking in through the back door? The guy walked us the same route as in the movie. We went right in, even though there was a line in front of us. The Copa stage was on the same floor as the tables. They actually put a table for us on what was the stage area. Now, when the show started, nobody got served drinks, except for us. And when Bobby Darin came out, he sees us, stops, dances across the floor, and says, 'Oh no, I know who these guys are.' He came right over to our table. We were treated like kings. That was the atmosphere in those days. The bottom line is that all those entertainers had no choice if they were going to do anything. So you can't say they're with organized crime. It was the nature of the beast. It was like any other industry: take the garbage industry. Not every garbageman is with organized crime, but certainly they all had to acquiesce to it during those days. Or they got killed."

The Cosa Nostra was then in its heyday in that region of New Jersey where Jimmy Roselli was raised. The five New York families—Genovese, Gambino, Lucchese, Bonnano, and Colombo—all nestled in the same area, working together during the 1950s and 1960s, when there was a strong, friendly relationship between the law enforcement community, politicians, and the mob. In addition, there was the Bruno family from Philadelphia and New Jersey's very own de Cavalcante family.

When he was going through his teens, Buccino was in awe of these mobsters. He would see Angelo (Gyp) De Carlo and his crew in the neighborhood. Gyp was a powerful capo of the Genovese crime family and New Jersey boss of Mafia loan sharking, gambling, and stolen securities operations. "Gyp got control of Jimmy Roselli soon after that," Buccino recalled. "Gyp was kinda husky, had a big nose. A homely guy, on the fat side. He was kind of laid-back, not a flamboyant guy like John Gotti. If you went into a bar you'd think he was your uncle. I saw him many times when I was a kid and I never saw him angry. People would show him respect, but he was never loud."

There was Anthony (Little Pussy) Russo, and all the wiseguys with their pink Cadillacs. During the holidays, the young Buccino would watch the police at traffic crossings. As Daniel (Red) Cecere, De Carlo's trusted soldier, drove around, the police officers would stand at attention as he pulled over at each stop and gave them an envelope. "I thought these guys were the greatest in the world," recalled Buccino. "We'd borrow shylock money from them and they didn't charge us interest because we were neighborhood kids. They were breaking us in; it was like a training program. They took care of you." The neighborhood was so wide open that the mobsters ran monte games in the basement of the local Catholic church. There would be an adult monte game and a monte game for the kids. It was a widespread phenomenon.

The wiseguys also ran the pinball machines. Red Cecere or Gyp De Carlo would come into the candy stores and put a bunch of nickels on the machines for the kids to play. The local kids looked up to them and regarded them as superstars. The wiseguys made sure they went to every wake when an Italian person passed away, and they put five dollars in the kitty. They politicked, and they were great at it. Everyone paid homage to them. If they wanted landscaping done, they just picked up the phone. There were stories about one of the soldiers calling an electrician to do some work on his house without financial compensation. A couple of days later one of the wires shorted out, and he called the electrician over and gave him a beating, saying, "You coulda burned down my house." Numbers men walked down the street calling out, "Number man, number man." In the 1960s there were over twenty crews of perhaps 160 to 200 made members operating in North Jersey alone. Today six to ten members remain in the same area.

"Everybody loved them," Buccino said, "but then I found out what they were really like. Jimmy Roselli? He learned. Because he wanted to be part of it. He was part of it. He got burnt by it. He realized their true colors. They didn't say to him, 'Okay, Jimmy, you don't wanna play, that's all right, you have a good voice, you're gonna make it.' No, it was 'You play ball with us, or you don't make it.' "

"As soon as they get wind of who you are and you happen to be Italian, they push themselves on you," recalled publicist Harriet Wasser. "They want to see you, meet me upstairs, meet me here, meet me there. And, of course, if you played the clubs, you got involved anyway. They just did it in a roundabout way. Every club imaginable had some kind of protection, I believe. In New York, it became the main topic of conversation: who their connections were and what kind of criminals they were involved with during their careers, after their careers. You can't avoid them [wiseguys]. Because they are your people.

"But it's funny," Wasser continued. "One guy used to say to me, 'There's no such thing as a Mafia.' But whenever somebody would get him upset, he'd always threaten them with his friends: 'They don't know who they're getting involved with when they get involved with me.' You don't even know if it's true. But the point is, they're ashamed and proud both at the same time. They deny it, but then when a situation comes up where they have to be tough, they're very proud of the fact that they are Italian and that they're connected. It's a real double thing."

It was at Leon and Eddie's, the jumping 52nd Street cabaret, that Roselli made his fateful connection to Gyp De Carlo in 1955. "When I sang on Sunday night at Leon and Eddie's, there was a guy there who worked for a big man known as Gyp the Collar. 'Come back next week and I'll introduce you to Gyp,' he said. That was the worst fucking thing that could have happened to me."

Gyp took a liking to Roselli, and Jimmy started doing odd jobs for him. De Carlo owned a large restaurant, the Mountainside, on Route 22 in Springfield, New Jersey, and Roselli would go up there to work.

Jimmy discovered one of his best songs through De Carlo. "Every wiseguy had a song that they loved. Every guy's song I did I later recorded. Because I thought they were good songs, not because I wanted to please them. Gyp's was 'I Lost All My Love for You.' We would ride in his car and he would sing this song to me. 'That's a good song,' I thought. 'Someday if I get the chance I'm going to record it.' They weren't tired songs that everybody did. That's really a great song. I did record it on my very first album. I loved it then and I still do."

The lyrics of the song, which was written by Harry Akst, Samuel Lewis, Joseph Young, and Al Piantadosi, may suggest why Gyp the Collar found it so captivating:

> *Revenge may be sweet*
> *After all I've been through,*
> *But why should I hurt you,*
> *What good would it do?*

Despite his budding singing career, Roselli took his marital responsibilities very seriously, and opened a luncheonette in Hoboken to support himself and Angie. Their daughter, Anne, was born October 10, 1957. On the day of her birth, Jimmy went running to the bar where his father worked, wanting to share his joy. Phil Roselli said laconically, "Babies are born every day." Jimmy replied, "What did I expect from you? If I didn't mean nothing to you, what could she mean to you? You're a piece of shit and that's all you'll ever be," and he turned and walked out.

Later, when Roselli sang professionally at the Stanley Theater in Jersey City, his father came to see him perform. "I said, 'I dedicate this song to my father sitting there.' And I sang, 'Daddy, You've Been a Mother to Me.' The lyrics went, 'Daddy, dear old daddy . . . way up above she can see. You were more than a dad, you're the best friend I had.' My father was crying, he got up and walked out. I was going to tell him, you got no guts."

In the period between Anne's birthday and the episode at the Stanley Theater, Jimmy's relationship with wiseguys began to intensify. "These greaseballs just adored this kid," said Al Certo, "because he spoke beautiful Italian. He liked to be around them, and they liked for him to be around them. That's how he learned how to cook, by cooking for them. And for Jimmy they were like having his grandfather around."

Jimmy had started the luncheonette, Mickey's, in 1956. He watched the wiseguys place bets on the phone in the back of his restaurant. Smoothly dressed, holding thick rolls of bills, they excited Jimmy's envy and curiosity. They were like a family, making jokes, kissing each other, having a good time, free and easy. They would put their arms paternally around Jimmy. He was comfortable with them, having known their likes from early childhood.

While some may have reminded him physically of his grand-father, they broke all the codes of morality and responsibility that his grandfather instilled in him. In reality, they bore closer resemblance to Jimmy's father, who abandoned him and lived his life outside any standard of morality.

While still running the luncheonette, Roselli signed a five-year contract with De Carlo in 1957, making him his manager. Gyp played a cat-and-mouse game with Roselli, keeping him on a string, getting him small jobs for a hundred dollars a week: not enough to live on. Roselli's independence and feistiness were a challenge to De Carlo, as they would be to other wiseguys. De Carlo wanted to break Jimmy down before building him up into a lucrative property. "Do me a favor," Roselli finally said. "Don't give me no more jobs. Forget about me. I'll get my own fucking jobs." Gyp responded, "You're a fucking prima donna. You'll never get anywhere."

"No," Roselli said, "not with you I'll never get anywhere. I'll wind up in a fucking cemetery with you."

"I'm gonna kill you someday, kid. I'll take a bat—"

"Big fucking deal," Roselli said. "What am I, a tough guy? You'll put me out of my misery."

Gyp continued to drop by Jimmy's luncheonette, taking his seat in the back. Other wiseguys would arrive with satchels of money from crap games. One would ask how much was in the bags. "How the fuck I know?" the other would respond. "It's spillin' over."

Jimmy overheard other bits of their conversations:

"Henry Bunion disappeared."

"How? Under water?"

"In concrete."

Then Gyp would try to reason with Jimmy—in his own way: "I see you breaking your balls here, it breaks my heart. You got more brains than all these guys. Why should they be makin' real money and you ain't?"

For all of Jimmy's tough talk, his career was drifting. He had had the luncheonette for three years, he worked hard, but he never made any money. He would leave at three, and then Angie's uncle came in, a horse player. "There was never any money," Jimmy recalled. "It disappeared."

He was still playing the joints and took jobs where he could find them. In 1959, still billed then as Mickey Roselli, he could be found at Derrig's Prevue Lounge in Cliffside Park, New Jersey. The advertisement for him included pictures of Jimmy with Jimmy Durante at the Latin Quarter and at the Beachcomber in Miami Beach when Betty Hutton visited him backstage.

That's when he started to hang out with wiseguy bookmakers. "I see them making all this money. One day I said to Lee Salomon [later Roselli's agent at William Morris], who was trying to put a bet in, 'You want to bet?' He said, 'Yes.' 'Give me the money,' I said. 'You got it.' I take the money and bring it to Gyp. That's how I started becoming a bookmaker."

Despite his disillusionment about doing business with the wiseguys, Roselli's experiences with Gyp were far from over. "He was a fucking sicko," Roselli says. "He once said they never shoulda killed this guy Willy the way they shot him; Gyp said they should have threw him off a fucking bridge in a car. What the fuck is the difference how you kill a guy? Come on. Fucking heartless cocksucker he was.

"He used to say, 'You'll never get nowhere. You gotta be a fag. You wanna be a fag, you'll be a big star.' 'No, I don't wanna be no fag.' 'Sex glands know no profession,' I used to tell Gyp. Oh, he used to get mad! He promised me he'd kill me. He used to want me to sing at his place in Springfield. They had banquets. I'd say, 'What the fuck, I'm gonna sing for the guys who come to collect the garbage or bring the linen to the joint? What are they gonna do for me?' He called me a prima donna again. 'If I'm gonna sing for somebody,' I told him, 'I'm gonna sing for somebody that's going to do something for me.'"

Soon after the break with Gyp in 1962, Roselli finally experienced some luck. His brother-in-law, Matthew Rega, came to his rescue and from his profits as a bookmaker financed Jimmy's first recording session at a cost of $5,000. "Matty bankrolled everything in those days," related composer and arranger George Siravo. "After rehearsals, Matty was counting out the bills, throwing them at the bartender. No matter where we went, it was always Matty, Matty, Matty."

But now Gyp wanted a new contract, to which Jimmy said it's all over, there's nothing left. Gyp was furious. He kept, Jimmy said, his photograph on the bottom of his toilet seat.

"Many times I didn't know if I was gonna get home, if I was gonna get killed on the way. Those were tough times: bob and weave and duck. You never knew when they're gonna get you. They follow you; they knew where you hung out. They could come at any time. A lot of these guys, when they had a few drinks, told me I almost got killed. What I can't figure is how I didn't. Why didn't they go to work on me? If not kill me, at least give me a fucking beating? They had all the assets. They didn't have to do it in broad daylight. They could get me in a fucking saloon, say somebody bumped into me."

In fact, after Jimmy broke from Gyp, Gyp sent a couple of goons down to South Jersey to go to work on him. One of them was Johnnie Di Gilio, whom Al Certo happened to grow up with. But when they saw Al too, "like a brother to Jimmy," they knew they couldn't lay a hand on Jimmy.

Years later, in 1965, Robert Buccino was selected from the task force formed by the state police to be the undercover gambling investigator in North Jersey. He had search warrants for

some ten locations, including De Carlo's. Buccino focused the
investigation on De Carlo and his crew, and attacked the gambling enterprises in Essex County under De Carlo's control. It
was called Operation Godfather. "The Hudson County Genovese crew was the one that was supposed to have the hook
on Jimmy Roselli," said Buccino. "The nucleus of their operation was in Hoboken, and John Di Gilio was the soldier in
charge of that crew. And he was under Bobby Manna."

As a result of Operation Godfather, in 1969 De Carlo was
put on trial in New Jersey on charges of extortion. The FBI
released some twenty-one thousand pages of recorded conversations De Carlo had had with other Mafiosi.

The tapes gave a clear picture of the extent of Mafia control
in New Jersey. One recording was a conversation between
De Carlo and one of his aides, Joseph (Little Joe) De Bene-
dictis, in which it was revealed that the mayor of Newark,
Hugh J. Addonizio, "helped us along. He gave us the city." A
year later, on July 22, 1970, Addonizio was sentenced to ten
years in prison on kickback conspiracy charges involving the
Mafia.

Other conversations revealed widespread Mafia collusion
with law enforcement authorities and politicians. In another
recording, Anthony (Little Pussy) Russo and De Carlo com-
plain that the head of the state police was demanding $1,000
a month from wiseguys to protect gambling in Long Branch,
another $1,000 for Asbury Park, and another $1,000 for the
county, a sum Capello wanted doubled during the summer
season.

The tapes also gave a chilling picture of life at a great stone
mansion owned by another Mafia boss with whom De Carlo
worked. Ruggiero (Richie the Boot) Boiardo, the reigning pa-
triarch of organized crime in New Jersey, lived on a wooded
plot of several acres in Livingston, New Jersey, known as "the

barn." The sprawling mansion was guarded by wrought-iron gates and stone pillars topped with bronze swans and was hidden from the road by trees and shrubbery.

Life magazine ran a spread about the house, calling its design "Transylvanian traditional," which was true in more ways than one. For in the rear of the estate, behind a greenhouse, was Richie the Boot's incinerator for human bodies, his very own private crematorium.

Several transcripts deal with De Carlo's murder of a victim identified only as "the Jew":

De Carlo: . . . I picked the Jew up in front of the Grotto [restaurant] in the afternoon. I ride him up, real nice, . . . take him up there, real nice, go through the door, I got the pistol, I walk in then—we're supposed to talk over a deal. . . . Johnny comes from behind the door, hits him on the head with a butt, the guy goes down, as he goes down, the kid drops his pistol. . . . I grab for the pistol, I get it just in time and then when I hit him, the kid grabs the pistol from Johnny, then Johnny hits him with a crowbar in the head and the kid hits him in the head. Now the guy is gettin' up again. As he's getting up, I hit him. I hit him and I picked him up; I got a chain and put it around his throat . . . lugged him and I put him in the garage. Threw him in the back of the car, his car . . . put him in the tank and then they were done with it.

D [unidentified]: What did you do? Start the fire right then?

De Carlo: Oh, everything was [set] . . . good hot fire—matches and everything, you know.

D: [He must have] burned like a bastard.

Other transcripts revealed the extent of De Carlo's involvement with Roselli. In one conversation between De Carlo and Richie Fusco that took place on April 4, 1961, Richie Fusco says that he "has an interest" in a singer named Manaro and that he persuaded comic Joey Bishop, when he was a substitute host on the Tonight Show, to have Manaro on the show. According to a summary passage within the transcript, De Carlo "identifies his [own] singer as Mickey Roselli and doubts that Manaro could sing as well as Roselli. He then played three of Roselli's records [by way of proof]."

In the same transcript, the informant "advised that for the past five years Ray [Gyp] De Carlo has had about $1,500 invested in the career of popular singer Mickey Roselli. Only recently [Roselli] has made what Ray believes may be a good record, 'You're in Love with Everyone.' " Roselli, according to this informant, originally aspired to be a bookmaker.

De Carlo was denounced by U.S. attorney Herbert J. Stern as a "brutal, sadistic" man who "would violate any laws." Convicted of extortion and conspiracy, he was sentenced to twelve years' imprisonment in 1969. He served nineteen months of the sentence. But after the intervention of Spiro Agnew, President Nixon, incredibly enough, commuted De Carlo's sentence on December 20, 1972.

Following these events, Stern again attempted to have De Carlo jailed, this time for failing to pay an outstanding $20,000 fine. U.S. marshals arrived at De Carlo's lavish home and threatened to break down the door. When they were admitted, they had to place an ailing De Carlo on a stretcher and deliver him to court.

Once in the courtroom, De Carlo began spitting up blood and was released. During this period he sent one of his goons to Roselli, pleading to see him.

"Gyp sent one of his boys, Augie, to find me," Jimmy said.

"Augie said Gyp wanted me to come and see him. He was dying. I said, 'Tell him to go fuck himself.' Just like that. 'The guy loves ya,' Augie said. 'Loves me?' I said. 'That kind of love I don't need.'"

Gyp died weeks later.

5

IGLOO BALLS

FRANK SINATRA AND JIMMY ROSELLI ENTERED THE 1960s from vastly different directions. Sinatra had suffered a catastrophic decline in the early 1950s. "People dropped him like a bomb in those days," Roselli recalled. News reports of his extramarital affairs, his volatile outbursts at the press, and his associations with mobsters (he was photographed with Lucky Luciano in 1947) had their effect on public opinion. The emergence of rock and roll had cut heavily into his record sales, and Columbia Records refused to renew his contract. In addition, he was dropped by his agent, the Music Corporation of America, his network, and his movie studio. The breakup of his short and highly publicized marriage to Ava Gardner had led him into bouts of deep depression, heavy drinking, and insomnia. Most critically, Sinatra was experiencing serious problems with his voice.

Yet by 1953 he was back on top again as a result of his Academy Award–winning performance in *From Here to Eter-*

nity. Mitch Miller, who had been his boss at Columbia Records, quipped, "By getting stomped to death in that movie, [it was like] he did a public penance for all [the wrongs he had done]. You can chart it. From the day that movie came out, his records began to sell." Sinatra was a *Time* cover story in 1955. From 1958 through 1966, he had twenty albums in the Top Ten. His 1959 album *Come Dance with Me* stayed on the charts for 140 weeks. Sinatra's Rat Pack image was fully formed by 1960; it was captured on film that year in *Ocean's Eleven* with Dean Martin, Sammy Davis, Jr., and Peter Lawford. At the same time Sinatra was burnishing his Presidential Buddy image as producer of President Kennedy's Inaugural Gala.

If the 1960s marked the apogee of Sinatra's fame, the start of the decade would see Roselli flirt with national fame as well. Despite his father, despite Gyp, Roselli had landed on his feet by 1963. He had a child he dearly loved, and his voice had been powerfully caught on the spellbinding records he made that year with the financial backing of his brother-in-law, Matty Rega—"Mala Femmena" and three other singles—and two albums in 1964: *Showcase: Jimmy Roselli* and *This Heart of Mine.* The two albums, independently released on Lenox/Ric, did not have the distribution or promotion a major label could give them, but they attracted attention, and "Mala Femmena" created a stir. He had been saved, not by the "family," but by a member of his real family, Matty, and his Hoboken pal Al Certo. And what truly kept him afloat was his transcendent talent.

"Jimmy believed, I think sincerely," said Bob Gans, Roselli's first manager and record producer, "that when he finally became close to being a star, he should have been that star twenty years ago. Like he's always been that, they're just seeing it now? What's the matter with these assholes? So therefore he was a little bit more brittle and a little bit more rigid than Sinatra. 'What's the matter with you jackasses out there? Don't you see the talent that I have?' "

Sinatra rose swiftly to the top. But while Jimmy admired Sinatra, he couldn't emulate him. He wouldn't trust the pros— the managers and agents—who could advise him, open doors for him, teach him, and provide access to the right places. Jimmy thought his native common sense was better than the advice of the smooth-talking, high-flown types who might very well screw him. And he did not want anyone to profit from his talent, even those who were working hard on his behalf, believed in him, and were advancing his career. When a composer who contributed significantly to Jimmy's growth and whom Jimmy admired asked him one day for a contract, some guarantee of financial security, Jimmy shook his head: "Not in my religion," he said. The composer, who felt betrayed, would not work with him again for years. As Jimmy put it, he had done things alone since he was a child, from the time he was crawling on the floor. If he trusted anyone, it would be the wiseguys, because they felt like family. Their betrayal only increased his bitterness and isolation.

A real source of joy for Jimmy in those years was his relationship with his young daughter, Anne. "My father and I were very, very close," she recalled. "I remember we were on 42nd Street and Broadway and they had these stores with the biggest stuffed animals. Dad would take me into the city three or four times a week; we were always together. Every time he said, 'Pick the one you want. Go on, sweetheart.' He'd find me the biggest ones and I could barely fit them in the car, and my room at home was full of them. I have so many good memories of him. I went everywhere with him. I was his little tchotchke, his little pal. When I was a little girl he took me on his lap onstage and sang 'Daddy's Little Girl' to me."

But Jimmy's marriage was in trouble. Anne recalled being about five years old and trying to get her parents to hold hands, begging them to be affectionate toward each other just while she was in the room. "I think they probably stayed together as long as they did because of me," she said. "My father's biggest claim is always that he wouldn't have ever gotten a divorce. It's that Italian thing: they want to have their cake and to eat it too. My mom was this sweet, docile little woman he could tell what to do. But in his defense, I can't remember my mother preparing a meal for him: my grandmother was the one who did that. She lived with us: a very strong woman, and they had a personality clash, as much as my grandmother adored my father. My mother was passive; she'd sit at the table and my grandmother would serve her. I wish the divorce had come about years before. I wouldn't have endured the years of pain. They fought when he didn't come home. She had emotional and physical problems; my dad was fat for years because he was eating his troubles away."

Despite a constricting home life, Jimmy's career was on the upswing. He had recorded his first singles in 1960, and from the start, Roselli utilized some of the most gifted arrangers in the business: Ralph Burns and George Siravo. His first singles for Lenox/Ric Records in 1960–63 included two obscure ballads, "I Can't Stop Crying" and "You're in Love," arranged by Siravo; swinging versions of the Smith-Wheeler-Snyder classic, "The Sheik of Araby," arranged by Siravo; and Frank Loesser's "Slow Boat to China," also arranged by Siravo. "Mala Femmena" was arranged by Ralph Burns, as were Marcy Klauber and Harry Stoddard's "I Get the Blues When It Rains" and Arthur Freed and Harry Warren's "This Heart of Mine."

Jimmy was not shy about letting the world know about these records either. Joe Farda, host of the *American Italian Music Hall* on WRTN-FM in the New York metropolitan area, remembered seeing Jimmy at 116th Street and First Avenue in Italian Harlem selling his records from the trunk of his car. "Oh, everybody knew him," Farda said. "Jimmy would be out on the street with the guys. He'd say, 'Hey, I got my record. C'mon, buy my record . . .' He was one of the guys, one of the young guys singing. You see, what made Jimmy was the guys love him, not only the girls. He's a man's man that sang; he was a tough guy. The last of the saloon singers: the others are too namby-pamby."

It was the single of "Mala Femmena" that put Jimmy on the charts. Roselli surfaced on *Billboard*'s "Hot 100 Singles—Bubbling Under" chart with "Mala Femmena" at number 135 on August 10, 1963. The record captured Roselli's very clean sound, which was not unlike that of the classic Neapolitan singers. His phrasing was impeccable, his pitch exceptional, and his mastery of the song revealed a startling passion.

What gave Ralph Burns's arrangement such appeal was the constant pulsation of the beat and the bolero against the legato line that Roselli was singing. Scott Harlan commented, "You get the sense of somebody smiling as he says (and I'm inventing here; I don't understand Italian), 'Kill him; he hurt my child.' The first part of the record is backphrased; then it goes completely on top of the beat. In the tradition of the classical singers, he is phrasing it with the lyric and not with the musical line. Roselli's is consistently right in the middle of every note, intonation-wise."

The song also demonstrated Jimmy's incredible breath control as he sang eight-measure lines. "You have to know what you're doing," averred Harlan. "He could be singing *Pagliacci*. He could be singing in Italian opera houses in Rome. It's that good an instrument. It's a huge, extraordinary voice. And so passionate."

Roselli's first album, *Showcase: Jimmy Roselli*, was produced by Bob Gans and released by Lenox/Ric in 1964. It included his singles as well as "Her Eyes Shone Like Diamonds," "I Wish You Love," and several other songs which Roselli sings with aching clarity to this day: Tannen-Hickey's "It Takes But a Moment (to Fall in Love)" and "The Way You Look To-night."

The background research Roselli did for "Mala Femmena," for "Passione" (which was originally sung by Caruso), and for his other Neapolitan classics began in the late 1950s. Jimmy used to frequent a store on Mulberry Street called the Italian Book Company. The couple who owned it, Frank Tudisco and his wife, were Neapolitans. Roselli asked for their help in pronunciation and the phrasing of lyrics. They gave him records from Italy with the melodies he was searching for. He learned the classics, what Jimmy calls the "stardust" of the Italian catalogue.

Jimmy would sit on the floor night and day with a tape recorder, listening to different lyrics and melodies, different pronunciations. The Neapolitan songs were difficult, "like operas," he said. If he couldn't get them right, he would rather not do them. One time he heard an Italian song recorded by Dean Martin. "He didn't really sing the lyric at all," Roselli remarked. "He was double-talking. I had to pinch myself. As for 'Mala Femmena,' [it] hit me the first time I heard it. The man who wrote it was a Neapolitan, Toto, the most famous Italian comic. Like Fernandel in France. And when I recorded it, it hit like you wouldn't believe. A lot of Italian singers learned songs phonetically. I was brought up a Neapolitan. To sing Neapolitan songs, you have to be a Neapolitan."

And you have to rehearse. Billy Dennison, who began working with Jimmy in 1961 and remains his musical conductor to this day, summed up the routine. "He'd outline around thirty-five songs. He'd break them down and at showtime it would be about twenty. That would take an hour or so. Out of the huge repertoire, he had a lot to choose from. I showed him the previous show's lineup of twenty songs, and he'd pick about fifteen to seventeen alternates. During the rehearsal we'd try three or four alternates. By the end of the rehearsal, which took every bit of four hours, he'd say, 'Okay, here's the lineup.' So then, on the spot, I had to make sure the men were straight on what we're gonna play that night. We always started out with so much more than we ended up with."

In the beginning, there were only ten men in the band: a six-man front consisting of four trombones; then, on the side of the bass trombone, the baritone sax, which also had to double on the flute and clarinet. On the other end, there would be a trumpet player who would also play flügelhorn. As Jimmy got more popular, said Dennison, "we added banks of strings. A typical arrangement would be four violins, a viola, and a cello. So that would be six."

Roselli's first recordings benefited from the creative efforts of Burns (who initially arranged most of his Italian-language records) and composer and arranger George Siravo. According to Will Friedwald in his book *Sinatra! The Song Is You*, Siravo was "perhaps the most underrated of Sinatra's collaborators." Siravo had produced the groundbreaking 1950 Sinatra album for Columbia, *Swing and Dance with Frank Sinatra*, and had worked closely with Tony Bennett.

"Jimmy knew that I knew the business and had entree into record companies," Siravo recalled. "I broke my ass to get a guy to listen to him; his name was Bob Gans. We eventually formed a record company, Ad Lib Records [the original name, later Lenox/Ric Records], and one of the first guys we recorded was Roselli in 1964."

Gans remembered taking George Siravo out to Elizabeth, New Jersey, to see Jimmy for the first time at a club. "The place was what Roselli frequently described as a sewer. I was very impressed. The guy was talented and he sang beautifully. He had a sense of humor too that got to me. Some of his banter was funny; he was kind of Runyonesque. A natural.

"I changed his name from Mickey. I thought that was too juvenile, like Mickey Mouse or Mickey Rooney. At that point I think he would have gone with anything I suggested. He was very, very willing to please. He needed something to make that leap. I was the vehicle. And that 'something' turned out to be 'Mala Femmena,' which would go like wildfire."

For Gans, Roselli's uniqueness had much to do with his ability to communicate with an audience—as an actor and comedian—that hadn't really been tapped because of Roselli's unease with the professional world. "I think Jimmy had a way of reaching an audience that had never been done before," Gans explained. "So much of his persona could have been developed beyond what it was in those years, had I had a little more time with him. There were so many untapped things about him. He needed direction.

"I think that beneath whatever layers Jimmy puts over his soul and his feelings," Gans related, "he really is a sentimental, feeling human being. If he weren't, I don't think his message would be a genuine one. And I think the true Italian, especially the older generation, would see through it."

Despite Roselli's growing popularity as a nightclub performer, his was not always a polished act. In the beginning, he had a lot to learn. "He was terrible as a showman," said George Siravo unequivocally. "He didn't know what to do with his arms, his hands. But Rosie (that's what I called him) was born with this emotion that he had in him. He gave the people a sense that this guy is clumsy, and you start to feel sorry for him—you look for a way to get out of the place, you're so uncomfortable. You gotta get in there where the performer is so relaxed and you're enjoying it.

"I would put blocks of thoughts into Rosie's head and give him confidence. He was never overly confident. I think a shrink would say that's why he comes out with being overly aggressive—to hide his insufficiencies."

Driving across the George Washington Bridge one night into New Jersey, the lights of Manhattan in the distance, Siravo turned to Roselli. "I just got an idea," he said.

" 'What's that?' Jimmy replied.

"I said, 'Your personality is shit.'

"He starts stuttering. 'Explain that,' he finally says.

"I said, 'What you gotta learn is how to become the boss.'

"He says, 'How the fuck am I gonna do that?'

" 'Easy,' I said.

"He said, 'Well, explain it to me.'

"I said, 'You see those lights out there, thousands and thousands of lights. You see them, right?'

"He said, 'Yeah, I see them.'

"I said, 'What you've got to begin to realize now is how to acquire poise. How to get out there and act. Just think that God created every one of those lights as disciples, and that he sent them down here to listen to you sing.' They were there for him. *For him!* That was how important he should feel about it. You gotta be impressed that if God did this for you, it's gotta give you confidence. It's gotta make you feel like somebody put eight million dollars in your bank account. The size of your balls gotta get like the size of igloos, that big.

"All of a sudden he put his arm down and rested his hand on his thigh. It sunk in. He's quick to pick things up that he was unknowledgeable about. Right after that he learned how to be a performer."

It was Bob Gans who suggested that Roselli record some Italian songs, even though everyone else counseled against it. "When he sang that stuff," said Gans, "I saw people in little clubs in Little Italy with tears in their eyes, with expressions on their faces like God was in the middle of the room. They didn't just applaud and scream, they stood on tables. I mean, this was his *soul*."

But it was not an auspicious time for a singer like Roselli to break through, and recording 'Mala Femmena' in 1963 was a risk for two reasons: it was in Italian, and it ran over three minutes, which made it undesirable for radio play.

Gans agreed to let Jimmy include it on his album, "for your birthday," and Roselli's recording of the song went on to sell a million copies. But Roselli was entering a decade of musical, cultural, and political changes that would irretrievably alter the vocabulary and taste of an entire industry. Only a Sinatra, with his professional zeal, versatility, and single-minded ambition— and a stunning musical sound abetted by the brilliant Nelson Riddle that captured the swinging spirit of the times—could come back and tower over a business whose traditional foundations were crumbling. He had the capacity to reinvent himself. Following his Oscar in 1954 for best supporting actor, Sinatra built a legacy of seven seminal albums with Riddle in the 1950s that were masterpieces: *Songs for Young Lovers* (1953), *Swing Easy* (1954), *In the Wee Small Hours* (1955), *Songs for Swingin' Lovers!* (1955–56), *Close to You* (1956), *A Swingin' Affair* (1956), and *Only the Lonely* (1956). Will Friedwald characterizes these albums as "the greatest extended works in all of popular music."

Italian singers of the 1950s were among the most popular performers on the scene, especially ballad singers. Music critic Arnold Shaw pointed out in 1952 that their musical arrangements were characterized by an "undercurrent of swirling strings, woollen woodwinds, and light rhythm," whereas mainstream pop was "a pasta of Neapolitan bel canto and pseudo-operatic singing." Those he had in mind included Sinatra,

Dean Martin, Tony Bennett, Mario Lanza, Jerry Vale, Perry Como, Vic Damone, Frankie Laine, Al Martino, Lou Monte, Toni Arden, Connie Francis, Julius LaRosa, and Alan Dale.

Jimmy assumed the spirit of the 1950s would go on forever and began to record albums that harked back to that era. But the signs of erosion were all around him, and almost overnight it would all be gone.

Jimmy's paternal grandfather,
Michael Roselli, age fifty, 1929

*Jimmy's mother, Anna Lavella Roselli,
age eighteen, 1925*

*Jimmy's father, Philip
Roselli (right)*

Jimmy Roselli, age four, 1930.
"He was the apple of my father's eye," said Jimmy's Aunt Etts

Jimmy, age five, with his half sister, Joan, 1931

Jimmy delivering telegrams in Hoboken, age eleven, 1937

Jimmy's First Holy Communion, age seven, 1933

Jimmy (left) with friends in Hoboken, age twelve, 1938. By this time, says Jimmy, "I got the shine box and used to sneak into the saloons at night . . . I started singing regular in saloons"

Jimmy winning the Major Bowes' Original Amateur Hour *radio show contest, age thirteen, 1939, for singing "Pocketful of Dreams." Major Bowes rewarded him with forty cents*

Jimmy at Camp Rucker, Alabama, age eighteen, 1944.
Jimmy served in Company E, 266th Infantry, 66th Division

An early publicity shot of Jimmy Roselli, age twenty-one, 1947

6

STRANGER IN A STRANGE LAND

ROCK AND ROLL WAS A MUSICAL AMALGAM THAT COM-
prised many strains of American music: rhythm and blues,
country and western, gospel, jazz, folk, and swing. Its strong
sexual overtones (in the black community "rock and roll" had
been a common term for both dancing and sexual intercourse)
made rock highly suspect to the parents of the white teenagers
who were rapidly falling under its spell.

Frank Sinatra joined the chorus of disapproval in an over-
heated attack in 1957. With a covert swipe at his chief rival,
Elvis Presley, Sinatra said of rock and roll:

> It is sung, played and written for the most part by
> cretinous goons and by means of its almost imbecilic
> reiterations and sly, lewd, in fact plain dirty—lyrics
> . . . it manages to be the martial music of every side-
> burned delinquent on the face of the earth.

Others clearly felt differently. Critic Jeff Greenfield described listening to the music as an adolescent in the late 1950s: "Each night, sprawled on my bed on Manhattan's Upper West Side, I would listen to the world that [disc jockey] Alan Freed created. To a twelve- or thirteen-year-old, it was a world of unbearable sexuality and celebration: a world of citizens under sixteen in a constant state of joy or sweet sorrow. . . . New to sexual sensations, driven by the impulses that every new adolescent generation knows, we were the first to have a music rooted in uncoated sexuality."

In 1954, "Sh-Boom," a rock-and-roll song recorded by both a black group, the Chords, and a white one, the Crew Cuts, became the fifth-best-selling song of the year and the first rock-and-roll hit. In 1955, twelve of the year's top fifty hits were rock-and-roll songs. That was when Bill Haley and the Comets' "Rock Around the Clock," which was featured in the teen film *Blackboard Jungle*, went to the top of the charts and sold some fifteen million copies by the late 1960s, becoming one of the best-selling single records of all time. Rock and roll was here to stay.

Rock and roll was more than a change of musical direction: it signaled a youth rebellion against the sexual and social status quo that would affect sexual behavior as well as race relations. From 1956 to 1960 black artists such as Chuck Berry, Ray Charles, Little Richard, Little Willie John, Fats Domino, the Platters, and Sam Cooke rose to fame and fortune. White singers, most notably Elvis, borrowed black styles and utilized them to catapult themselves into the ranks of the new icons. And the white rock-and-roll singers, like Presley, Jerry Lee Lewis, Buddy Holly, and Pat Boone, were popular, sometimes far more popular than the original black artists. Presley rose to instant fame after the release of his 1956 record "Heartbreak Hotel" and his appearance on *The Ed Sullivan Show*, where his swaying hips and tremolo voice sent his teenage audience into a frenzy. His blend of rhythm and blues, rockabilly, and country-and-western music led to fourteen consecutive gold records from 1956 to 1968.

Record sales soared. With the success of the new music, annual revenues climbed from $219 million in 1953 to $277 million in 1955, reaching a staggering $600 million in 1960. The transformation taking place was cultural, social, and po- litical, but it was economic as well: the baby boomers had enor- mous buying power. America even had a new image in the presidency, with such a "young," glamorous President as John F. Kennedy.

For a while, the older music survived side by side. In 1954, Sinatra, then at the height of his powers, was declared top male singer by *Billboard*, most popular vocalist by *Downbeat*, and singer of the year by *Metronome*.

Nevertheless, by 1955 the ballad singers were already begin- ning to lose their hold on the public. "In 1955 it changed," Tony Bennett said. "[The record companies] started going for this obsolescence idea. They didn't want records that would last, they didn't want lasting artists, they wanted lots of [con- secutive] artists. It became like a supermarket: Go with the next, the next. So they started discarding people like me and Duke Ellington and Leonard Bernstein. The marketing boys took over. It took a big step away from melodic music. It sud- denly became very professional to be unprofessional. Which was very neurotic."

At issue was the value of enduring art. As Carmen McRae put it to jazz critic Leonard Feather in 1965: "It's a shame that so many good records today of good old standard tunes done by really fine artists are bypassed for things like 'Sh-Boom.' I don't think it takes any talent at all to sing 'Sh-Boom,' but it takes talent to sing things by Cole Porter and Gershwin and

Rodgers and Hart. The people today are on a different trend, and I guess there's nothing you can do but just bat your brains out. But I think any of us who delve into standards, or good original tunes, should stick by our guns."

Alas, the composers of many of the most popular standards were themselves beginning to pass away, and the New York they once celebrated was now heading into decline. Oscar Hammerstein II died in 1960, Cole Porter in 1964. The lights were going out on Broadway, while Times Square became a haven for pornography, burlesque shows, and prostitution; the New Amsterdam Theater, home of the Ziegfeld Follies, was long shuttered, dark and abandoned; the Automats, once eating palaces for the working class with slogans like "Less Work for Mother," were desolate.

Record companies, artists, composers, and musicians gradually moved to the West Coast, where Tin Pan Alley regrouped on Sunset Boulevard. But as Bob Dylan would soon sing prophetically in a little club called the Gaslight in New York City's Greenwich Village: "The Times They Are A-Changin'." As Neil Gabler wrote of Walter Winchell, quoting a press agent's comment to the *Daily News*: "It wasn't so much that [Winchell] finally quit. The world he lived in and helped shape quit on him." In a sense, the same could be said of Jimmy Roselli.

The changes in popular music were twofold, remarked Gerald Early in *One Nation Under a Groove*: "First, a movement away from the Tin Pan Alley–type popular songs of the Berlin-Gershwin-Arlen ilk to a music that was more obviously and overtly influenced by, and openly mimicked, black Rhythm and Blues; second, a shift away from middle-aged or mature-sounding Italian male singers as kings of the popular roost toward white southerners, adolescent Jewish songwriters, and blacks as the trendsetters in popular music, a major ethnic shift that had a profound impact on the culture at large." Irving

Berlin, one of Roselli's favorite songwriters, was out. Elvis, Bill Haley, Roy Orbison, Chubby Checker, and Little Richard were in.

Within a few years, the impact of rhythm and blues had totally transformed American popular music, and Tin Pan Alley was displaced as the music center of the universe. According to Gerald Mast in *Can't Help Singin': The American Musical on Stage and Screen,* rock and country-and-western songs deliberately reverted to archaic eight- and sixteen-bar forms, "suggesting the aspiration to sincerity, purity and 'naturalness' by rejecting the urban and urbane song structure of white European immigrants."

Roselli's second album, *This Heart of Mine,* which he produced himself for Lenox/Ric in 1964, reprised some of the material from his first album (including "Mala Femmena" and "The Sheik of Araby") and contained some of the new singles he had recorded since then: "A Beggar in Love," Ciervo-Delle and Grotte-Baratta's "Statte Vicino Amme," and one of his Neapolitan masterpieces by Bovio, Valenti, and Tagliaferri, "Passione." "Passione" is very operatic; this could be Puccini in the street. Roselli uses a lot of vocal tricks that come from classical opera: trills and glissandos, in which he slides from one note to another.

Also in the mix was a haunting version of "I Lost All My Love for You," the song with which Gyp the Collar had serenaded Jimmy in his car. Even though the song is about the tantalizing possibilities of revenge, Roselli is so at home with it, so comfortable, easy, and nonthreatening, that if the listener didn't pay attention to the words, one would think it was a warm love song. Right before the line about revenge, in a transition from the bridge to the chorus, Roselli holds a very bluesy note—although it's a B natural—for a long time, so perfectly pitched it's like a dart hitting a bull's-eye.

A third album produced by Roselli, *Life and Love Italian Style*, was also issued by Lenox/Ric Records in 1964. Once again, Ralph Burns was arranger and conductor, this time of a forty-man orchestra. Roselli's first fully Italian-language album, it surged beyond language barriers with powerhouse renditions by Roselli of standards like "O Sole Mio" ("There's No Tomorrow"), by Al Hoffman, Leo Corday, and Leon Carr, and "Oh Marie," by Vincenzo Russo and Eduardo di Capua-Casa. Not even Louis Prima's orgasmic version of "Oh Marie" transcends Roselli's jaunty and swinging interpretation. The album featured two of his greatest recordings: the passionate love song "Anema e Core" ("Soul and Heart") by D'Esposito, Manilo, Curis, and Akst, as well as the superlative "Just Say I Love Her" ("Dicitencello Vuie") by Kalmanoff, Falvo, Dale, Ward, and Val.

These were superb albums, but the times were not auspicious, for in 1964 came the Beatles, and "the musical world," remarked Stan Martin, who was with radio station WNEW-AM in the 1960s, "was never the same again."

The Beatles had nineteen singles in the Top Forty of 1964. The next year Roselli had his hit with "There Must Be a Way." But by then some of the major singers, including Johnny Hartman, Steve Lawrence and Eydie Gormé, Kay Starr, Della Reese, and Dakota Staton among many others, no longer had major-label contracts. The only Italian on the Top Forty was the young Dion. This did not make the veteran Italian balladeers extinct: they still had their major niches and they still sold records. But it was a new world.

Bob Taylor, who was a programmer at WNEW-AM when the music industry was undergoing these seismic shifts, noted that "good singers like Steve Lawrence and Vic Damone weren't becoming big like Sinatra and Nat 'King' Cole, and not because of lack of voice. Music just changed."

An African-American, Taylor believes that Roselli was vic-
timized in a way by his times. "When WNEW meant something [the 1950s and 1960s], we'd take the labels off the records
when they came into the station. We didn't want to know who
the composer or the artist was. And a group of us would just
be sitting in the office listening for a certain sound. So we
became pretty attuned to what sound we wanted. There could
be a brand-new singer, it didn't matter who, but we got that
sound we wanted. I got it from the first record Carmen McRae
made, 'In Love in Vain.' I listened and said, 'Whoa, this is
something.' We had a show called *The Music Hall* and we
played the record. The switchboard just lit up. Just a simple
ballad delivered with this saloon intimacy.

"When I first heard Jimmy, I said, 'Oh, this guy has a sound.'
I could just sit down and have a sip of Jack Daniel's and I could
hear that guy singing away. One of the first songs I heard was
his version of Irving Berlin's 'When I Lost You.' You tell me
if that isn't going to reach in and grab you right between your
rib cage. That's Roselli.

"I really think Roselli could have been one of the greatest
saloon singers of all time. He has that mood, he has that feeling
of a song. And you kind of think he's singing right to *you*,
which is such an important thing for a performer. Even on a
record.

"But WNEW had managers who were ratings-conscious as
opposed to the tradition of the station. And they were trying
to get a piece of the new action. Jimmy was a victim of that.
He came along at a bad time. Earlier he would have had a
much broader impact: he would have been right up there."

Jerry Vale, another Italian-American singer who recorded
"Mala Femmena" and achieved considerable recognition in the
late 1950s, quipped: "Unless you were a young kid with a lot
of hair, they really didn't pay much attention to you. We had

our fans, don't misunderstand me. But it was a matter of timing. Jimmy Roselli came on the scene even after I did. If it had been earlier he might be a lot bigger. It's a shame; he deserved to be bigger. It certainly wasn't due to a lack of talent. I love Jimmy. He's a great singer.

"But I had more hit records than Jimmy, records that were popular all over the country. Jimmy wasn't that lucky. Right up until today, I go to Jimmy's rehearsals to hear him sing 'Mala Femmena.' I wait until he sings it and I leave. My day is complete, I'll see you later. I just want to hear him sing it."

Despite a cultural sea change, some of the traditional ballad singers were continuing to break through. Sinatra, Dean Martin, and Sammy Davis, Jr., were not suffering—nor were Louis Prima or Bobby Darin. "Keep in mind," Bob Taylor recalled, "Tony Bennett came out in the 1950s and made it, and he's one of the finest singers of all time. And he's still going." In August 1964, Dean Martin's "Everybody Loves Somebody Sometime" managed to bump the Beatles' "A Hard Day's Night" off the number one spot on the charts and was the biggest hit in America. In 1964, Martin also had two albums on the Top Twenty charts; one of the two, *Everybody Loves Somebody*, reached number two and stayed on the charts for forty-nine weeks. And it was on just that turf that Roselli was contending. It would be difficult, but if he could learn the ropes, acquire poise and confidence onstage, and soften the edges of his volatile personality, he had a shot. His phrasing could not match Sinatra's, but he had a rich, warm lyric tenor voice, superb articulation, and a vast range. As composer Sammy Cahn told *The Wall Street Journal*: "[Roselli] has a larger, richer voice than Frank. He's a miracle." Tony Bennett lacked Roselli's range, but he had a far more flexible, adventurous, and open personality than Roselli. If Roselli came out

of a tradition of Neapolitan singers, in Bennett's gravelly singing voice you can literally hear, as Whitney Balliett has pointed
out, the Manhattan streets.

But there is an emotional forthrightness and simplicity to
Bennett's phrasing that bears some resemblance to Roselli's,
although Roselli's passion was rawer, more unrestrained,
whereas Bennett's was usually a model of affability, even pol-
itesse. George Siravo recalled, "Tony Bennett could say, 'I'm
going to kill you,' and have a smile on his face. Tony was dating
a girl in those days who everybody thought was a high-class
hooker from Sherman Oaks. I used to call her Coke Bottles
because she used to hit Tony on the head with them. I don't
think he had the balls to chase her off. As beautiful as she was,
she was as cold as ice. What he took from that broad! If it were
Roselli, never mind. A year later, even a minute later, she'd
have had the bottle in her skull. Hey, the guy is a man.

"Tony didn't have that blood and guts that Rosie [Roselli]
had. The hunger he had. The hunger is what does it. That's
the catalyst of desire. Of wanting something so bad."

With the success of "Mala Femmena," Roselli was hot. "I
had just gotten a book written with arrangements for ten men:
four trombones, one trumpet, one saxophone, and four rhythm.
So wherever I was going to go to work, they only had to pay
for the ten musicians," Jimmy figured.

Roselli's success bred success, and one of his lifetime dreams
soon came true: in 1965 he was signed up by a major label,
United Artists Records (UA). In a news story entitled "UA
Inks Jimmy Roselli, Lena Horne . . . ," *Variety* wrote on March
24, 1965: "Jimmy Roselli, the virtually unknown singer who
scored at the boxoffice during his recent stand at the Copacabana, N.Y., has been signed to a longterm deal by United
Artists Records. Roselli, who is a popular figure in the Italian

colony around the metropolitan area, has already been signed by the Copa for additional appearances over the next five years while Ed Sullivan wrapped him up for three guest shots."

In 1965 and 1966 there was still a major battery of nightclubs remaining in Manhattan. In addition to the Copa and the Latin Quarter, leading clubs included Basin Street East, El Morocco, the Five Spot, the Americana Hotel, the Plaza, the Waldorf-Astoria, La Chansonette, the Playboy Club, the Rainbow Grill, the Riverboat, the Village Gate, and the Village Vanguard.

Before the Copa engagement, Roselli had begun to headline at bigger clubs around the Italian communities in Brooklyn and Long Island, but he had yet to break into Manhattan. He was tremendously popular in Bensonhurst, Bay Ridge, and Carroll Gardens, as well as Mineola, Rockaway, Massapequa, and Westbury, where he headlined at the Westbury Music Fair. In Westchester he starred at the Westchester County Center and the Westchester Premiere Theater. As always, the wiseguys were there, waiting impatiently outside, even starting fights with one another.

"I played the San Su San nightclub on Long Island," Roselli recalled with pride. "They were throwing punches outside to get in. It seated seven hundred people. Then I wound up at the Boulevard on Queens Boulevard, which seated about eleven hundred." Roselli began to earn as much as $30,000 a week at these venues, as well as at the Club Bene and the Garden State Arts Center in New Jersey. His success in these personal appearances showed that his gift differed from that of Sinatra, Bennett, or Vic Damone; he was not abandoning Italian. And the music's soulfulness transcended language barriers. Roselli was cornering a market; at the same time, he had the potential for crossover appeal.

Mala Femmena, Roselli's first big-time album, which he produced for United Artists in 1965 with arrangements by Ralph
Burns, was a reissue of his 1964 *This Heart of Mine.* The cover
of the album showed an ebullient Jimmy in a tux, leaning backward, hitting the climactic notes of a song, arms outspread,
embracing the music and the world. In its review of standout
LPs on May 5, 1965, *Variety* wrote: "Jimmy Roselli, the young
singer of Italian background who packed the Copacabana,
N.Y., during his recent stand there even though unknown out
of neighborhood circles, impresses on this disk as a savvy performer. He exploits his powerful pipes in operatic style on the
title tune and a couple of other straight Italian numbers. But
he displays a lilting pop technique on ballads like 'I've Lost All
My Love for You,' 'On a Slow Boat to China' and 'The Way
You Look Tonight.' " Roselli soon followed this with his second album for UA, a reissue of *Life and Love Italian Style.*

Roselli had found a specific niche, not only in his Neapolitan
repertoire but also in his choices of American songs. Many of
them were old even when he heard them as a boy in the saloons
where he shined shoes. Contemporary ballad singers like Sinatra rarely sang them. They were a far cry from the more
complicated and subtle melodies and lyrics favored by Sinatra:
the Cole Porter, Jerome Kern, and Rodgers and Hart creations.

Roselli preferred Irving Berlin, Harry Warren, Harold Arlen, Buddy DeSylva, Lew Brown and Ray Henderson, and
Sammy Cahn. More often, his choices were the "saloon songs"
of the Gay Nineties, not the darker, brooding ballads of Sinatra
and company. More than a few stemmed from 1912: "My Gal
Sal," "When I Lost You," and composer Ernie Burnett's "My
Melancholy Baby." "My Gal Sal" was the most famous song
written by Theodore Dreiser's brother, song plugger/composer
Paul Dresser. The waltz "When I Lost You" was a ballad of

lost love written by Irving Berlin in 1912 when his twenty-year-old bride of two weeks, Dorothy Goetz, died of typhoid after their honeymoon in Cuba.

These were the types of songs he chose for his first *Saloon Songs* album, which he also produced in 1965, an album bursting with joy and gusto. "Jimmy knew those songs like he knew his own name," said George Siravo, who arranged and conducted the album. Roselli conjures up a vanished world in these songs. Rather than being out of date, the songs are full of life in Roselli's renditions, and he never camps them up: "Daddy's Little Girl," "That Old Gang of Mine," "Ace in the Hole," "If I Had My Way," "Maybe" (one of his great recordings), "Daddy, You've Been a Mother to Me," "Who's Sorry Now," and Irving Berlin's "When I Lost You" and "I'm Sorry I Made You Cry," among them. The album cover, which includes an encomium from comic Joe E. Lewis, features Jimmy seated on a barstool against a darkened background, his collar open. He looks downward, one hand extended, one hand holding a microphone, in a somber, contemplative mood.

Even when Roselli moved toward more contemporary music (although he infrequently ventures outside the post–Tin Pan Alley era), he would shy away from the familiar and come up with ballads that were out of the ordinary, from "A Million Dreams Ago" and Phil Badner's "Come Into My Life" to his friend Sol Parker's "It's Been Swell" and "It Doesn't Hurt to Say You're Sorry."

Another single, "When Your Old Wedding Ring Was New," arranged by George Siravo, was Roselli's masterpiece in English. It was a success in 1966, and later on Jimmy's 1967 album, *Saloon Songs, Vol. 2*. Astoundingly, it would hit the charts again in England in the late 1980s and early 1990s when it was rereleased. The entire first half of the song was sotto voce, with Jimmy holding his vowels as long as possible. In the second half, with its rising crescendo, the approach was one of tonal purity; Jimmy kept to the true middle of the tone, with a classical use of the vowel line. Here Roselli projected a loose, off-the-cuff, street-singer kind of style, and there was something for everyone in it.

His sense of intonation, like Streisand's, was intuitive, a gift he used to hit the middle of the pitch in a very powerful way. In this, he differed greatly from Sinatra, who would backphrase a song like "Wedding Ring." Roselli was right on the beat every time. It was a phrasing choice. Sinatra, who didn't like holding vowels, was a master of backphrasing, a looser, improvisational, conversational style in which the singer takes the note, plays with it, and pushes the lyrics over into the next measure.

The lyrics of "When Your Old Wedding Ring Was New" (written by Bert Douglas, Charles McCarthy, and Joseph Solieri) tell something about the world Roselli embraces in his music:

> *When your old wedding ring was new*
> *And each dream that I dreamed came true*
> *I remember with pride, how we stood side by side*
> *What a beautiful picture you made as my bride*
> *Even though silver crowns your hair*
> *I can still see the gold ringlets there*
> *Love's old flame is the same*
> *As the day I changed your name*
> *When your old wedding ring was new.*

The song encapsulates Roselli's view of the world, one with firm boundaries. Romance and fidelity, the sanctity of love and marriage, the enduring nature of passion: these were the old sentimental truths that the 1960s ripped apart.

Another Roselli favorite, "If I Had You," by Ted Shapiro, Jimmy Campbell, and Reginald Connelly, went:

> *I could show the world how to smile*
> *I could be glad, all of the while*
> *I could change the grey skies to blue*
> *If I had you.*
> *I could leave the old days behind*
> *Leave all my pals, I'd never mind*
> *I could start my life all anew*
> *If I had you.*
> *I could climb the snow-capped mountains*
> *Sail the mighty ocean wide*
> *I could cross the burning desert*
> *If I had you by my side. . . .*

One can imagine a bow-tied young man, perhaps Mickey Rooney, in a white suit, poised on one knee in the Peoria moonlight, an apple tree overhead, the sounds of crickets and wind chimes and scent of roses and honeysuckle, as he proposes to a young lady (Judy Garland?). It's a vision of turn-of-the-century America before Hemingway's Nick Adams has returned from the trenches of World War I to question the reality he has known, before the Holocaust, before the debacles of Vietnam and Cambodia.

Roselli would never stray from that vision.

Musically, "Roselli's just got a very, very pure sound," Scott Harlan noted. "When he finally gets wherever he's going in any musical phrase, it's in an amazingly beautiful place—elegant, with clarity, a kind of simplicity in terms of being true to the music, whether he's singing full-out classical lines or sotto voce, soft voice. I'm talking about an enormous versatility. He can sing on the beat; he can sing off the beat; he can phrase with the lyric; he can phrase with the musical line. He can sing dark, he can sing focused, he can sing legit, he can sing sotto voce and off the voice. It's like many different instruments wrapped into one, and his choices are very carefully controlled. It's not just showing off."

As singers—not performers—there are parallels, noted Harlan, between Roselli and Roselli's lifelong idol, Al Jolson. "The similarity between them," Harlan explained, "is in the pureness in the lyric line, the phrasing, and in the directness. Roselli is not phrasing anything musically in these ballads. He's thinking about what he's saying. The words are more important than the musical line. That's the difference between the ballads and his Neapolitan songs, where he's thinking about the vowels and the music. He's got the capability to do both."

With all his talent, Jimmy's choice of such dated material reflected his own beliefs and priorities, but it could not have been very helpful in building his career as a recording star. The public would rarely be able to look to him for new material. His tastes in music were old-fashioned, and so were the values he lived by. Unlike Sinatra, that lovable "Pal Joey" heel—hip, cavalier, capricious, and cruel—Roselli was not really of the era, and his behavior reflected it.

"When I was struggling," he recalled, "I used to go in a joint called Trenchy's on City Island. Trenchy always treated me real good, always treated me nice early on in my career. Then I started moving up with 'Mala Femmena.'

"Trenchy never gave me a tab when I went in there. One time I went in with four people and asked for the tab. No check. This is after I became a would-be star. So I said to him, 'I want to come in here and do a show for you for a week. I don't want no money, but you gotta pay the orchestra.' I was drinking that night and I was pretty drunk, unusual for me. I went home. In the morning the phone rang. It was Trenchy.

He said, 'You were feeling pretty good last night.' I said, 'I remember what I said. You go ahead and advertise the shows for a week, you pay the band and that's it.' I said to him, 'You didn't even ask me. I asked to do this.' And I did it."

Roselli continued: "Then Trenchy made an announcement on the floor that I'm gonna follow Jerry Vale. He got all excited on the floor. People called out, 'I want a table for ten,' 'I want a table for twenty.' When I appeared there, you couldn't get near the place, it was mobbed. At the end of the run Trenchy took me in the back. He wanted to give me five thousand. I said, 'I don't want it. I told you I wanted to do this for you and I did it.' Thank you very much, buh buh buh, he paid the band, and that was the end of the story. He always treated me good, Trenchy."

But the price of his measure of success was discovering the hypocrisy of some former friends.

In 1963, when Jimmy started making records, everything started to pop, people started coming back. Jimmy recalled the situation: "I told them what I thought of them fucking pieces of shit. Just like that. When I gotta say something, I say it. I give my heart open, wide open. But when I gotta tell you something, you'll know it. You won't get it from her, from him, you'll get it right from me." To this day Roselli remains deeply hurt at the way fame and recognition work: the ambivalence of fans who both love him and sometimes try to consume him.

With the success of his records and performances at major clubs, Roselli's popularity surged in 1965—and with no one more than the wiseguys. And while they professed to love him, their moods could change overnight. There was always an element of danger, even in the friendliest of times. "We were working the San Su San on Long Island again in 1965," said Skinny Skelly, Roselli's chauffeur and assistant at the time. "Jimmy finds a thirty-eight in my drawer in the bathroom. He says, 'Hey, what the fuck is going on here?' I said, 'Put it down. It's loaded.'

"Jimmy asked me, 'You know how to handle it?' I said, 'Yeah, I know how to handle it.' Jimmy said, 'What are you doing with it anyway? You gonna give me a lotta fucking trouble with this?' "

Skinny Skelly looked at Jimmy and said, "Roselli, you know all these fucking wiseguys that come to your dressing room? They want to knock the fucking door down. I can't control them. They see this little thing in my hip, they're gonna think twice. I'm not carrying it for your protection. I'm a small guy. I'm doing it for me."

Skinny Skelly explained, "Because once a couple of guys came into the dressing room and I said, 'Jimmy can't see you right now. Who are you anyway?' They tried to shove me down the stairs. I got my jacket off and said, 'Take it easy, pal, what are you pushing for?' As the guy talks to me, he sees the gun. I said, 'You want to push me down the steps? That ain't nice.' He says, 'I'm sorry.' I said, 'There's nobody pushing me.'

"So this is what I told Roselli that day. He said, 'Okay, but hey, if you get caught with it—' I said to him, 'Don't worry; there's a hundred guys out there, they're all carrying fucking cannons.' These guys always had their guns. 'What's the big deal?' I said. 'You got seven hundred people in the audience. I bet you a hundred guys are carrying guns.' He threw a look at me. 'You son of a bitch,' he said. He laughed and just walked away."

It was not just the lower-level wiseguys who took an interest in Roselli. The godfathers themselves had begun to notice him and even follow him. In addition to Larry Gallo, Carmine Galante, Sam Giancana, Joseph Colombo, and Carlo Gambino became avid fans.

From 1965 through 1968 Roselli released one outstanding

album after the other: *Right From the Heart* (1965), *Mala Femmena* (1965), *Saloon Songs, Vol. 1* (1965), *There Must Be a Way* (1966), *New York: My Port of Call* (1966, later retitled *Lullaby of Broadway*), *Sold Out: Carnegie Hall Concert* (1966), *Life and Love Italian Style* (1966), *Saloon Songs, Vol. 2* (1967), *The Italian Album* (1967), *The Great Ones* (1967, later retitled *Rock-A-Bye Your Baby*), *Core Spezzato* (1968), and *The Christmas Album* (1968). In 1967 he recorded "Who Can Say?" for the soundtrack of the film *Africa Addio,* and in 1969 the title song for the soundtrack of the film *Buona Sera, Mrs. Campbell,* starring Gina Lollobrigida.

As Roselli moved up, he continued to act as if he were living in an encircled tent, in a permanent state of volatility, and he was. He still could not help surrounding himself with his old pals from the neighborhood and wiseguy wannabes and hangers-on even though he could not trust them. He seemed to be more comfortable with them *because* he could not trust them: it was what he was familiar with. To him, professional and show business types were "phonies" who spoke in a coded language; wiseguys and pals from the old neighborhood were "real people." And they liked him because they could freeload off him—but also because he was talented, quick-witted, funny, and tough, which was the way they saw themselves.

Following a performance, Roselli would have a few drinks to come off his high and to relax. He never lost his fast wit. One night after a concert, exhausted, he was driving home and fell asleep. His Cadillac hit a tree. A police car appeared right behind him.

Jimmy got out of the car as the policeman was coming up to him. He turned to the cop and shouted, "What took you so long?"

"What?" the cop said.

"Did you see that guy cut right in front of me and swerve? Why don't you go get him? He made me go into this tree!"

The policeman looked at Jimmy. "Let me see your license," he said.

Jimmy handed him the license. The cop looked up. "You're the singer."

"Didn't you see that guy?" Jimmy repeated.

"No, I didn't see any guy. Jimmy, how's your car?"

"I can drive it. Ya know."

Jimmy drove off, merrily waving.

As a result of that incident, however, he never drove when he was high. One of his Hoboken pals would drive him home. He'd hole up in the back of the car with a bottle of brandy. But with these kinds of pals, you had to protect yourself. "I'd get in my car," he reminisced, "put my hands in my jacket on my money to protect it while I slept; ya know, some of the guys around me, they'd rob your pockets."

Yet to Jimmy they were still family.

7

MAKING IT

IN RETROSPECT, ROSELLI AT LEAST PLAYS UP HIS "DE-fiance" of the wiseguys. But in reality he was in the wiseguys' grip in those years. And having freed himself from his entanglement with Gyp De Carlo, Roselli dove in again. It began with a chance meeting. "I was walking in Harlem," he remembered, "and I saw this big wiseguy, Buckalo. I waved hello. We talked, and it started all over again. I used to hang out in that neighborhood [East 116th Street, First Avenue, and Pleasant Avenue] looking to get a little work. I met the crew. I believed these guys were really gonna help me. I put myself in my own trap. I accepted their help, so now I was obligated."

Buckalo, whose real name was Anthony Ferra, ran the East Harlem Mafiosi. He held out two glittering prizes for Roselli: bookings at the Copacabana, the top nightclub venue for singers in the country, and Carnegie Hall, America's most prestigious concert hall. They were the opportunities of a life-time.

As always, Roselli wanted the prize, but he didn't want to pay the price: financial and psychological subjugation. And unlike some singers who faced the same dilemma, Roselli did not have the inner flexibility to maneuver his way through the maze. Over and over again, he reenacted the scenario of his youth, hoping the outcome would finally be different, hungry for the love his father never gave him, sensing, nonetheless, that he would be betrayed.

"They dangled the Copa in front of his eyes," said Pete Cavallo. "Like with any aspiring singer, you show him a big nightspot like that, it's hard to resist. And whatever you say about these guys, they did open up his career there."

Just as this was happening, the Italian branch of the Chicago Patrolmen's Benevolent Association flew Roselli out to sing at a benefit in Chicago at the Edgewater Beach Hotel on Lake Michigan. "This was my very first appearance in Chicago," Jimmy related. "I told them I wanted forty musicians, a certain set of speakers. I said if they're not there, I won't sing, so don't give me a hard time. 'No problem.'

"I got off the plane, they come to pick me up at the airport. I said to the captain, 'Somebody gave me a horse in Vegas. Do me a favor, I want to put two hundred on him.' He said, 'You can't bet horses here.' I said, 'Are you kiddin', the fucking cradle of gangsterism? Who you bullshitting?' I told the cop, just like that. I said, 'Get away from me, don't even talk to me while I'm here.'

"Now I get to the hotel. I hear the sound system. I said, 'Listen to me: I don't want no problems. I'm going upstairs. I'm gonna take a shower, lay down for half an hour, whatever. When I come down, if you don't have this sound system with the speakers I asked for, I'm getting on the next plane.' They said, 'The stores are closed, it's Sunday.' 'Break in the joints,' I said. 'I don't care what you do.'

"They got the speakers. At the start of the show, they put guns to my head. 'You cocksucker,' they said, 'you broke our balls. You better sing like you never sung before.' I said, 'You got everything I asked for. Just sit down and relax. Enjoy the show.'

"I enter the auditorium. They were waiting for me. I didn't sing a note; I got an ovation for ten minutes. Ten minutes they stood and applauded. I got on the mike and said, 'Jesus, if I knew it was gonna be like this, I'd of gotten here sooner.' I did an hour and a half. They wouldn't let me off."

Roselli's big break, the Copa, came later in 1965. He was thirty-nine. This was the event that marked his entry into the big time. Like so many of his triumphs, this one, too, would be bittersweet.

The Copacabana, which had been created by gangster Frank Costello, was more than a "big nightspot." It was one of the most famous nightclubs in the world. Named for the resort hotel in Rio de Janeiro, the 700-seat club had a star roster that included the biggest names in show business: Frank Sinatra, Martin and Lewis, Sammy Davis, Jr., Lena Horne, Sophie Tucker, Bobby Darin, and Ted Lewis among them. The Copa's legendary chorus line, called the Copacabana Girls, wore their hair upswept and dyed it orange, purple, pink, and green to match their sequined outfits. On occasion they also wore mink brassieres and panties and fruited turbans.

The Copa had been run since its inception in 1940 by Jules Podell, a former bootlegger with a police record, who originally fronted for Costello. The club had been investigated in 1944 by Mayor La Guardia for its ties to Costello. The investigation sought to prove that "there were known racketeers or gangsters frequenting the Copacabana," not to mention "persons interested or part owners who are disreputable persons engaged in unlawful enterprise." Costello was subpoenaed at his home, but refused to testify on the grounds he had not been summoned in good faith. The Copa, while admitting to no relationship with Costello, eventually agreed to "terminate and sever" any connection that Costello may have had with the club.

Lee Salomon, one of Roselli's two William Morris agents, described not long before he died in 1995 how Roselli's first engagement at the Copacabana in 1965 came about: "Julie [Jules Podell] says one night, 'I gotta use this guy in Jersey named Jimmy Roselli. See what's he like.' For me to go out on a Saturday night is like Hitler attending a Seder. It's a fucking blizzard that night. There's not a car going across the bridge. Finally I reach the place, the Chateau Pelham. Not a soul on the street. And I walk in. And there's three thousand people sitting at banquet tables.

"I couldn't believe it. All the husbands are there, the wives with the buns, the gold teeth. They sit me down at a table with Buckalo. A comic comes up. Did his whole act in Italian. I'm so fucking bored. Then somebody says, 'Jimmy Roselli.' This is not Rock Hudson, okay? Nice-looking guy—on a scale of one to ten, maybe a six and a half or a seven. By the time he got through, he was an eleven. I'm not saying Jimmy was homely. But he got so good-looking. And one song after another, not a fucking word in English. He hit notes the last time I heard was Mario Lanza. He keeps getting standing ovations. And as he sings, Buckalo put his arm around me and says, 'Let me translate: The donkey goes over the hill to take a shit. Suddenly a beautiful girl appears. . . . The barber can't find his razor in time to cut the throat of the guy who's fucking his wife. It's sad. But he finds a way.'

"Each time Jimmy finished a song, Buckalo stood up. Three thousand people stood up. Buckalo sat down. So three thousand people sat down. Everybody was looking at Jimmy with adoration. And the guy keeps getting better-looking and better-looking. I told Podell he was fucking great."

Roselli had his debut at the Copacabana on February 25, 1965. Sammy Davis, Jr., introduced him. Busloads of people came from around the country, lining the streets outside the club for blocks. "The table captains came over to me and said, 'We never made so much money in our lives with Sinatra, Martin and Lewis, Sammy Davis,'" recalled Salomon. "Every wiseguy was there, the bottles, the booze; it was like—unbelievable. And he absolutely killed them. Killed them. Everybody was talking about Roselli now."

Louie the Fireman, a younger Hoboken friend of Jimmy's, was at the opening: "I seen him when I was seventeen years old. I'd never heard of him. My older brother said if your girlfriend is Italian (she was) you will really want to hear this singer at the Copa. You will never hear a man sing songs the way this man sings them. When we got there, there was a line all the way down Madison Avenue, all the way up 60th Street. The lights dim. All of a sudden ten violinists stand up and play. Spotlights are jumping all over. A blue light hits this man, whom I've never seen. He started singing 'Mala Femmena.' Every girl in the place, including mine, was standing on the tables trying to see this man. I've never seen this happen before or since. It was something that gave me goose bumps and went right through me."

Two weeks later, on March 10, *Variety* headlined its front-page story "Roselli's Unique Show Biz Impact":

> Jimmy Roselli, a virtual unknown outside of the Italian colony on Long Island and Brooklyn, until he came into the Copacabana, New York, two weeks ago, has done the biggest business at the Jules Podell

spot since the recent engagement of Sammy Davis, Jr. . . . Roselli's business boxoffice is regarded as the miracle of the current nitery season. . . . Granted that Roselli was supported largely by the Italian residents of the area, it's likely that his b.o. [box office] pull will transcend [*sic*] other nationality groups the next time around. . . . Another benefit accruing to Roselli was a contract for three firm shows on the *Ed Sullivan Show* with options for an additional three. Sullivan came to the Copa Saturday night and sent him a mash note which he urged the singer to read from the floor. . . .

Apparently, there's plenty of loot behind Roselli. At the Copa he brought in his own nucleus of musicians and his own conductor. . . . His salary at the Copa wasn't revealed, but one insider indicated that he had to spend more on musicians than his own salary called for. . . . According to one spokesman at the William Morris Agency, Roselli has no formal manager, but has friends aiding and advising him. . . . Another indication of the lengths that were gone into to make the Roselli engagement successful is the outside advertising that was done by the singer or his management. There was a full-page ad in a recent issue of the *Illustrated News* . . . and there is a huge neon sign on upper First Avenue spelling out Roselli's Copa stint.

Variety's writer could not know that the advertising, including the neon signs (which were on both the East and West Sides of Manhattan), had all been purchased (as had the musicians and the arrangements they were working with) by Roselli himself.

Billboard wrote that Roselli "showed warmth, determination, knowhow and one of the richest voices to come along in a long time. He captivated the audience. Backed by a band the likes of which the Copa has never seen, Roselli had everything going for him. . . ."

Nick Lapole of the *New York Journal-American* added, "It's always exciting to be in on the birth of a new star and last night, at Jules Podell's Copacabana, a cheering audience . . . gave singer Jimmy Roselli a standing ovation as he concluded his premiere appearance on Manhattan's big time. . . . Last night, Mr. Podell gave him his chance for stardom and Jimmy made good in a big way. . . . You're going to hear more and more of Jimmy Roselli."

Down front at every show—and there were three a night— were the wiseguys, including the "biggest of the big," the godfathers. No one adored Jimmy more than they. First of all, he was Italian and sang the Neapolitan classics the way no one else could. In addition they had taken Roselli's version of the 1929 chestnut "Little Pal" (written by Al Jolson, Lew Born, Buddy DeSylva, and Ray Henderson) to their hearts. This treacly song brought tears to their eyes. They sang it to their young sons and wanted Jimmy to sing it at their grown sons' weddings. Carmine (the Snake) Persico told Jimmy he had "bawled like a funny boy" at the song. It was easy to see why: in the song, the narrator is about to go off to prison and tells his son he wants him to take care of his mother, be a good man, and accomplish the things for which the father has never had time. Jimmy made the wiseguys weep as he sang:

> *Little Pal, if Daddy goes away*
> *Promise you'll be good from day to day*
> *Do as Mommy says and never sin*
> *Just be the man your daddy might have been*

Your daddy didn't have an easy start
So here's one wish that's dearest in my heart:
What I couldn't be, Little Pal
I want you to be, Little Pal
I want you to sing, be happy and gay
Be good to your mommy while your daddy's away. . . .
And if someday, you should be on a new daddy's knee
Think about me, just now and then,
Little Pal.

Sam (Momo) Giancana, kingpin of the Chicago mob, came to Jimmy's dressing room after a show and said, "I heard you was a prick. The way you sing you got a right to be a prick." When Jimmy admired Giancana's wristwatch, Giancana took it off and handed it to him.

A frequent visitor to the Copa was Carlo Gambino, an old man who physically reminded Jimmy of his beloved grandfather. One day during the engagement, Gambino sent a chauffeured limousine for Jimmy, and Jimmy and Pete Cavallo were driven to the don's home in Massapequa, Long Island. Gambino served them dinner and they reminisced about the old country.

"We went to Carlo's house. Now we're there with the boss of bosses," recalled Pete Cavallo. "This man was in his seventies, he's sitting in his rocking chair. You thought, you're at your grandfather's house. His wife did the cooking, not the maids. It was a feast. And he was so warm. As far as what he did, and whatever killings and all that, we don't know. It's all hearsay. But he had his *gumba* who lived next door with his wife. And he made a typical Italian dinner—started off with the antipasto, and the pasta, with all the meat, and then the fresh ham, then all the celery, the olives, the cake with the cheese, the Italian espresso. I *loved* it there. He took us down to his wine cellar. He loved Jimmy. Not at any time did he give an appearance of being a wiseguy. You see, the bigger they were, the nicer they were. All I know is that the man was a perfect gentleman."

"Wherever I worked from then on," Jimmy said, "Carlo was there. He would come backstage. He couldn't make the steps to my dressing room. He would say, 'Just tell Jimmy I said hello. Don't bother him. He's tired.' He was a good man. One time I was in a restaurant and he was in the back. I didn't know it, so he sent one of his guys to get me and we went in the back. He said, 'Whatsamatta, you don't want to sit with me?' I says, 'I didn't even know you were here, Carlo. I'd love to sit with you.' 'Sit down and have dinner with me.' Then I sit and bullshit with him, crack in Italian. He used to fall on the floor, he got a kick out of my Neapolitan dialect. He had a great sense of humor. He never tried to control. He said to me, 'If you want to sing, you sing; if you don't wanna, you don't have to sing for anybody.'"

"Now three months later, we had a subpoena," recounted Cavallo. "About Carlo. And the thing is, they want to catch you in a lie. They say, 'Were you ever in his house?' They want you to say no. They don't know you're aware they're taking movies.

"We say, 'Yeah,' we both say, 'Yeah.' We both went on the stand differently. That's why [Jimmy] kept calling his lawyer in. Me, I didn't have to call a lawyer. I sez look, I'm [Jimmy's] manager. All I know is the man comes to see us. He's a perfect gentleman, he's a big man, he couldn't be nicer. I had the perfect answer. 'Don't you know—' they said. I said, 'Look, I told you I only believe five percent of what I read and hear. I don't know what you say, I know nothing. All I know was the man was a perfect gentleman, like other fans . . .'"

Carlo Gambino was hardly alone among Mafia dons in his

admiration for Roselli. "This guy [Jimmy] had godfather after godfather," said Tony (Skinny Skelly) Petrazelli. "Gambino. Carmine Galante loved him. Carmine Persico. Sam Giancana. They all loved him. But there are a lot of guys don't talk with Roselli. Sometimes this guy reminds me of Sinatra. Personally, they're both arrogant. I know. I've cut his hair, put the wig on him, took care of him like he was a baby.

"Whatever happened was like, to Jimmy, 'I don't need them, fuck them.' He had, like, an attitude. Buckalo, forget about Buckalo. You talk about Buckalo—Buckalo's a sweetheart of a guy. I thought Buckalo was going to put him away a couple of times. That whole crew, I thought they were going to put him away.

"We used to pal out in Amen's Bar in the Bronx. And there were a group of people, big people, all right? Buckalo asked him to do a wedding, some wiseguy's daughter. Roselli said he couldn't do it, his pianist was away. Later on, Buckalo was a little pissed and he said to me, 'Tony, is this kid actually trying to tell me he can't—' I said, 'Buck, I don't know what to tell ya. I can't talk against him. I'm with him.'

"I said to Roselli, 'How come you refuse this guy?' He says, 'Oh, fuck them. I don't need them.' Come on, if it wasn't for these guys, where would he go? Where would he be? So you go there, so you do a tune! He could have named any price he wanted. If he really wanted the money, you understand? Look, if you think any singer can get anywhere without the help of these people . . . They could make you or break you anytime they want. But he was just a lucky guy, and he is to this day. He can knock people. His attitude hasn't changed.

"But when a time came when somebody would say, 'Let's do away with this rotten son of a bitch,' this godfather or that godfather would jump in: 'Oh no, nobody touches Roselli.' He was always protected."

Skinny Skelly ruefully recalled the time he was losing money "gambling, gambling, gambling, and shooting crap. I was going berserk, and Jimmy knew it. He liked to play the horses but he was just a lucky guy; he never lost."

Needing $1,000 to pay off a loan shark, Skelly approached Roselli. "Ya gotta help me out, pal," he pleaded. "I'm in fucking trouble. I owe Amiel a G note, or he's gonna break my fucking legs."

Roselli looked at him and replied, "Do me a favor: go see him. Let him kill ya. You're no fucking good. I told you before: When it comes to your family, I'll do everything I can for you. But you're a sick son of a bitch. You'll bet on anything. You come to me looking for money for that, I got no pity for you."

Skelly said, "All right, ya prick ya," and walked away.

Later that day Jimmy called Skelly and told him to pick him up with the car and make reservations for fourteen people at the House of Chan, a Manhattan restaurant. "At the restaurant," Skelly said, "there's music, record people, everybody's having a good time except me. Roselli says, 'Get the check.' It's for $1,200. He takes the money from a roll of bills.

"Now we're heading back to Jersey. He's feeling good. He says, 'What's the matter, what's on your fucking mind?' I said, 'You know. Let me tell you something,' I sez, 'you creepy son of a bitch. These fucking people at the restaurant, you don't even know them. And you're a fucking big shot, $1,200. And here I am, your buddy's all fouled up, I'm jammed up, and you tell me let them kill me, you rat bastard.' He said, 'I told you, Tony, when it comes to gambling I'm not gonna help you out.'

"Now we get through the Lincoln Tunnel, there's an underpass there. I'm so fucking disgusted, this cocksucker, I'd like to rob him, I thought, the way I feel right now. All of a sudden I put on the brake and put the car in neutral. He said, 'What are you doing?' I said, 'Look, I've had it with you.' I get out of the car, get on the sidewalk, and I start walkin' away.

"Roselli's lookin', I'm wavin'. He's behind the wheel. You ever see a guy when he's trying to make a broad from a car? It looked like a guy going after a broad. There he is driving alongside me: 'Come on, Tony. Cut the shit, take me home.' I said, 'I gotta borrow some money, get out of here. I gotta see some people.' He says, 'What do ya want me to do, have an accident?' I say, 'Ya fucking bum, I hope you hit a bridge.' I picked up a stone. 'If you don't get the fuck out of here, I'm gonna hit you with this.' He drove home, I seen him go over the bridge."

Jimmy's brutal rejection of Skelly drove the two men apart for a time, but their zigzagging relationship would continue over the years. As long as Roselli was the one with a career and access to large sums of money, he held the reins over those who were basically hangers-on. But they resented it, and they quickly disappeared when things did not go well for him.

Skinny Skelly's complaints about Roselli's lack of gratitude toward the wiseguys also have a certain narrow truth. The mob made you or destroyed you. Roselli's engagements at the Copacabana and Carnegie Hall made him a prime contender for stardom, or even superstardom. Yet he felt the mob did nothing for him but rob him.

Sinatra, for one, understood when it was time to show the wiseguys some appreciation—whether his actions were voluntary or not. His performances at the 500 Club in Atlantic City are a case in point. The venue was one of the major nightclubs in the country from the 1940s through the 1970s. It was built by Marco Reginelli, a Mafia underboss from Philadelphia. Reginelli's successor, Angelo Bruno, chose Paul (Skinny) D'Amato to front the club for him much as Julie Podell fronted the Copacabana. Bruno was particularly fond of D'Amato, who had served time in Lewisburg Penitentiary for white slavery. The club featured the biggest names in show business, including Jimmy Durante, Joe E. Lewis, Sophie Tucker, Dean Martin and Jerry Lewis—and Jimmy Roselli. It also was known for prostitution and gambling. In his book about the Mafia in Atlantic City, *The Boardwalk Jungle*, Ovid Demaris wrote that Sinatra appeared at the club for five engagements over a period of a half dozen years in the 1960s. "What is amazing about Sinatra's appearances at the 500," Demaris remarked, "is that he performed free of charge, doing as many as four shows a night. Skinny D'Amato says that it was because Frank loved him 'like a brother,' but then Skinny seemed to feel that way about everybody he knew."

If Roselli refused to play up to the wiseguys as Sinatra did, he had company in Dean Martin, who actually defied Sam Giancana. In *Dino*, his biography of Dean Martin, Nick Tosches documents Martin's refusal of Giancana's demand in 1962 for a "command performance" at the Villa Venice, Giancana's secretly owned roadhouse club located northwest of Chicago. This led to an angry conversation between Sam Giancana and Johnny Formosa, a henchman who served as Giancana's emissary between Chicago and the West Coast. Giancana, furious that Martin had defied him, now demanded a free performance by Sinatra, Martin, and Sammy Davis, Jr. "Let's show 'em," Formosa said to Giancana. "Let's show those asshole Hollywood fruitcakes that they can't get away with it as if nothing's happened. Let's hit Sinatra. Or I could whack out a couple of those other guys, [Peter] Lawford and that Martin, and I could take the nigger and put his other eye out." Giancana replied, "No, I got other plans for them." And he did. Sinatra, Martin, and Sammy Davis, Jr., performed gratis on November 26, 1962, at the Villa Venice. Sinatra told the FBI he was performing as a favor for the club's owner of record, Leo Olsen.

Roselli's stubbornness had become as well known as his physical stamina during the Copa years. Carmine the Peddler, one of Roselli's drivers during this time, said simply: "The guy's an animal. He wouldn't let you sleep. You'd get home seven or eight in the morning after driving him to his house, and this guy's calling you at ten o'clock. I mean the sheets weren't even getting warm.

"As for drinking, he would start with a beer, anisette, brandy. Never got sick, not even a headache. Only one time he got drunk, and he was heavy then, about two hundred ten pounds. I had to put him on my shoulder and carry him. I take him up the steps to his house. I'm ringing the doorbell and his wife came out. When I started to put him down, I lost my balance and he fell and hit his head up against the railing."

Carmine recalled: "One time he got sick at the Copa. Laryngitis. He couldn't talk at all. Julie Podell suggested this little Jewish doctor. The doctor looks down Jimmy's throat and says, 'What vocal cords you have! Best I've ever seen, bar nobody. I seen Frank, Dean, Sammy. Yours are just wonderful.' The doctor said to lie down and relax. The show went on. Jimmy came out; he sings first from the back. Chandeliers were shaking; that's how powerful he was that night. Chills; you could see the hair stick up. Standing ovations, maybe fifteen minutes. The man was sick, he came out strong like that. He's an animal; he really is.

"I had to deal with the women too," Carmine remembered. "Those who wanted to meet him had to come to me first: 'Oh, please, I'll do anything . . . let me touch him, kiss him . . .' But Jimmy would turn his back to that stuff."

Another neighborhood guy whom Roselli employed during the Copa years was his valet, Gennarine. "He couldn't read or write," Jimmy remembered. "Joe Colombo had given me a pair of cuff links with diamonds in them. I took 'em off and said to Gennarine, 'Hold these.' I'm all wet in the elevator, I'm taking my shirt off. I got to my room, I get in the shower, then I put a terry-cloth robe on. Then I get dressed for the next show. I put a clean shirt on, and ask Gennarine for my cuff links. He gives me one, he can't find the other one. I said, 'Look, before I blow my top and start screaming and lose my voice, do me a favor, get out of my sight.' As he opens the door to leave, my friend Hank is coming in. Gennarine says to him, 'What's he mad about? I only lost one cuff link.'

"Another time he walks into the hotel lobby and he's stopped by a guard. 'It's okay. I'm Jimmy Roselli's ballet,' he says. I was always surrounded by rocket scientists."

The Copa engagement may have been prestigious, but financially Roselli was losing badly under the Buckalo contract. "They told me I had to work in the Copa. Not only that; they didn't give me any money. That fucking job used to cost me money. Seven years! Everybody made money, the waiters, the captains. Everybody but me. I said, 'When you [wise-guys] come to me with a job, don't come with a bat in your hand, browbeat me, hit me on the fucking head. You gotta talk to me and say this is the place that wants you; how much do you want? Not what they want to give me, what I want!' "

Jimmy received only $1,250 a week at the Copa, a mere fraction of what he would have earned otherwise. He had to shell out thousands for musical arrangements alone. But he did understand the value of the exposure the Copacabana engagements were giving him; he also purchased (in addition to the neon signs) billboard signs all over the city advertising his appearance. Still, once again Roselli eventually wanted out of the contract and told Buckalo so.

"Nobody had put up any money for me, like they did for Tony Bennett for his first album. They had a *right* to have a piece of the guy. That's why nobody ever bothered me; because I didn't owe nobody nothing. I didn't make them put up ten, twenty thousand, then try to run away."

Whatever the conflicts, 1965 continued to be a ground-breaking year for Roselli. On August 13, he began another major engagement at the 500 Club in Atlantic City. *Variety* (August 18, 1965) noted: "Roselli, who has a big and powerful voice, is out front for 40 minutes doing 14 numbers. They range from Italian songs through a variety of pop standards." In December, Jimmy was back at the Copacabana for a return engagement. In its review on December 15, 1965, *Variety* wrote:

> Jules Podell has embarked on a program of better relations with the Via Veneto and Mulberry Street with this bill. The tenor of the show was first enunciated by Pat Henry who got one of the top hands of the evening with the simple statement, "I'm Italian." Hardly anything could top this on the current Copa show. Yet even for the non-Latin trade, it's an entertaining layout through which Podell is attempting to reprise the surprise boxoffice bonanza when Jimmy Roselli pulled record business during a previous engagement.
>
> Roselli was a virtual unknown, except among the Italians. During his first Copa date, his paesanos lined up outside on the street seeking admission. There was no accounting for it, except maybe the tremendous ardor of one Latin for another. . . . Roselli has that extreme Italianate air. He is a schmaltzy saloon singer who just overflows with his vigor and passions. Although he pitches for his compatriots, he snags all in the room.

Leonard Harris of the *New York World-Telegram* and Nick Lapole of the *New York Journal-American*, both of whom had reviewed Roselli's first stint at the Copa, went back for a second look. On December 10, 1965, Harris wrote:

> A new Jimmy Roselli has come back to the Copacabana. The glossy voice has new sheen and range; the Tony Bennett dynamics have an overlay of Jolson warmth. Roselli, who is no kid—he appears to be in his late 30s—[is] back for four weeks, bigger and bolder.
>
> Sometimes a little too big. Fighting for dominance with a 24-piece orchestra—Jimmy usually wins—he overpowers one number after another. This is impressive, but occasionally it tends to overpower the listener as well as the song. A pianissimo here and there would render the high points the more Olympian.
>
> No other complaints. . . . He does 16 numbers, 11 in English, five in Italian, and leaves you feeling he's given his best. And Jimmy's Roselli's best is mighty good.

Nick Lapole wrote on December 10:

> It was just a scant 10 months ago that a young baritone with a powerful voice, Jimmy Roselli, virtually unknown to Manhattan nightlifers, became an overnight sensation with an exciting debut at the Copacabana. Last night the handsome youth from New Jersey returned to Mr. Podell's club and once again took over as if he owned it. Again a well-crowded room applauded each of his numbers madly, roared

and whistled its approval as he concluded his performance. . . . [His] robust voice . . . improves with
each hearing. Obviously he is working hard at his
trade, the singing of popular songs, and the improve-
ment in his technique attests that he is not wasting
his time. . . .

He has the backing of a 24-piece orchestra conducted by Billy Dennison, but I believe that's about
16 more musicians than he needs. His voice is so
powerful and full that it often drowned out his accompaniment. . . . He bowed off with "Rock-A-Bye
Your Baby," and if you don't think the entire
crowded Copa wasn't rocking with his catchy
rhythms, you just weren't there, Charley!

Despite the ongoing conflict between Buckalo and Roselli,
Buckalo went about arranging Roselli's Carnegie Hall booking.
He turned to Ray Muscarella, who was a show business pro-
moter connected to wiseguys.

Muscarella rented Carnegie Hall for the night of Jimmy's
two concerts. Roselli wanted to play Carnegie Hall, but, char-
acteristically, insisted he wanted out of the relationship with
both Buckalo and Muscarella and said so, a circumstance he
blames for what happened next.

The September 12, 1966, concerts were triumphs, the highlight of his career up to that point. Roselli did two sets, finish-
ing at 3 a.m. after several ovations. But it was not a typical
glittering night at Carnegie Hall. "You could usually spot a
Roselli operation," an observer told me, "by its homemade
quality, 'the boys' standing around counting the money." In
this case, Carnegie Hall, following its standard procedures,
gave the promoter, Muscarella, a check for the box office re-
ceipts. Muscarella, in turn, took off with the check, which

would be divvied up with Buckalo. When Roselli walked off-stage, he learned what had happened.

Two of Muscarella's men were waiting for him backstage with the news. Jimmy's friend Al Certo, who was there at the time, recalled the moment: "They says to him, 'Look, we're not gonna help you, and we're not gonna hurt you. You're on your own.' 'What about the money?' Roselli asked them. 'You get nothin'.' " Roselli was left owing his musicians almost $40,000. He spoke to the president of the musicians' union and arranged to pay them back with the money he made in his next concerts.

Although Roselli denied this incident in his interview with *The Wall Street Journal* in 1991, he later admitted the truth. "They took the money and scrammed," he told me. "I knew beforehand they were gonna rob me. But I knew that was a cheap way to get out for me. Not only was I alive but I got rid of them. They got rid of me, I got rid of them."

"Jimmy was the thing then, the rage," said Pete Cavallo. "That's the way these guys operated. They always took your money. They figured it was a good score; it was like going on a hijack. But it was legit in their eyes. Who was going to come to them and say, 'You gotta pay the union'? Who was going to put the muscle on them? They made a ton of money.

"Jimmy always says he don't know why he got involved with these guys, why he kept doing it. He kept being led by the nose, thinking, 'Well, this group are good guys.' The other guys are pieces of shit, but these are good. He figured, 'Let me go with them, then I'll get my break and I'll go on my own,' but it wasn't that easy to break away. And when he did, it cost him. One reason he opted for the wiseguys is that the wiseguys would give him his twenty-four men for the band. The legit agents would say no, we only give fourteen men. He wanted the twenty-four men. He had his own mind. He was set in his ways.

"So he kept figuring maybe these new guys would help," Pete said. "But then he had had it. He said, 'I can't do this no more.' And in the back of his mind, he was scared of them too. 'Cause these guys were bad guys. The only thing is, they had a problem killing him because all the Italian people loved him. Then later on he met Carlo Gambino, who said, 'Nobody can bother you.' When Carlo got acquainted with Jimmy and fell in love with him, he was Jimmy's ace."

Buckalo had also obtained an important gig for Jimmy after Carnegie Hall at the Celebrity Theater, the lounge of the Sands in Las Vegas, for three weeks beginning October 19, 1966, and Jimmy honored it residually. The pay was small, and he was playing the lounge, not the main room, but the gig had importance; it was part of the momentum that was building for him.

Roselli's career was definitely on the rise now, but an incident at the Sands could not have improved the connection, such as it was, between him and Frank Sinatra. After the show, Jimmy walked out and bumped into comedian Joe E. Lewis and Sinatra, who was working the main room. Joe E. and Frank were coming toward him. Joe E. Lewis grabbed Jimmy in a headlock and said to Frank, "*This* is a singer, ya fucking bum." Recalled Roselli: "Nobody else could have got away with that with Frank. Frank loved Joe. I hadda love him too, the way he was talking to Frank."

But although Roselli and Sinatra were appearing at the same hotel, Sinatra never came to hear him sing. Mia Farrow, Sinatra's young wife, came to watch Jimmy every night. Billy Dennison recalled: "I remember one night Frank came over to us in the lobby, kind of stoned. He put his arm around Jimmy, they went in the elevator, and Frank said, 'Oh, I'll be there [at Jimmy's show] tomorrow night.' Never came. Gentle put-down. Same hotel at the same time. Kind of disconcerting in that they're both from the same town, same Italian background, knew each other."

The what-ifs about Roselli's career center on two factors: Sinatra's influence and wiseguy connections. "What would have happened," deputy chief investigator Robert Buccino wonders, "if [the mob] gave him a movie, let him make it big in Vegas, start really doing the things like the Sinatras and everybody else did? But he pissed them off. They tried to break him and it didn't work. And that's what hurt him. As long as they know they're going to continually earn with somebody, they'll leave him alone. But if he's defiant, they'll bleed him to death, like the Carnegie Hall incident. That's the style. And if he made a stink, then they'd kill him.

"There was a rumor in those days that Jimmy saw Sinatra at the Copa and opened the door for him and said, 'Hi, Frank,' and that Frank replied, 'I'm Mr. Sinatra to you.' Jimmy wanted to be like Sinatra. And now you get insulted by Sinatra. Then you try to play tough with the wiseguys. But the wiseguys are basically taking the money and saying, 'Go —— yourself.' Now, of course, Jimmy's going to say [about the Carnegie Hall incident], 'I wanted this to happen because I didn't want to be part of those guys.' If he had had the opportunity, he'd be right with them—if he was able to eat some of that [abuse] and go on."

Roselli believes (and many others like Lefty Jimmy Geritano attest to it) that there is another crucial reason he survived: the protection of Italian women. "When I started singing big," he remembered, "the tough guys were there in the front row with the big cigars. They loved me so much they wanted to kill me, some of them. But their mothers and sisters and their wives wouldn't allow it. One or two guys, when they had a few drinks, would tell me, 'Do you know how many times you woulda been killed if it weren't for this guy's wife, this guy's mother?' "

Why didn't they kill Jimmy?

"He got whacked on the head, nothing too severe, but he walked out of it," Dennis Della Fave, Jimmy's cousin, reported. "You know why? This is crazy. *Their mothers.* Their mothers were going to be in the audiences. They said, 'If anything happens to this guy, my mother's going to kill me. She wants to see him.' This is the craziest thing in the world. And he knows it. That's why every little Italian lady who comes to a performance he hugs and kisses. And this guy doesn't do that with anybody else. He doesn't sign autographs; it's embarrassing to him."

Once Anne Bucko, a woman in a wheelchair from Jimmy's neighborhood, went to see him at the Copa. "She'd never seen him perform," said Carmine the Peddler. "My wife and daughter came with Anne and some of her children. Now, that night, Jimmy came down the steps and was about to sing his opening number. The corsage girl came by and he took ten dollars out and bought one.

"Now, when he starts singing the opening number from backstage, you don't see him. If you've never been to his show before, you turn around: you don't know where it's coming from. And then you see him running down the steps. But this time we look up and he's on his knee, pinning a corsage on this seventy-five-year-old woman. You never seen six hundred people crying for what he done. He dedicated the whole show to her. And when the Bucko family went to pay the tab, there was none. He picked up the whole tab for them and my wife and daughter."

But even with the women, Roselli could be his usual feisty self. Donna Roselli, Jimmy's second wife, recalled the night when Jimmy was appearing at the Copacabana in 1966. A woman was waiting for him to come off the stage and walk down the stairs. When she saw him she asked him if he would take a picture with her. Suddenly she put her arm around him and said, "Oh my, you've gained weight."

Jimmy replied, "What did you come here for, to fuck me or hear me sing?"

And there's no question that Jimmy aroused the jealousy of Italian men because Italian women loved him. "The men liked him but they didn't like him, if you know what I mean," said Buccino. "Sinatra and Dean played to the men in the audience. Look at Tony Bennett, macho-looking guy. Tony stayed popular, because he played to the men as well as the women."

The strength of Mafia control, according to Pete Cavallo, was due not so much to their ownership of nightclubs as to the fear they instilled and the services they provided for the clubs. "The controlling aspect was that the owners were afraid of wiseguys," Pete explained. "That was the gangster era, the '50s and '60s. They were feared, and they also had control with the linen service, their control of unions, all that. They would make everyone go out on strike and destroy a club. Also, they spent a lot of money at the clubs and had pull that way. They had to sit in the front row; it was a circus."

There are horror stories about show business personalities trying to break free of the Mafia. When the comic Joe E. Lewis left the club where he was appearing and crossed the street to perform at a competing nightclub for better pay, the mob slit his throat. He spent years in hospitals recuperating.

"The thing about Jimmy," said Dennis Della Fave, "is how he was able to break free and come out with his skin. When Al Martino, for example, had a problem, he tried to switch agents. He didn't know the guy he was with was very well connected. The guy said, 'You want to switch? Fine, but you have a contract with me. You've still got to give me ten percent of whatever you do.' Well, Al didn't know, he didn't give them the cut. He wasn't a street-smart guy. They broke every bone in his body. He had to go to Europe to live for twelve years. That's how he learned his lesson. Jimmy did it with respect, and he never put himself in that position. He never carried it that far. He would never in a million years get to the point where he made these guys so crazy."

Despite the fact that he didn't get paid, Roselli's Carnegie Hall concerts were a major landmark in his career. He paid off the musicians, he was rid, for the moment, of the wiseguys' control, and he was solidly established within the Italian community. The singer most venerated in that community, Enrico Caruso, remained remote, worshipped from afar. Roselli was in their midst, accessible, one of them.

And with the Copacabana and Carnegie Hall successes and his new prestigious recording contract with United Artists, Roselli was on his way to national recognition.

Buckalo did let Roselli back out of the Copa deal. The terms of the split were that Roselli would honor his obligation to play the Copacabana each year for seven years, but in all other ways he was no longer under Buckalo's control. At that point Roselli switched to legitimate representation. From 1966 to 1971 his manager was Harry Steinman, and his agent was Larry Spellman at William Morris, who was working under the direction of Lee Salomon.

Roselli would get his freedom, and his own direct business involvement with the Mafia would finally be over. But he could not have known the intensity of the animosity he was creating, and he had no idea what that would do to him in monetary terms.

While Roselli was appearing at the Copa, Ed Sullivan, host of the most powerful show on television, was begging him to appear on his program. Critic Steven D. Stark summed up Sullivan's influence in a *New York Times* article: "As the country's leading television impresario—and thus the national arbiter of taste—Sullivan appeared on CBS on Sunday night for 23 years and sold the masses on everyone from Dean Martin and Jerry Lewis to Elvis Presley and the Beatles. . . . [His] influence on popular culture was enormous. . . . It's fair to say that by putting his version of the Good Housekeeping seal on Elvis and the Beatles, Sullivan instantly made them national icons, helping them sell millions of records."

Roselli claimed that Sullivan "used to run after me every night at the Copa with his wife. They stood up after every song screaming and applauding. I told him I didn't like his show. And I didn't. It was a bullshit show. The main thing is he didn't pay no fucking money. He kept it all." One day Sullivan raced after Jimmy to the Copa elevator, shouting, "When are you coming on my show?" As the doors were closing, Jimmy shouted, "With a little luck, never."

Roselli eventually signed to do the Sullivan show, but on his own terms. "This is what I want," he said. "Three songs, no commercial. You're revving the people up, then you hit them with commercials. And I want the orchestra onstage behind me, not in the pit."

"It's exposure, Jimmy," Sullivan said in his defense. "Yeah?" Jimmy replied. "I got so much exposure, I'm gonna catch pneumonia."

Jimmy finally caved in, buoyed by the fact that Sullivan agreed to some of his conditions. But he was in for a letdown. "On the morning of the taping of the Sullivan show," he said, "I'd done three shows the previous night at the Copa, and Sunday night was closing night. It had been a four-week engagement.

"I had to be at the CBS theater at seven o'clock Sunday

morning. My throat was hanging out. I was *tired*. At the Copa, I got no money. It cost me forty thousand dollars every engagement. I was up to here with these Popeyes. And now Sullivan paid me no money. So I go there. I'm sitting there [at CBS] like an hour and a half. I could have been sleepin'. 'Roselli!' they holler. So I get up. I was beefing and screaming. Leo, a wiseguy from Boston, was there with me; he was riling me up even more.

"I said, 'Who's the fucking boss here? I'm gonna get aggravated and walk out of here. I don't want to do this Mickey Mouse show to begin with. You follow a tiger, a lamb, an elephant—who needs that? And you ain't paying me nothing.' Sullivan comes over. 'What's your problem?' he says. I said, 'I got no problem. This is what I want.' He says, 'What's your name, Georgie Raft?' I said, 'Listen to me, Mr. Sullivan. I'm not Georgie Raft. It took me a lot of years to get this little bit of recognition. I ain't gonna let you put me out of the fucking business with this Mickey Mouse show.'"

Roselli continued: "I turned around and started abusing two of my agents, Larry Spellman and a guy named Wolfson. I said to Sullivan, 'See these guys? These are two pimps. Because they're supposed to be doing all the screaming, not me. I'm supposed to be a nice guy.' I called them everything. Then I said, 'Let's get the fuck out of here.' Spellman comes running up to me. '[Ed Sullivan] loves you,' he said. 'He don't want you to leave.' I said, 'With all that bullshit I gave him?' 'Yeah!' Spellman says.

"So now they tape everything, and I walk in the control room. I sit down in Sullivan's chair, which I don't know. A guy tells me. I'm about to get up, and Sullivan comes over and says, 'Stay there.' He puts his hand on my shoulder. 'You know,' he says, 'that's a great idea, with the orchestra on the stage.' 'Whatever you say,' I reply. And Sullivan says, 'Yeah, as long as it coincides with your thinking.' Loved me! Loved me! Couldn't do no wrong with this guy. But there was no money there. What was I fucking knocking myself out for?"

Roselli appeared on the Sullivan show on March 14, 1965, and then two more times. Even though Sullivan caved in to accepting all of Jimmy's conditions, Roselli canceled the last four scheduled performances. The issue was money.

"His belief was why was he going on TV for nothing?" Pete Cavallo explained. " 'Millions of people see me, and the show don't pay for it.' He didn't understand that the show would make him famous."

At the end of his last performance Roselli told Sullivan, "Forget my phone number. Never call it again." The staff of the show presented him with a bottle of Chivas Regal in a velvet sack with a big ribbon because he had talked back to Sullivan. "Jesus, you must really hate this guy," he told them.

In later years Roselli also turned down Johnny Carson's *Tonight Show* (which paid $450, or scale) and *Regis and Kathie Lee*, and he also walked off *The Merv Griffin Show*. "The guy said, 'What do you want to sing?' " Roselli recalled. "The fucking piano book was thick like this. I threw it on the piano like that, *boom*. 'I sing 'em all,' I said. 'You pick whatever you want.' We rehearsed the camera, the songs, the music. Now Larry Spellman again, this fucking scumbag from William Morris, said to me, 'I want you to know you're not gonna sit down with Merv. When you're done you're gonna get off.' I was getting $320 for this?"

Roselli told one of Griffin's producers, "When I invite you to my home, and you knock on my door, we don't talk while you're standing outside the door. I invite you in and you sit on the couch. You're inviting me to come and sing; I want to sit down on your couch and feel at home. You tell me I can't sit on the couch, then I'm not welcome in your home." At the time, Jimmy had Carmine the Peddler working for him. "Pick up the music," he said to Carmine. "Let's get the fuck out of here." And he walked out.

From Jimmy's point of view, Sullivan was not helping him survive as an artist by paying him a thousand dollars when he could be earning thirty thousand or more for one night in a club. The fact that the program was the era's number one launching pad to fame and fortune eluded him. To Jimmy's mind, the amount of money you make tells you what the world thinks of you. If an entertainer accepts a small salary the first time, the proprietor of the club will feel no need to pay him more the next time.

But Roselli was not the only singer to feel this way. In 1955, at the time *Guys and Dolls* was released with Frank Sinatra in a starring role, Sullivan asked Sinatra to appear on his show. Sinatra would also be paid scale—especially since the purpose would be to publicize the movie. Sinatra refused. Sullivan denounced him publicly, and Sinatra took out a full-page ad in the *Hollywood Reporter* that said:

> *Dear Ed:*
> *You're sick.*
> *Frankie.*
> *PS: Sick, sick, sick.*

The obvious difference between Sinatra's behavior and Roselli's was that Sinatra, already a superstar, could afford to behave that way; Roselli, a rising singer unknown to the national TV audience, was committing professional suicide.

But underlying Roselli's reasoning was an anxiety that he might not be able to cross over and achieve a national audience beyond the Italian community. If he felt confident of his own ability to appeal to the American public, he would know that his audience would multiply exponentially from such massive exposure.

The late Lee Salomon said of his time as Jimmy's agent: "Jimmy aggravated me to death. Every suggestion I would make, not one would be even considered by him. He has his own mind, and that's it. Right or wrong, he's right. To this very day. Julie Podell of the Copa came up with a fucking line once. I said to him, I don't believe it, Julie, this guy Roselli, he don't want this, he don't want that. Julie said to me, 'He don't want to be a big star. Leave him alone.'"

But Roselli's closest friends, among them Pete Cavallo, childhood pals Al Certo and Johnny Marotta, Dennis Della Fave, his physician, Dr. Daniel Macken, and his wife, Donna, believe it's not so simple.

"The man knew he had a voice," Dennis Della Fave explained, "and at one time he wanted the world to hear his voice. But not from the point of view of stardom. He didn't want to be a star; that was not his goal. He was never comfortable being in the limelight. If he never got seen, it wouldn't have bothered him. That's why he walked off *The Ed Sullivan Show*. And I think part of it was that he never thought he was a good-looking guy. Because he always used to say to me, 'I'm not a Clark Gable, you know.' 'Jimmy,' I'd say, 'you're not ugly.' He's five foot eight, not the tallest guy in the world, but he's not ugly. And he had the smile: he got up on the stage and he was the best-looking guy up there. He was magic. He didn't understand that. He was always afraid of TV. You know, it wasn't the wiseguys who hurt Jimmy's career so much as the legitimate guys—because of the way he handled the Sullivan show."

Reflecting on Jimmy's aversion to exposure, Al Certo noted, "I've always thought, and so do a lot of his close friends, that Jimmy feared success. You know, success is a tough thing to handle. It's like a fighter being a champion; you never want to be knocked off. They want to knock you off the hill: you become a target for everyone."

Certo continued: "You can blame Sinatra, this guy or that, but I think you can blame Jimmy Roselli more than anything else. I think it's one of the reasons he demands so much money; it's a way of backing out for him. Because if you ever perform in an auditorium that's got ten thousand seats, and you only wind up with five hundred people in there, you're off the hill already. He tries to control his career that way [with infrequent appearances]. So he's sure he'll have a sellout."

If he tries and fails, observes Dr. Daniel Macken, "it will be a confirmation of what his father always thought. So he wants to keep it this way. It's a very self-protective mechanism."

8

IT WAS
A VERY GOOD YEAR

BY 1966, EVERYTHING SEEMED TO BE HAPPENING AT once. Roselli's UA contract stipulated that he record three albums a year, and this he did with astonishing versatility and imagination. *New York: My Port of Call* (1966), later retitled *Lullaby of Broadway*, was arranged by Ralph Burns and produced by Roselli. It contained one of Jimmy's bravura performances: his version of Jolson's longtime hit "Give My Regards to Broadway." Roselli belts it out as even Jolson never sang it, conjuring up a Broadway of innocence and lights; Damon Runyon and Moss Hart and Eugene O'Neill; Belle Baker and Nora Bayes; the RKO Palace reborn as it was with Judy Garland; the New Amsterdam Theater and the Ziegfeld Follies ablaze and alive again.

Two singles from the album, "This Is My Kind of Love" and "New York: My Port of Call," had been released earlier, in December 1965, and *Variety* had selected them as "top sin-

gles of the week"—the "best bets" of the week's 100-plus re-
leases: "Jimmy Roselli's 'This Is My Kind of Love,' from the
musical 'Anya,' is a classy adaptation of a familiar Rachmani-
noff melody delivered very effectively by this singer. 'New York:
My Port of Call' is a well-written piece of atmospheric material
with potential as a performance song."

On the album cover, a tuxedoed Jimmy stands singing, his
arms outstretched with love, in front of the thrilling Manhattan
skyline at night.

Of *New York: My Port of Call, Variety* wrote: "What Tony
Bennett has done recently for San Francisco, Jimmy Roselli
may be doing for New York. This is a neatly planned songalog
pegged to the Big City. Roselli, a big-voiced singer with great
flexibility, belts this stanza with power and style. The title song,
a new piece of material, is an excellent intro to a musical bus
ride around 'Give My Regards to Broadway,' 'Chinatown, My
Chinatown,' 'Lullaby of Broadway,' 'Manhattan,' 'Brooklyn
Bridge,' 'Meet Me at Jilly's' [a song of tribute to Sinatra's hang-
out bar in Manhattan owned by Jilly Rizzo], 'Autumn in New
York,' and the oldie 'The Sidewalks of New York.' Ralph
Burns' backgrounds are topflight."

The liner notes for the album were written by WNEW-
AM's legendary disc jockey William B. Williams, host of its
premiere show, *Make Believe Ballroom*. Williams was Sinatra's
favorite disc jockey and number one champion on radio in the
1950s and 1960s, and was the first to crown the singer "Chairman of the Board." Of Roselli, Williams wrote: "I suppose to
some, Jimmy Roselli may be one of those proverbial overnight
sensations; but in reality to those of us who have known Jimmy
and watched his career over the past couple of decades, the
road to his present success has been a long and arduous one.
. . . The basic training that Jimmy had working in all media

and before all kinds of audiences in small saloons around the country has given him the kind of poise and assurance that mark the star who has staying power."

Roselli's *Right From the Heart* had appeared in 1965. Here's Jimmy as the up-and-coming romantic singer, standing, on the album cover, within a large red heart. His arms again ready to embrace, he wears a red ascot and a white shirt. A lovely brunette in a black dress lies seductively on the red heart, her back to him, as he sings to her.

The album contained what would become one of Roselli's romantic signature songs, "Come Into My Life," written by his friend, the composer Phil Badner, and the haunting "A Million Dreams Ago" by Quadling, Howard, and Jergen. Roselli renders beautiful versions of Newman and Wrubel's "Why Don't We Do This More Often," "Sleepy Time Gal" by Alden, Egan, and Lorenzio, Skylar and Holmes's "The Dancing Has Ended," as well as singular interpretations of the unusual, relatively unknown material he would uncover and make his own throughout his career: DiMinno and Athena's "Right From the Heart" and Ruben and Badner's "Laugh It Off." *Variety* had already cited two singles from the album as "Best Bets" on May 19, 1965: "Jimmy Roselli's 'Why Don't We Do This More Often' showcases this singer in a savvy workover of a fine standard. 'Laugh It Off' is another standout rendition with overtones of Tony Bennett which will not hurt the spins."

Several albums followed in rapid succession in the next two years. The cover of *There Must Be a Way* features a loosely rendered charcoal drawing by Frank Gauna of a smiling Jimmy in a bow tie on a white background. The album's title song by Gallop and Saxon was already a hit single that year. This was one of Roselli's more commercial efforts, and on it, Jimmy sings with and above the chorus. The song sounds very arranged, as if an outsider had come in and styled it, until Roselli moves into the real melody and his voice soars. Simply put, his voice is better than the song. Commercial though it was (it reached number 13 on the *Billboard* charts), Roselli somehow managed to transcend it with his captivating and melodic voice.

Produced by Henry Jerome and arranged by Arnold Goland and Hutch Davies, the album displays a diversity that is characteristic of Roselli's repertoire. It included the World War II standard by Frank Loesser and Jules Styne "I Don't Want to Walk Without You," DeSylva, Brown, and Henderson's "Walkin' My Baby Back Home," "Oh What It Seemed to Be," by Benjamin, Weiss, and Carle, and the rousing "You Wanted Someone to Play With, I Wanted Someone to Love," by McConnell, Osborne, Capana, and Morris.

Then came *The Italian Album* and *The Best of Jimmy Roselli*, Roselli's first all-Italian-language albums. Pitched to his burgeoning Italian-American audience, the cover of *The Italian Album* features Roselli in a rural Italian setting. Beside him, an Italian beauty with black hair plays a guitar. Behind them is a full moon and the sky. The cover related to a song on the album: " 'Na Voce, 'na Chitarra e 'o Pogo e Luna" ("A Voice, a Guitar, and a Little Bit of the Moon"), inspired by Jimmy's beloved Aunt Frieda, who had discovered the song when she was in Italy. Jimmy had promised he would record it for her someday, and he did. The singer of the song says that a voice, a guitar, and a little bit of the moon are enough to serenade his girl and to make her kiss him and love him.

This stunning album includes the "stardust" of the Italian musical catalogue: "Torna a Surriento" ("Come Back to Sorrento"), "Innamorata," "Scapricciatiello," and the song with which he always begins his concerts by intoning his grandfather's words, "*Cante, guaglione, cante*": "Aggio Perduto o Suonno" ("Since I Lost You I Can't Sleep"). As in so much of Roselli's work, a recurrent theme is the pain of unrequited love.

In "Innamorata," the singer cries, "Please don't go! You are for me my first love. I dream of you night and day, and I am chained to you for the rest of my life." In "Scapricciatiello," a mother prays every morning for her young son, who is involved with the wrong girl, who will surely lead him into a bad life. In "Torna a Surriento," the singer implores, "Come back to Sorrento, come back to me! How can you depart from this lovely sea? Don't leave me, come back and let me live again!" And in "Aggio Perduto o Suonno," he laments, "Since I met you, I have loved you. I cannot sleep anymore. I am jealous; I am afraid of losing you. One day you say you love me, the next you say you don't. Why do you torment me?"

But what is most transcendent in the album is a song that for Jimmy must have strongly evoked his grandfather and his love for Naples: " 'O Paese d' 'o Sole." Here an exile returns to Naples, and is so overjoyed that he cries. The mandolins, the bright sun, and the blue sea tell him once again that Naples is the land of love. Roselli has never made a more thrilling record.

In its review of the album on September 7, 1966, *Variety* asked, "What could be more natural than a session of Italian favorites by Jimmy Roselli, who has an extensive ethnic following in the U.S.? Roselli belts this material with wide-ranging tenor pipes, using all the stops and sentiment that are required by these songs."

There is some overlap in songs between *The Italian Album* and *The Best of Jimmy Roselli* ("Innamorata," "Catena," "Rusella 'e Maggio!" and "Scapricciatiello" are on both albums). But *The Best of Jimmy Roselli*, which was produced by Roselli with music arranged and conducted by Ralph Burns, also contains other Roselli classics: "Mala Femmena," "Guaglione," "Anema e Core," and "Statte Vicino Amme," among them.

These two albums assured him his place in the Italian-

American community. In fact, it seemed as if every Italian organization wanted him to sing for them.

But Frank Sinatra was clearly in the ascendant. In 1966, he was named top male vocalist by *Playboy,* and his LPs *Strangers in the Night* and *Sinatra: A Man and His Music* won Grammy Awards. He also married Mia Farrow that year. Sinatra appeared in three films in 1966: *Cast a Giant Shadow, The Oscar,* and *Assault on a Queen.* He also staged the Inaugural Gala for California governor Edmund G. Brown.

In spite of Sinatra's successes, it was rock and roll that topped the *Billboard* charts: the Monkees claimed the number one spot with "I'm a Believer"; the Righteous Brothers took fourth place with "(You're My) Soul and Inspiration"; the Mamas and the Papas were fifth with "Monday, Monday"; and the Beatles were sixth with "We Can Work It Out."

The next year Roselli released a single, "Aneme e Core" ("Soul and Heart"), a love song mostly in Italian, in which the singer vows to "love you with all my heart, with all my soul, my whole life through." When Jimmy sang in English, he sang full vowels, with no variation from the Neapolitan intonation. "What he does in this record is what singers today call 'the mix,' " Scott Harlan explained, "something which many singers study for years. It's a good illustration of going from register breaks. At the end of the record he went into a totally different placement of his voice, a head placement, which is a very operatic thing to do. Men today who can do that are pop singers who sing way up high, like Michael Bolton. We call it a head tone: it's a way of using the falsetto of the male in a full-voiced way. A very difficult thing to do: Roselli went from a full voice to a head tone."

This was followed by *Saloon Songs, Vol. 2,* which included liner notes by the Copacabana's Jules Podell: "I've seen so-called saloon singers come and go and I must say that Jimmy Roselli ranks right up there with the best of them. When he's singing his heart out, you know he means it. Jimmy's got more emotion per pound than any other singer around and the people love it." The album was produced by Roselli and arranged and conducted by George Siravo. Here again, Roselli managed to make the past fresh and evocative without embellishing or camping up his versions of such chestnuts as "Somebody Stole My Gal," "Nobody's Sweetheart," and "Please Don't Talk About Me When I'm Gone." The real standouts, however, are "When Your Old Wedding Ring Was New," the song that follows Roselli everywhere to this day, and a particularly moving version of Allan Flynn and Frank Madden's standard "Maybe." What distinguishes "Maybe" is the amazing sostenuto, the very unusual length of time Jimmy can sustain a note with such fullness. You don't hear him breathing; he just holds the note and keeps going and going. It's not segmented; Jimmy takes you on a journey all in one mood and all in one tone. It's very melodic, very smooth and sexy. There's great strength in his being able to sing a ballad with such intensity. As with many of his favorite songs, Roselli sings "Maybe" the same way today that he sang it in 1967. When he knows he has something, he doesn't play with it. And he's aware that his audiences want it that way.

Variety again singled out the album for special mention as a "top LP" on October 9, 1967: "Jimmy Roselli continues to offer a solid output of swingers and ballads . . . in a forthright manner that catches 'saloon' intimacy. . . ."

The Great Ones (now called *Rock-A-Bye Your Baby*) was also released in 1967, an homage to the singers Roselli admired most. Produced by Roselli and conducted and arranged by George Siravo, it includes songs identified with Jolson, Tony Bennett ("Somewhere Along the Way"), Mario Lanza ("Because You're Mine"), Sinatra ("You Make Me Feel So Young"), Nat "King" Cole ("Sweet Lorraine"), Johnny Ray ("Cry"), Eddie Cantor ("Ida"), Billy Eckstine ("I Apologize"), Perry Como ("Prisoner of Love"), and Bing Crosby ("I Surrender, Dear"). The album is revealing too for Jimmy's own assessment of the various artists. Of Tony Bennett he remarked in the liner notes: "One of the warmest voices ever." Jolson: "My favorite performer and entertainer of all time. He had more heart than anyone and the ability to make an audience laugh, cry or sing along with him." On Billy Eckstine: "A musician's musician—a highly underrated talent. I'll never forget the enjoyment he gave me with this song."

Roselli would cap 1967 with his live recording, *Sold Out: Carnegie Hall Concert*. Produced by Roselli, conducted by Ralph Burns, and with arrangements by Burns and Larry Wilcox, the album captures the intense excitement of the September 12, 1966, concerts. There are standout versions of "You're Nobody 'til Somebody Loves You," by Russ Morgan, Larry Stock, and James Cavanaugh, "Vesti la Giubba," adapted by Roselli from *Pagliacci*, and one of Roselli's all-time finest performances: McQueen and Lippman's "A Fool in Love." The recording catches three brief snippets of dialogue from Roselli that night: an aside to his personal conductor and pianist, Billy Dennison, a joyful comment to the audience, "This is better than a nightclub, isn't it?" and an encore chorus of "A Fool in Love" that was preceded by his telling the audience, "This one's for you." For Jimmy, nothing could say more than the songs he sang.

Variety remarked: "Jimmy Roselli's concert at Carnegie Hall, N.Y., last September has been preserved in an excellent live performance. The transition of Roselli from a big-voiced belter into a savvy performer is markedly evident in his challenging songalog. Roselli impresses on such tunes as 'I Get a Kick Out

of You,' 'A Foggy Day,' 'Strangers in the Night,' 'You're Nobody 'til Somebody Loves You,' and, just to prove that he can
hit all the notes, 'Vesti la Giubba,' from *Pagliacci*."

But *Variety*'s close coverage of almost everything Roselli was
doing in the 1960s would disappear permanently in the 1970s,
when the wiseguys helped turn him into an invisible man.

9

BLACKBALLED

IN 1967 AND 1968 THE SENSE OF JOYFUL COMMUNALISM generated in the early protest years of the 1960s gave way to a mood of darkening violence and pessimism in the United States about the possibilities of genuine social change. The Tet Offensive of January 30, 1968, had permanently altered American perceptions of the war at home. Then came the March 16 massacre at My Lai, its inhabitants killed by a battalion of the U.S. 11th Infantry Brigade. Less than a month later, Dr. Martin Luther King, Jr., was assassinated by James Earl Ray in Memphis, and on June 5 Robert Kennedy was shot in Los Angeles by Sirhan Sirhan. On October 7, the Baltimore trial of the Catonsville Nine—priests, nuns, and social workers who had burned 1-A induction files—began. Five days later, but across the country, five hundred GIs, many in uniform, participated in a San Francisco peace march from Golden Gate Park. Finally, on November 7, Richard Nixon was elected to the presidency.

As Todd Gitlin wrote: "Everything was at stake, anything seemed possible. . . . For every face of authority, there was someone to slap it." Each side, Gitlin noted, believed that the final showdown of good and evil, order and chaos, was looming.

With the Vietnam War still raging in 1968–69, there were over one hundred campus bombings and attempted bombings, as well as incidents of arson across the country—targeting ROTC buildings, campus and government buildings, and high schools. Each week brought arrests, trials, antiwar demonstrations, and demonstrations by GIs opposed to the war. On November 15, 1969, three-quarters of a million people marched through the streets of Washington, D.C., to the Washington Monument to hear Senators George McGovern and Charles Goodell speak and John Denver, Arlo Guthrie, Pete Seeger, and the touring cast of *Hair* sing. It was the largest single protest in American history.

At the same time, several thousand militants led by Jerry Rubin and Abbie Hoffman, who were on trial as part of the Chicago Eight, marched on the Justice Department, carrying NLF (National Liberation Front of the Vietcong) flags. They tossed smoke bombs, bottles, and rocks, and were greeted with tear gas. They tore down the American flag and raised the flag of the NLF in its place. "The once-solid core of American life," Gitlin commented, "the cement of loyalty that people tender to institutions, certifying that the correct order is going to last and deserves to—this loyalty, in select sectors, was decomposing."[13]

Popular music, meanwhile, was blasting itself free from its last vestigial links with the old-time nightclub and music industry and its visions of Fred Astaire putting on his top hat and tails. On January 14, 1967, in San Francisco's Golden Gate Park, Allen Ginsberg, Gary Snyder, and Timothy Leary had presided over the First Human Be-In. Music was provided by Quicksilver Messenger Service, the Jefferson Airplane, and the Grateful Dead, among others. *Newsweek* called it a love feast, a psychedelic picnic, and a happening. It was, in the view of 1960s historian Allen J. Matusow, the moment when America discovered the hippie.

As historian Richard Gid Powers noted: "If the hipster was, in Norman Mailer's terms, the 'white Negro,' reveling in the victim psychology as a symbol of alienation from success-oriented America, the hippie demanded all the trappings and pleasures of success without subjecting himself to the corrupting co-optation of participation in the system that created that wealth. The hippie believed himself entitled to all the freedom, pleasure, and power that had always been the trappings of winning in America, but without conforming to the values it had taken to wrest that victory from the Darwinian concrete jungle of modern America.

"Popular crooners," Powers continued, "were still dressing in tuxedos, their audience in business suits, and their music honed the moneyed lifestyle into a thing of grace and beauty. The hippies dressed in rags, not the rags of Chaplin's tramp, but outrageous garb that mocked businessmen's dress, in colors that derived from the circus clown. The hipster transformed the elegance of the urban aristocracy into a cool that showed how ordinary life could be heightened through aesthetic form. For the hippie, the goal was Norman O. Brown's 'polymorphous perversity,' the union of many bodies, the Dionysian ego that reunifies male and female, Self and Other, life and death."[14]

Still, the hippie movement liberated sustained bursts of creativity, and Bob Dylan, who had outraged the Newport Folk Festival in July 1965 by playing an electric guitar, was not the only genius to be energized by the counterculture. Black artists, including the Staple Singers, Sly and the Family Stone, and the Chambers Brothers, combined spirituality with a social message. But the message often took a more violent turn. "We'd rather die on our feet than keep living on our knees," asserted James Brown in "Say It Loud, I'm Black and I'm Proud." The fires raging in the streets—in Watts, Newark, and elsewhere—were alluded to in the Rolling Stones' "Street Fighting Man" and Sly and the Family Stone's "There's a Riot Goin' On." What was celebratory in the early 1960s now took on a darker hue. "Summer's here and the time is right for fighting in the streets," Mick Jagger sang in 1968, parodying Martha and the Vandellas' 1964 song "Dancing in the Streets."

Of course, Woodstock was the seminal event of the late 1960s, "the greatest event in countercultural history," according to historian William O'Neill, which drew half a million members of the "love generation."

Then came the catastrophe of Altamont. "That fall," Richard Gid Powers remarked, "the music that rejected all limits and structures found that it had liberated the forces of Thanatos as well as Eros." The December 6, 1969, concert headlined by the Rolling Stones was held at a racetrack forty miles outside San Francisco, and it was marked by escalating violence. A young black man, Meredith Hunger, who was allegedly holding a gun, was hacked to death in front of the stage by members of the Hell's Angels motorcycle gang (who had been hired as security guards for the concert) as Mick Jagger sang "Sympathy for the Devil," "Under My Thumb," and "Brown Sugar." The scene was actually caught on camera in the film made for the event, *Gimme Shelter*, released in 1972. The Stones made no expression of remorse. "The violence seemed just another stage setting for the Stones' routine," wrote Sol Stern. "They continued to play, mostly uninterrupted, while the fights flared

again and again across the front of the stage."¹⁵ Altamont
would be regarded as the end of an era. "Who could any longer
harbor the illusion," commented Gitlin, "that these hundreds
of thousands of spoiled star-hungry children of the Lonely
Crowd were the harbingers of a good society?"

In Jimmy Roselli's world, none of this meant very much—
except for its impact on his career. Clearly these various shifts
signaled that the musical market open to him would be a
smaller, shrunken one. Yet in reality he was on the charts, he
was moving up, and no one disproved the common wisdom
about making it in a countercultural musical climate more than
the group to which he rightfully belonged: the gifted Italian
singers. At that very moment, two of them were on top of the
heap, and they would stay there for a long, long time: Frank
Sinatra and Dean Martin.

By the late 1960s, Roselli was becoming a star—and he acted
like it. On April 30, 1966, he hit *Billboard*'s "Top Adult Contemporary" chart at number 29 with his single "I'm Gonna
Change Everything," and on August 12, 1967, he appeared on
Billboard's "Top Pop Singles" chart at number 93 with "There
Must Be a Way." He reached number 13 on its "Top Adult
Contemporary" chart with the same song on July 8, 1967.
"There Must Be a Way" remained on the charts for thirteen
weeks. Four other Roselli singles were also on the *Billboard*
charts: "All the Time" reached number 19 on October 14,
1967, and stayed on the charts for nine weeks; "Please Believe
Me" was listed at number 31 on January 13, 1968, and remained for four weeks; "Oh What It Seemed to Be" reached
number 35 on May 25, 1968, and "Buona Sera, Mrs. Campbell" appeared at number 38 on March 1, 1969, and stayed for
four weeks.

Four Roselli albums for United Artists also appeared on *Billboard*'s charts from 1965 through 1969. *Life and Love Italian Style* stayed on the charts for eleven weeks and achieved a peak position of number 96 on June 26, 1965; *The Great Ones* reached number 145 on September 11, 1965; *There Must Be a Way* appeared at number 191 on November 18, 1967; and *Core Spezzato* reached number 184 on June 21, 1969.

Jimmy was earning up to $5,000 per performance at major venues like Palumbo's in Philadelphia, though not at the Copacabana, where the Buckalo deal remained in effect. Roselli continued to play the Copa each year and felt thoroughly ripped off. The Buckalo crew took his records out of jukeboxes and made his life as miserable as possible. His recording contract with United Artists gave him major exposure, but he received no royalties from the company until much later, after he threatened to sue.

During this period, Roselli got a call from Mexico. The caller stated that he would like Jimmy to fly there to sing at the wedding of the daughter of the President of Mexico. Jimmy asked the caller if he was kidding. "The guy says, 'Hold on, somebody wants to talk to you,' " remembered Jimmy. "A voice says, 'How's that wristwatch?' It was Sam Giancana. 'Oh, hello, Doc,' I said. I used to call him Doc. 'How are you, Doctor? How ya feelin'?'

"He says, 'Jeez, I'd like for you to sing for the President.' I say, 'What about Frank?' Sam says, 'I told him you were better.' 'I'll be on the next plane,' I says.

"Sam says, 'Take Morty Storm [the comic] with you,' and I did. Sam was waiting at the airport when I arrived. He had a big, beautiful home in Cuernavaca—eighteen acres. All walled-in but beautiful.

"The concert for the daughter's wedding was all Mexicans. I sang Italian songs. Morty got up and told jokes and nobody paid any attention. They didn't understand him. But Sam was there crying. 'This is funny,' he said. I said to him, 'You got a sick sense of humor. The guy is dyin', he's bleeding to death out there, you think it's funny.' "

A source who has asked to remain anonymous remarked, "You can imagine how Frank reacted when the story about Jimmy singing for the President got back to him. Particularly the part about Sam saying Jimmy was the better singer. Frank wouldn't forget that—ever." Roselli, who frequently resented wiseguy demands on him, complied readily in this case. It was part of Jimmy's mercurial evaluation process: Giancana was on his list of "sweethearts" and "beautiful individuals."

Roselli spent much of 1969 and 1970 building a palatial mansion in Watchung, New Jersey, for his wife, Angie, and his daughter, Anne. He also spent much of his time driving back and forth between his girlfriend Donna's Manhattan apartment and the new house. Jimmy distrusted professionals, and, probably hoping for a bargain, he hired a "good Italian contractor" who eventually walked out of his contract for the Watchung house, taking a large chunk of the money with him. Jimmy was stranded. Having relied on "the guys from the corner," he had once again been betrayed. Pete Cavallo came to his rescue, locating a professional architect who successfully completed the building of the house.

Its construction cost him almost a million dollars, but Jimmy's new thirty-five-room home brought him little happiness. Watchung, an upper-class suburb forty-five minutes from Hoboken, was a symbol to Roselli of his rise in the world and a way of telling the wiseguys he had made it on his own.

"It was hands down the biggest house in town, a palace, about two and a half acres of land," recalled Dr. Daniel Macken. "The main floor had an enormous living room that was probably the size of my apartment. He had thirty-foot-high ceilings, and it made you feel as if you were in a tunnel. It was kind of sad. The carpets were red plush; he had a lot of red furniture, deep wine red, Romanesque statues."

"The ceilings were thirty feet high," recalled Jimmy's daughter, Anne. "When I got a little older, I would say, 'All these rooms are filled with nothing.'

"Only a shell of him was at home. I knew something was keeping him away all week except the weekend. My father tried to keep it together. He invited a couple of bachelor uncles to live with us. He made these gestures. My mother, though, was such an emotionally weak woman married to such an emotionally strong man. He needed somebody more like himself."

According to Anne, Jimmy would come home in the early hours of the morning. He would jump on her bed and smother her with kisses. "He would reek of booze," recalled Anne. "He wasn't drunk, but he'd been out having a good time. He could hold booze with the best of them; a good solid drinking man's drinker. I remember saying, 'Daddy, you smell. I love you too, but go away.' "

"There was no warmth," said Dennis Della Fave. "The only time there was any fun was when Jimmy had his friends over. He had to have them over because that was his only life. Angie never participated. She and her mother would stay in the kitchen. They locked themselves in. They were like hermits. There was nothing to come home to for this guy. When he left Donna's, and sat in the car going back to Watchung, he got quiet. He dreaded going there. He was caverned off. He had his own bedroom, his own music room. Angie and her mother never came out. He bought them this beautiful place they never took advantage of. They never walked around the property. The dogs weren't allowed to go out; they were afraid the dogs would catch cold."

"It was always fucking combat," Jimmy remembered. "I

couldn't wait to run out of the house. Angie and her mother were never happy in that house. They knocked that fucking house from day one. You'd think I'd brought them from a mansion and put them in a shithouse. I brought them from a shithouse and put them in a mansion. I said, 'You put a curse on this house, you're always knocking it.' The mother started coming at me. I said, 'If you were a man, I'd knock you dead.' She wanted to dominate me. I got a personality that Christ can't dominate. I told her to get the fuck out of there. She would go out the front door and come in the side.

"They wanted dogs. I bought two schnauzers. I had a beautiful patio with two big barbecues. In the daytime, I said, 'Open the sliding doors and let the dogs go out there, run around and play.' They were little; they couldn't go anywhere; and it was beautiful outside. Never let them out there. 'The mosquitoes will bite them.' The mosquitoes will bite them? I came home at night, when I did come home, shit and piss all over the floor. Sometimes I'd come in and step in it. Jesus Christ, I'd get like an animal. I'd come home from this motherfuckin' wiseguy, that wiseguy, and there was another big battle when I got home. The ones outside were amateur nights."

But Jimmy still wouldn't break up his marriage or break from his past. "I got married for better or for worse; I got the worst of it and I gotta live with it. But I didn't expect to get fucked every time I turned around."

Or as Pete Cavallo put it: "He got humped without bending over."

"A lot of times he'd push his mother-in-law out," his Hoboken pal Vito Pedesta recalled. "We'd put all her pots in the car. She'd be packed and I'd be ready to take her home. Jimmy would feel sorry. 'Bring her back,' he'd say. Then we'd have to go get her back."

During the same period, Charlie Guiffra, the brother of Angie's father, became seriously ill with cancer. Roselli arranged for his valet, Gennarine, to drive his uncle to the hospital for cobalt treatments three times a week. Roselli paid for all of it, about sixty thousand dollars.

Roselli's albums, which he usually produced himself, continued to tumble out rapidly. He loved nothing so much as the feeling of being in the studio with musicians and arrangers he admired, singing for himself. *The Christmas Album*, arranged and conducted by Ralph Burns, appeared in 1968. It contains all the standards, including a haunting "White Christmas" (Irving Berlin) and "I'll Be Home for Christmas" (Kim Gannon and Buck Ram); another standout is the song he sings in both Italian and English: "Buon Natale" (Saffer and Linale).

It's Been Swell (1968) was a contemplative album of ballads arranged and conducted by George Siravo. In the title song by Sol Parker, Roselli sings with sweet simplicity of first love and an entire universe springs up before one's eyes, of walking in Central Park in spring holding hands. But even when Roselli is saying, "It's been swell," there's an undertow of angst, an Italian weightiness. There's a sense here that as good as the experience he's singing about is, this is as good as it gets. He is deepened but limited by his sadness. The back cover includes an elegant picture of Roselli, his collar loosened, tie hanging down, his hands wrapped around a microphone, a slight smile on his face—a man in his forties at the peak of his powers, in love with what he is doing. The album represents the gentler, mellower side of Roselli—Roselli in the early hours of the morning—and it is one of his finest achievements.

The songs include "Try a Little Tenderness" (Woods and Campbell), "Maybe It's Because" (Irving Berlin), "My Funny Valentine" (Rodgers and Hart), and an unforgettable "For All We Know" (Lewis and Campbell). Jimmy sings of the purity and enduring nature of love in the face of the evanescence of life with heartbreaking emotion. Here he's doing his interpretation of a classic, playing with it more than he usually does. His approach is less straight and pure, less of a glide; he is more expressive, making the song his.

Core Spezzato, Roselli's Italian album, also appeared in 1968. The cover features a broken heart in red, with torn ribbons in the colors of Italy: white, red, and green. On the back cover, Jimmy, much heftier here in a checkered jacket, looks back over his shoulder at the camera, smiling. This release marked Jimmy's first album collaboration with another gifted arranger, Leroy Holmes, who produced and orchestrated. The orchestra was conducted by Billy Dennison.

Roselli's next album, *Core Napulitano* (*Neapolitan Heart*) in 1969, was a mix of English and Italian. Produced by Henry Jerome, it featured the work of three top arrangers: Arnold Goland, Larry Wilcox, and Ralph Burns. Roselli is especially successful here on two songs in which he mixes Italian and English, the Italian seeming to infuse the English with an elevated passion: "Love My Love" ("Love Senza Tramonto"), by DiMinno and Cardini, and "Please Believe Me," by Tenco and Stillman. The liner notes were written by Gertrude Katzman, music director at that time of WNEW-AM, the station that gave Roselli his greatest boost and would soon remove him entirely from the airwaves.

In 1968, a New Year's event occurred that Roselli has never forgotten, one that embodied his vacillating feelings about "half-assed" (or wannabe) wiseguys. It was also a powerful reminder of the ambivalence of hero worship: the relationship between a star and his fans, and Roselli's difficulty in maintaining some professional distance from the bedrock Italian community that spelled family for him.

The incident took place at a Catholic church in the Bronx. "At the rehearsal," Jimmy related, "everybody wants to take me home. My mother's going to cook for you, this and that. You can't believe what went on. Then it comes time to do the show in the evening. I did an hour and a half of singing. Well, when I got off, half the place wanted to strangle me. They didn't want me to leave.

"I went back on and did another fifteen minutes. When I came off, three or four guys wanted to fight me. Some had guns. They were nuts, all juiced up. I tell you, it was a madhouse. I got like a crazy man: 'You guys are doing a lot of talking. But nobody's movin'! *Come on. Come on.*' " The same people who had wanted to take him home with them to meet their mothers, the ones that wanted to cook for him, make pasta for him, now wanted to kill him. He walked out. "I got in the car," remembered Jimmy, "and I was furious all night. Furious! They didn't want me to leave. They wanted me to go home and sleep with them."

For similar reasons, Roselli was reluctant to appear at various religious feasts because of his experience with wiseguys who had been known to pop up in key roles at these events and then try to exploit him. Al Certo recalled the time Roselli was asked to appear at the Feast of Nole. "They said, 'You're close with Jimmy. We love him, and this is the Feast of Nole, his feast, where his grandfather came from.'

"I told them if I could get Jimmy to come there, forget about singing. 'Forget it!' I said, 'Those days are over.' They said, 'No! Forget about it! Don't even think about it! No singin'!'

"So I told Jimmy about it. He hears it's his hometown. I knew he was going to go. He said, 'Yeah, but no singin'!' I said, 'Don't worry, they ain't gonna ask you.'

"So it was a big event in Cliffside, New Jersey, in the streets, in the summertime. They carried around the saints. Then they saw Jimmy and they went wild. 'Hey, Jimmy!' they yelled. They pulled up in a car and grabbed him, threw him on top of the ojee [the movable platform]."

Then some "greaseball," Jimmy recalled, "announced into the microphone: 'Jimmy Roselli's going to sing a song for us.' I said, 'You wanna start that shit?' The guy kept hopping the people up that I'm gonna sing. I said, 'You announce that once more and I'm gonna put that mike right in the middle of your head.'"

"This went on for five or ten minutes," Al Certo recalled. "People screaming, 'Come on, Jimmy, sing!' There were thousands of people now. It was like the *Godfather* scene with the statue. But now the people started getting on his ass: 'Come on, Jimmy.' Jimmy's fighting back and forth with the guy at the mike.

"I started panicking. All of a sudden the people turned: 'Get him off there! Get Roselli the fuck off there!' They wanted to hang him. We had to get a cop escort. They shouted, 'We'll never buy your records.' They spat at us."

It was a volatile time for Jimmy, whose own behavior was sometimes on the edge of rationality.

Frank Gauna, who was in charge of the art department at United Artists Records when Roselli was under contract, was in a position to see many of Jimmy's mood swings. "Jimmy and I got in a fight," Gauna told me. "My boss said, 'Where the hell is Roselli? Get him in here.' So I did.

"The next day Jimmy walks in with his bodyguard, Carmine the Peddler. I'm on the phone. Jimmy grabs the phone out of my hand and calls me a squealer. I say, 'Hey, man, what are ya doin'?' He grabs me by my shirt, slams me down on the table. I fell against the steel edge and I cut my back. 'Hey, man, what's happenin'?' I say.

"So Jimmy gets up on the couch and dives off it at me. As

he dives I grabbed him by the head and he crashed into the doorknob. I put him right into it. The guy goes down and he ain't moving. I thought he was dead. I said to Carmine, 'Hey, Carmine, did you see that? He fell on the floor.' We picked Jimmy up and put him on the couch. Then he opened his eyes and said he wanted to go to sleep.

"Another day," Gauna went on, "I'm getting into Jimmy's car, so Carmine opened the door for me. Jimmy throws the car keys to Carmine, and they hit him in the chest and fell on the ground. I got down and picked up the keys and handed them to Carmine. Jimmy says, 'Hey, Frankie, put the keys back on the ground. He picks them up. He's my valet.' "

Gauna recalled a typical bar scene with Jimmy's pals in which a drunk started a fracas, and the person Gauna was talking to stood up, and without a word, went over to the drunk, knocked him out cold, and then returned to his conversation with Gauna as if nothing had happened.

Gauna went on to point out a side of Roselli's personality he admired: his wit and pithy way with a phrase. "I was seated with Jimmy and some guys in a restaurant on Broadway," Gauna recalled, "and they were talking about this bookie named Sal, Jimmy's friend. Sal had hired a kid named Tony to teach his chick, Marie, to sing. But Tony didn't do the right thing. They were always talking about 'doin' the right t'ing.'

"One of the guys says that Sal came home and found Tony in bed with Marie. Apparently Tony looked up and said to Sal, 'You got the wrong impression.'

"As we're talking, Tony himself, who's about twenty, enters the restaurant, looks around wildly, and spots Jimmy. Everybody looks down at their plates. Tony walks up to Jimmy and says, 'Jimmy, please tell Sal that he got the wrong impression last night.'

" 'I heard you were in bed with her,' Jimmy says.

" 'That's why Sal got the wrong impression, Jimmy,' Tony says. 'Jimmy, I swear if I'm lyin', you can find me in the river.'

"Jimmy looks up at Tony and says, 'I looked for you there this morning.' "

Even Jimmy's critics concede he was an affable drinker, even to the point of befriending his enemies, and one thing he refused to do was to eat alone. "I'd get a message," said Gauna, " 'Jimmy wants to eat,' and we'd all join him. If you sat beside him and he didn't like what you said, you found yourself moved. Your silverware was gone, it was at the end of the table. The favorite expression of these guys was, 'You're not doing the right t'ing.' "

One friend who lasted because he could tolerate Roselli's abrasiveness was Pete Cavallo, who met Jimmy in 1968. At the time, Cavallo was running live stage shows at Loew's 46th Street Theater in Brooklyn. The venture was highly unusual and inventive for the late 1960s: it was big-time vaudeville in Brooklyn in an era when vaudeville had been long dead.

"We'd lost money on shows with Buddy Greco, Lou Monte, and Jack E. Leonard," recalled Pete. "So I decided, forget about it, I gotta get Jimmy Durante. A friend of mine who was a connected person but a neighborhood guy was close to Durante. So I went up to him and asked him if he could help me get Durante.

"But meanwhile, my partner said there's a guy named Jimmy Roselli who's killing them. I said, 'Who's Jimmy Roselli?' We went up to the Concord Hotel to meet him. He was having a drink in the lounge. He said, 'Where do you want me to work?' I told him. 'I never heard of the place,' he said. 'Who worked there?' I said Lou Monte, et cetera. He said 'Who?' This was his sense of humor. He said he wanted twenty thousand a show, a lot of money then. My partner said, 'What are you, crazy?' So Jimmy says, 'Hey, I didn't ask you to come up here.

You asked me to give you a price. Furthermore, I won't work there because nobody worked there.' Jimmy turned to my partner and said, 'To begin with, you I don't like. And he looked at me. 'Him I like.' And that was that.

"A couple of months later I went to see Durante where he was playing at Palumbo's in Philadelphia and he agreed to play my theater. After his show I go to the bar and I saw Roselli there. He made a motion to me, and I thought he was calling my friend, who started to go over. Jimmy made a motion: 'Not him.' So I go over. He said, 'What are you doin' here?' And I told him about getting Durante. 'Durante's going to do your theater? When?'

" 'February.'

" 'You want me to come in in March?' And that was that.

"We didn't sell out with Durante. It was amazing. Roselli was coming in next. Now, we don't know from Roselli. When I sold tickets, they used to come in for six, eight, ten tickets; if I got a row of fourteen, it was great. I advertised. People coming in: 'I need fifty-two tickets.' 'Two tickets?' I said. 'No, fifty-two. Can I buy the whole loge?' We sell out both shows. I tell my partners, we gotta do another two shows. 'What are you, crazy?' they said again. We added the shows. We did ten thousand people in two days. Screaming, yelling, standing on the seats. The men love him as much as the women, if not more. That's amazing. He has a following from both sexes. I'm Italian. I don't really understand the language, a word here and there. But he would so control your feelings and your mind when he's singing, you get emotionally involved in what you're hearing. You put in your own words."

After that engagement, Cavallo moved on to the Walker Theater in Brooklyn and booked Jimmy again. The response was the same. The theater had no parking facilities and people were forced to park as far as twenty blocks away. They walked into the theater furious. "But when they walked out, you saw on their faces it was worth it," recounted Cavallo.

"One night Jimmy ran late and twenty-five hundred people were waiting in the rain for the second show. I walked up to him on the stage and told him. He said, 'Sure.' But then he turned to the audience and said, 'How do you like this guy? Takes your money and wants to cut the show.' That's part of his sense of humor. He constantly outdid every show I ever did: Tony Bennett, Bobby Darin, Don Rickles."

As Pete and Jimmy worked together, a deep bond grew between them. When they went on the road, they would sit for hours in their hotel room together and Jimmy would confide in him. "I never forgot what he told me," Pete said. "He went through so much rejection as a child. The amazing thing about his story, I think, is that he basically has gotten so far with his own way of doing things. I know him better than anybody. I know his moods, his motives. Never tell Jimmy he has to do something. You're dead."

As Jimmy himself has said, "You can't tell me I gotta. The only thing I gotta do is die."

"He wanted to be his own man," Pete explained. "He couldn't see doing weddings and things like that. He didn't want to be told what to do, or be under the gun. All he wanted to do is go and sing, and get paid for it properly. He wanted to make his own decisions. He wanted to say, 'I can't work three shows a night. My voice won't stand for it.' He wanted to go out and break away from everybody. Which wasn't an easy thing to do in those days."

Just as Pete came along, Roselli made more powerful enemies—enemies whose reach went even further than that of Gyp De Carlo and Buckalo. First came the Sinatras in 1969— Frank's mother, Dolly, then Frank himself. "It happened in my shop," Al Certo said. "Two bookmakers come to me; one of them says, 'Tony Pro [Provenzano] has got this baby charity [St. Joseph's School for the Blind] he does every year. But Tony is in jail. We're looking to help him out. Dolly's the chairman. She wants Jimmy to be there. Could you ask Jimmy to make an appearance?' I said, 'Well, okay.' Jimmy had sung for Dolly many times before, including Nancy, Jr.'s fifteenth birthday. So he had a closeness to the family to a certain extent. That was a time when Jimmy was really getting hot. He had 'Mala Femmena' out, he was breaking records at the Copa. When you get to a certain level, everybody wants you to make an appearance at a garage or whatever.

"That's where the cockiness came in," said Certo. "Jimmy, now, he's on top of the pedestal; his balls got a little big. He says, 'Dolly knows my number; why don't she call me like she's always done before?' Jimmy took it as an insult. By the time the story got to Frank, he thought that Jimmy refused his mother. But Jimmy just wanted to be asked personally." In her biography of Sinatra, *His Way*, Kitty Kelley confirmed Sinatra's version of events. She quoted Nancy Siracuse, a journalist with the *Hudson Dispatch*, as stating: "Frank got so mad at [Roselli] for turning down his mother that he never spoke to him again."

Some people believe that Sinatra, furious at the insult to his mother, had Roselli blackballed. "This fucking guy was always a thorn in my side," Roselli confided. "I guess I was a thorn in his side too."

He added slyly, "I worship the ground that's coming to him."

Certo recalled, "There was a time we walked into Jilly's. Sinatra walked over to Jimmy, put his hand on him, and said, 'How ya doin', *star*? How's the star? How ya been, star?' Didn't call him Jimmy. Jimmy looked at him and said, 'I'm not the star. You're the star.' 'Whyn't you have a drink with me, star?' He tried to put Jimmy down. You know, Frank always surrounded himself with guys, as far as voices go, lesser than him: Dean Martin, Sammy Davis."

Shortly after he refused to sing at Dolly's charity, there occurred an event that was even more damaging to Roselli. Joseph Colombo, head of the Profaci crime family, had formed the Italian-American Anti-Defamation League (which would later evolve into the Italian-American Civil Rights League), claiming that he wanted to unify the Italian-American community.

Historian Richard Gambino has written that the stereotype of Italians as violent, cunning, and criminal "grates against every nerve ending in the Italian-American ego, which desires respect and honor. Instead not only are they ignored and ridiculed, but they are also held in contempt."[16] Whatever Colombo's motives, the formation of the league tapped into a deep reservoir of long-pent-up anger and hurt within the Italian community over the derogatory way in which Italians were depicted in the media.

Of course, Italians were engaged in organized crime, but their number was comparatively small. It was rare to find a genuine acknowledgment of the contributions made by the great majority of Italian-Americans whose hard work and integrity were vital to the building of America. Writing of a meeting of the league he attended at the time, historian Michael Novak noted that "Italians have been symbolic villains in the American imagination ever since the puppet shows that Huck Finn went to see: those swarthy characters in black puppet capes, with thin mustaches, so threatening to milk-white maidens. Joe Colombo was tired of the mockery. He sensed that Poles, Sicilians, Italians, Greeks, Armenians, Croats, Serbs, Portuguese, Russians, Spaniards, Lithuanians, and others were also losing the sharp lust to 'become American.' They looked around; the prospect did not enchant. One by one, hundreds and then thousands were deciding not to continue trying to become what they are not, can never be. They were beginning to love themselves a little better. . . . I watched Joe Colombo with fascination. He was (I thought) the wrong man for the job. But who else was doing it?"

The rage among Italian-Americans ran so deep that it mattered little that a Joe Colombo was the league's leader—at least he was trying, or so the feeling went. One can cite analogies in the Jewish community's toleration of a near-psychopath like Meir Kahane because his ideology and his "Never Again" refrain tapped into feelings stemming from or related to Holocaust memories. For not dissimilar reasons, segments of the black community tolerate a Louis Farrakhan or an Al Sharpton due to anger and a sense of vulnerability that has its roots in a long history of oppression.

A specific catalyst for the formation of the league was the impending production of Francis Ford Coppola's *The Godfather*, a film that was certain to perpetuate denigrating images of Italian-Americans. Italian-American organizations denounced both Mario Puzo's novel on which the movie was based and the proposed film. In fact, the league played a leading role in trying to disrupt the project, claiming it would cease its harassment if the filmmakers removed any references to "Mafia" or "Cosa Nostra," an agreement that was reached. The victory was little more than a semantic one. No one who saw the film doubted it was about the Mafia.

On June 29, 1970, fifty thousand Italian-Americans poured into Columbus Circle (Circolo di Colombo) in New York City to celebrate Italian-American Unity Day and to insist that the Mafia was a figment of the public imagination. The crowd gathered to protest discrimination, an acute sense of powerlessness, negative media, and a lack of urban services and programs for the Italian-American community. The climax of the demonstration was a march to the New York headquarters of the FBI, which protesters accused of persecuting them.

The circle was decorated with green, white, and red streamers, and the crowd wore buttons that declared: "Italian Power," "Italian Is Beautiful," and "Kiss Me, I'm Italian." Hand-painted banners proclaimed: *"Basta con la Mafia"* ("Enough of the Mafia") and "Just Because We Have Italian Names, It Doesn't Mean We Are Criminals."

The Unity Day program stated:

> We meet here not to rejoice, but rather to raise a unified voice of protest.
> We have been defamed in the press, on television and radio.
> We have been degraded and discriminated against, and now, we say, Enough! . . .
> We have been reduced to the status of second-class citizens and we say, Never! . . .
> Let this, our first Unity Day Rally, serve notice that the Italian-Americans will no longer tolerate that treatment. . . .

But the media, according to Richard Gambino, "turned the event into a circus without attempting to distinguish the legitimacy of the feelings of the protesters from the tainted reputation of the league's early leaders."

A year later, on June 28, 1971, Colombo would be fatally shot by an assassin at another Columbus Circle rally. The league faded away quickly, and was never heard from again. But in its own distorted way, the league had scored a real civil rights point, one that was undercut from the start because of the criminal background of its founders.

During the period of the league's formation, Roselli had

been the only celebrity who took an active role in promoting it. He even marched with the organization around the FBI building. With his deep roots in the heart of the Italian community, Roselli was its natural representative. At the Feast of San Gennaro in Little Italy, Jimmy made a rare appearance, signing up fans for the league.

Pete Cavallo recalled, "There had been an earlier incident with Colombo. He had come to Jimmy a year before and said, 'Do my son's wedding and I'll fill your whole house with furniture.'"

"He never gave me a chair," Jimmy said.

"Yes," Pete reminded him, "you got one black chair. A black chaise lounge."

Though after the incident Roselli should have been suspicious of Colombo's promises, he listened when Colombo asked him to sing at a huge concert the league was planning at Madison Square Garden's Felt Forum. As Roselli remembered it: "Colombo said to me, 'You gotta head the league, you gotta do this, you gotta do that.' I thought, 'How could I walk away? They're all Italian.'"

But at the next meeting, an aide to Colombo told Roselli that Sinatra had agreed to perform. This altered the picture. Jimmy asked how much time he would be allotted to sing. "Maybe ten minutes," the aide said. Roselli understood that Sinatra would get whatever he wanted; he asked how much time Sammy Davis, Jr., would have onstage. "Oh, he's going to do whatever he wants," Colombo's aide said, adding that the league would pay for eleven of Davis's musicians. Finally, Roselli asked for three musicians he always used at his concerts.

"He said to me, 'You can't have the musicians; you can't rehearse.' They put up all these obstacles," Roselli said. "Sinatra had come in with a pad and pencil and said he didn't want me or Jimmy Durante on the bill at all. Pete Cavallo said, 'Refusing to perform is what Sinatra wants you to do.' But my fucking guinea temper—I said, 'Tell Joe Colombo he can suck my prick in Macy's window.' "

Pete went to their planning meeting. "They said, 'By the way, Jimmy Roselli is not going to do the show.' They said he wanted twenty-five musicians. I couldn't believe what I'm hearing. They humped him, now they make him look like a fag. The guy says, 'It's more important to Roselli that he have twenty-five men than that we put a few bricks in a hospital or feed a few hungry kids.' Yelling: 'Boo! Take his fucking records out.' "

As the rumors about Roselli's refusal to sing spread, the number of musicians he supposedly demanded kept growing from twenty-five to thirty-five to forty-five. Nightclub and theater owners were pressured not to book him.

"Club owners affiliated with wiseguys couldn't put Jimmy in even if they wanted to," said Cavallo.

Recalled Jimmy, "Joe Columbo had said, go down the fucking aisle. But I told him, 'Fuck you, your Defamation League, and all the fucking wiseguys.' I don't know how I didn't get killed. But they didn't kill me because they knew I was right. They coulda got me in a fucking saloon, said somebody bumped into me, go to work on me. But nobody did—because basically I never hurt anybody and I never harmed anybody. And when I did tell somebody off, I was always right. I used to say to the wiseguys, 'You guys taught me all the fucking brains that I got. Now you're mad because I was a good pupil. Don't get angry. I learned from all you guys.' "

The wiseguys had found effective ways to punish him. Even before he had left the Copa in 1972 after seven years of performing there, the boycott of his records and other nightclub engagements began. Now it intensified. As Roselli explained: "It wasn't easy for me. They held me back, telling their people not to go and see me. But people still came. They couldn't stop them nohow."

"Sinatra was another factor," according to Roselli. "Because he was a jealous piece of shit and that's how he did things. Especially since I came from half a block away from him. See, Sinatra got jealous of me and it's not hearsay. I know. Because he was in the company of wiseguys and anytime he got in their company, my name came up. Because I was always the sweetheart of the wiseguys. If not them, their mothers, their wives.

"Much as he wanted to be a singer, Sinatra would have given up his whole career to be a don. That's my opinion. He had Jilly and everybody calling him 'the old man.'"

Not only was Jimmy being blackballed by club owners, his singles in jukeboxes were being boycotted as well. "The Genovese crime family controlled the vending industry," commented deputy chief investigator Robert Buccino. "And I say, *controlled it.* Not influenced it, controlled it. I remember that time period. Roselli was extremely popular. At first they called him the next Sinatra and he was going big time. Then all of a sudden, bing, it was just cut off. And that was it, that was his career. You didn't see him anywhere, not even on television. Nothing.

"Sinatra just totally ended him. There's no doubt about it. . . . Roselli sang at the 500 Club in Atlantic City [which was run by the Bruno crime family] and then it was all over. The thing is, these stories [circulate]. That was like common knowledge. Because one thing about organized crime is that they always want to make an example and let the people know it: 'see what happened to him.' In other words, so the next guy won't refuse them. [Roselli] insulted Carlo Gambino, he insulted Sinatra, he insulted the Brunos . . . He couldn't be controlled. There were also questions whether he was too cheap . . . that he wanted money every time he sang. He didn't want to do the gratis type of thing. He wanted to get paid."

When Roselli told Buckalo he wanted out of his contract, the mobster said, "You have to do this job [at the Copa]. But you're on your own otherwise. Don't say you're with us. Nobody's gonna bother you. But don't miss one engagement." Roselli explained Buckalo's willingness to release him by saying, "They felt I wasn't listening to them. So I got my freedom." By honoring the Copacabana engagements each year for seven years, Roselli was absolved of all other entanglements with Buckalo. His direct business involvement with the wiseguys was finally over.

"They felt he was too much of a headache anyway," explained Pete Cavallo. "He was always bitchin' and moanin', bitchin' and moanin', and they got tired of hearing it. He got his money up front, or he wouldn't sing. But his career was definitely sidetracked. They figured, well, you go on your own, you ain't going nowhere anyway. The average guy would have been down the toilet, could not have survived. Because of the peer pressure. But he disproved that by surviving on his own merit, winning over on his talent. He took the knockdowns."

But it wasn't easy. Cavallo estimated that Roselli lost between $50,000 and $75,000 a year in income in the early years of the boycott. And Lee Salomon recalled how one night in 1972, bombed, he walked into the Dream Bar on 79th Street and Collins Avenue in Miami Beach, "a real racket joint. There was the boss, a woman with a guy, and me. And all of a sudden I hear a Jimmy Roselli record. And I said, 'Boy, is this guy not the best fucking singer you ever heard in your life?' 'That cocksucker? I forgot to take his records out.' "

After June 21, 1969, Roselli's name would never again appear on the *Billboard* charts. The wiseguys did their work well.

But despite the mob's best efforts, Jimmy's spirit was not broken. "He would bend," Pete Cavallo said, "but you could never
break him. Oh, they wanted to break him. They thought they
could."

"You put me against the wall, forget about it," Jimmy said.
"You can kill me, but that's what you have to do."

10

DONNA: "A LID FOR EVERY POT"

AS ROSELLI'S REPUTATION GREW, HIS PERSONAL LIFE went through a violent upheaval. "The first eleven years of my marriage," Roselli recounted, "I never, never played around. First of all you get some fucking diseased broad, who needs all that shit? I'd look, I'd bullshit, but it ain't worth it. It really isn't. Everybody talks. They think I was a big cunt man. I wasn't. Never. And at the time when I was young, I enjoyed singing. My whole life was how I was going to sing and where I was to sing and when."

By the twelfth year of his marriage, the tensions between Jimmy and Angie had begun to harden. "Angie was too possessive," recalled Roselli's Aunt Etts. "She was always jealous. The female fans used to grab him and kiss him; it was the business. I guess she couldn't take it."

Things were not helped by the presence of Angie's mother in the home after Jimmy's father-in-law died. Jimmy felt Antonette Guiffra dominated Angie's life, and left the couple with little privacy. "She was a good kid. Her mother destroyed her," Roselli said. "The mother wouldn't let go. She was always in the house. She was a good woman, but a headache, very domineering. She'd come running at me. I said, 'If you were a man I'd hit you on the chin. You eat in my house and all you do is give me aggravation.' When I married Angie, her parents put a roof over my head. I fixed their whole house up, rooms, a driveway, and an office. Then I gave her mother three thousand in cash to try to reciprocate for all the things they did for me. There was a lot of family interference from the start.

"What happened with me and Angie: I've never even told this to my daughter. I came home one night and she was reading a letter from an old boyfriend of hers. I grabbed the letter, looked at it, and I gave it back to her. That was the end of my marriage. I lived there, but that was the end. I think they had a romance going with the mail. And it turned me completely off.

"After that, I ignored her," Roselli said. "She went her way and I went my way. I didn't leave, because that's my background. I got married for better or worse." Jimmy's interpretation of the letter illustrates the kind of spitfire overreaction he has been prone to over the years. Quick to take self-righteous offense and to justify his actions, he never had second thoughts about what he saw as Angie's betrayal. Quite possibly, Angie was seeking only a connection with an old friend, an innocent respite from life with her volatile husband.

In 1967, when Jimmy was appearing at the 500 Club in Atlantic City, he met the woman, twenty years his junior, who would become his confidante, best friend, and future wife: Donna Tumolo. But their first meeting did not suggest that this was to be the start of an enduring love. He was walking outside the club behind a fabulous blonde whose back zipper was undone. "Hey, girlie, your zipper is open," he said. She turned and looked at him. "Well then," she said, "why don't you fasten it for me?" He walked over to her and closed the zipper slowly.

He invited Donna to come to his dressing room the following day. When she arrived and knocked on the door, Jimmy greeted her in his bathrobe. He opened it and threw it on the bed. He was nude. "Okay, let's have lunch," he said. Donna fled from the room.

Their next meeting took place two years later, when Jimmy was appearing at Palumbo's in Philadelphia. "So help me Christ, this is how it happened," said Skinny Skelly. "Jimmy's ready to go onstage and I go out in the hall to get the announcer to announce Roselli. In the meantime I come across these two sisters. So help me Christ, I should drop dead, two more sisters!

"These two girls came from Italy, the whole family. They weren't in the country that long. When they came to me, they spoke broken English. They were pretty nice; Donna and Marie. They asked me, 'Do you speak Italian?' I said, 'Very well.' They said, 'We'd like to talk to Jimmy Roselli.' I liked the other one, Marie: I was always a snake in the grass. But this kid [Roselli], when he got married, never fooled around with other broads, I'd say for fifteen years. Whenever I'd suggest it, he'd say, 'Nah, I don't wanna.' Very faithful. He was always a straight guy.

"Anyway, these two sisters were built like brick shithouses. Me, I was a horny son of a bitch. So I said, 'Okay, baby, stay right here, I'll get Jimmy.' But Jimmy said, 'No.' Then, after the show, Jimmy said, 'Hey, Skelly, where's those two broads you mentioned to me?' "

Skelly brought the girls in and introduced them to Roselli. It wasn't until later that Skelly found out Jimmy had met

Donna once before. "So up we go to the suite," he said. "Jimmy just fell for Donna. He was hooked. The guy got hit like a ton of bricks. I don't know what the fuck happened. He told me to get the phonograph and his records. And the whole fucking night he played his records to her. That's all he did. I just wanted to fuck the other broad right away. But whenever I left his room, he said, 'Hey! Where ya goin'? Stick around.'

"There I am in the fucking chair listening to his records. How many fucking songs can I listen to? I was fucking annoyed and tired. I want to fuck this broad. I go in the other room, he comes in and says, 'Come back.' He was like Mussolini: 'you go here, you go there.' I said, 'Hey, Roselli, give me a fucking break.' 'Come on,' he says, 'you got plenty of time for that shit.' Oh yeah? I thought. I'll fix this fucking guy. So I told Marie to go in the bathroom. I went out the door and went in there, locked the two doors, but I never got to do my thing. Roselli hollered, 'Where's that fucking jerk?' I hollered from the bathroom, 'Go fuck yourself.' "

And so it started. Jimmy didn't touch her that night. Just a romance, listening to his records, holding hands. That was the beginning of the courtship.

Donna Tumolo had come to America from Italy on the *Andrea Doria* in the summer of 1956, when she was ten. (Later that year, on July 25, 1956, the 29,100-ton ship, 697 feet long and 90 feet wide, collided with a Swedish ship, the *Stockholm*, and ultimately sank; 1,662 passengers and crew were rescued out of the 1,706 who were on board, the most successful rescue operation in maritime history.) Donna's family had lived in the small town of Biccari, in the southern Italian province of Foggia. "I had four living siblings; six had died before I was born, three from rheumatic fever," she said. "There just wasn't any medicine at the time. When we came to America, the whole family (my parents, three brothers, and a sister) went at one time.

"We saw the Statue of Liberty. Everyone on the boat, all they talked about was '*la statua*,' 'the beautiful lady in the harbor.' It was like a dream come true. We all had looked up to America. When a person came here, I mean it was the greatest thing on earth. You were a pretty lucky individual to be able to do this."

Settling in South Philadelphia in an Italian neighborhood, Donna's parents worked as tailors. "We were able to mingle with our own kind," she explained. "Everyone at work spoke Italian, the same in the neighborhood. That's why my mom never learned to speak English."

After a while Donna's father wanted to go back to Italy, where he had been self-employed. "This was a comedown for him," she says. "But for my mother, it made a big difference to have a washing machine when you're used to washing clothing in the river."

Donna couldn't wait to be naturalized, and she became a citizen at fifteen. "My mother wanted to also, and started to study, but children can be very hurtful. She would try to study and we would make fun of her when she pronounced English words. She got so discouraged she put the books down and never went back to them again. Neither of my parents ever became citizens."

When she was a teenager, Donna began working in a dry-goods store after school and on Saturdays. "My parents taught us that in order to get ahead in life, you have to work," she said. "My seven-year-old brother sold pretzels, walking through the streets of the city with a little basket. We had to work; we were a big family. My parents didn't believe in us going dancing. But I was very stubborn. I felt if I worked all week, I deserved to go to a dance on the weekend. My mother would say to me, 'You should do what your sister does.' And I said, 'Oh no. She has one head and I have another.' "

It was a tough, but real love that her parents provided. While her parents were not demonstrative (there was little kissing or hugging), Donna and her siblings knew they were loved "by the way they protected us, the way they put food on the table for us. My mom used to say, 'I can't buy you the beautiful clothes that you want, but I will never let you starve.' She explained things to us. I remember when I was eighteen working in the beauty salon, women would say, 'Oh, I want to give everything to my kids.' And I turned around and said, 'Well, what don't your kids have?' I meant, the only thing they want is love."

In those days, the neighborhood was like an extended family. "There were four elderly couples near us without children or anyone—they were all alone," recalled Donna. "When my mother made dinner, she would be sure to make a plate for these couples too. In that period, that was what South Philly was all about. You'd sit on the stoop outside until three or four in the morning on hot summer nights. Everybody would take out their beach chairs. The whole block knew each other and helped one another. Only one couple could afford a TV set. So when *The Mickey Mouse Club* came on at five-thirty we all went over there."

Donna first saw Jimmy sing onstage when she was eighteen. He was singing songs she was raised with. "Such conviction, such feeling—I didn't understand how this man could not have been born in Italy. Then, at our next meeting two years later, we talked all night, and all week. Here was a girl talking Italian, and I was filling every gap in his life. I was bringing back his life with his grandfather. And I had spirit, I loved people. He couldn't believe what was happening to him."

"Next thing you know, Donna is working in Manhattan," said Skinny Skelly. "I was the beard, the guy who was supposed to be Donna's boyfriend so nobody found out about their relationship. I said to Roselli, 'Hey, I'm married, you got me holding [Donna's] hand.' 'What the fuck you worrying about?' he said. 'You're married.' I said, 'I gotta cover myself.' He said, 'For what? Who knows you?' So when we went into a club, I sat with Donna; Jimmy sat across. This went on for quite a while."

Roselli continued to live with his wife, but spent most of his time at Donna's apartment in Lincoln Towers. "Jimmy was not the type of guy to say, 'Look, honey, you be here for me,'" Donna Roselli explains. "He didn't have a gun to my head. From the beginning he said to me, 'I will never get a divorce. My family comes first. This is the situation.' His grandfather set certain principles in his mind that till this day he believes in."

Donna maintains that if she had really wanted marriage, she would have forced circumstances in a different direction. But she was comfortable as it was. "I had more than Angie did. Like I was the wife. The only thing that was missing in my life was the piece of paper. That didn't matter to me. But Angie had to be Mrs. Roselli. When Jimmy started to get recognition, Angie felt like she was a star."

The opposite was true of Donna. "To me, when he is onstage, he's the artist that I admire. But when he's sitting down at a table or we're walking, he's the man that I'm in love with. I mean, I won't think twice of telling him to go screw himself. I think this is why our relationship has lasted. At the end of the day he will do what he wants anyhow, but I will give him my opinion."

Jimmy's daughter, Anne, was twelve when Donna entered their lives, although Anne would not be sure of Donna's identity for six more years. "He was a very loving father until I was about twelve," Anne recalled. "He was affectionate with me; he was everything he wasn't with other people. When Donna came into his life, my relationship with him started to change. He became strange, dictatorial."

Jimmy's preoccupation was now with Donna. Even when he traveled abroad, if Jimmy needed her, she would come to him immediately. "Through the years, he'd be traveling on the road and he'd call me up," Donna noted. "He'd say, 'Meet me here and there.' And I'd get on the plane. In 1970 he took Anne and Angie to Italy. All of a sudden Angie got ill. Jimmy calls me up and says, 'Meet me in Rome.' I get in on the seven o'clock flight. Angie is going back on the same plane on the one o'clock flight."

Riding in a cab from Naples to the airport in Rome, Jimmy introduced the driver to his wife and daughter. He then asked the cabbie to wait for his return. "I left with Angie and Annie, and I came back with Donna and we got into the cab," recalled Jimmy. "In Naples they have a saying, 'When you come, bring your own blanket.' They called the girl the blanket. So I said to the driver in Neapolitan, 'This is my blanket.' The guy fell out of the car."

They traveled from Rome to Naples and arrived at the Excelsior Hotel. According to Donna, Jimmy suddenly became melancholy. It was disillusioning to find that Naples had such dire poverty. The gap between his grandfather's romantic memories of the city and the bitter reality was a painful blow. "We went to the restaurant and Jim started drinking brandy. Two musicians started singing. After hearing all the songs, he turned to me and said, 'I can't believe it. All my life I heard Naples was a paradise. My grandfather used to say, "See Naples and die." This place reminds me of my old neighborhood. The only thing that's missing is the underwear on the lines.' I told him, 'Your grandfather was right. Fifty years ago Naples *was* beautiful. But it's like everything else: it changes. Naples isn't the buildings, it's the people in them, the feeling.'"

The place, the situation, Jimmy's memories of his grandfather's stories—they were all too much to bear. He sobbed uncontrollably for hours. "He was shaking, he was crying so much," Donna says. "We rode in a horse and carriage for three hours and I kept saying to him, 'Don't feel that way, Jimmy, please.' But he couldn't stop his emotions. His whole childhood came back to him.

"The next day, we were walking toward our hotel. A small group of workers stood at a corner, singing and playing their mandolins. Jimmy stopped, looked, and listened. He said to them in Neapolitan, 'Did you eat?' Five minutes later they were seated at a table with us in our hotel room, talking, eating, and drinking wine. The men sang softly and played their mandolins. Jimmy joined in and sang with them, his arms around me. That's Jimmy."

Donna continued to hold down a job throughout the relationship. When they had had arguments at the start, Jimmy had thrown up to her that she wasn't working for a living. One day she went out and got a job in her sister's beauty salon and held it from then on.

For years some people would say, "Here's the whore," "She's the one that broke up the marriage." "I was always the bad person," she said. "Nobody knew what I really went through. There were times Jim was so proud. He didn't have a dime. I would lend him money to pay for his bills. We always looked after one another.

"I could cater to him forty-eight hours, not twenty-four, if there were forty-eight in a day, and he would still not be satisfied. But I understood that, because my father was that way. My father was the man of the house no matter what. My mother could express an opinion, but not in front of people. I could never show him up."

Donna's father was not happy about her arrangement with Jimmy. He felt she was depriving herself of the chance to start a family. "I couldn't discuss it with my parents until later on, where I just took a stand and I said to them, 'Whether it's right or wrong, this is what I want in my life.' And I think the last two years of my father's life he more or less accepted it. When he was ill I would go to Philly every weekend to sit with him. He said, 'Whatever you do, don't be a dummy; because you are more his wife than his real wife is.' He did understand at the end."

Donna didn't want to have a child out of wedlock; she felt she couldn't live with that. "I felt I was selfish enough to destroy my life; I didn't want to destroy my child's life. To be told he was an illegitimate child, he or she; I couldn't deal with that. Because I was called the whore, the woman on the side. Little did they know that I was making it possible for him to tolerate the lifestyle that he was living. I could have broken up the marriage very easily. But basically, I was always with him. The only thing I didn't share was the house, the name. But we shared a bond . . . *everything* he was to me. And till today he's that. Because I've never had any of my own kids.

"That's what happens in life: you get so involved with someone. I devoted my life to him," Donna said. "I don't think that I was forced to. It just happened that way. I don't know if it was my bringing up, that you were true to one and only one, even though we had our differences at times. But it was always unconditional.

"If Jimmy doesn't want to do something, I can stand on my head and he won't do it. I mean, I was worried about how he looked. I would do his makeup, put the hairpiece on. I'm standing with the hairpiece and he screamed at me, 'Are you starting with that fucking thing?' "

Jimmy never knew how to deal with disappointment, because he's had so many. "When you're hurt as a child, it stays with you until you die," Donna explained. "The older you get, the more your childhood preys on you. The things that happened in his life, this is why he became the way he is today. All the starch has been taken out of him. And he feels, what does it all mean? Because when he sings at this stage of the game, he treats it as a business. He doesn't give it to you for nothing. There were times when Jimmy would just sing because he enjoyed it."

There were incidents when Roselli tried to be trusting and it backfired on him, such as the time when the wiseguys wanted him to do the concert for the Italian-American Anti-Defamation League the second year in a row in 1970. "They came to my apartment," Donna recalled. "I said to Jimmy, 'They're fulla shit: don't fall for it again.' That night they said to him, 'Don't worry, this time is different.' He was suspicious but he took a liking to the individual or whatever. 'Okay,' he said, 'for the Italian people I'll do it, but don't screw me around.' They said to him, 'No problem, you have the say, you can pick your musicians,' etc. I don't know if it was this fatherly image he looked up to in certain guys, where he would trust them. Especially his own kind. I said to him, 'You don't learn, do you? Businessmen you don't give the time of day. But assholes, jerks like this, you look up to them. What are you trying to prove? I don't understand your thinking.' He said, 'Mind your business. You wanna get off my back? Leave me alone.' This was always his answer. So what happened? Sinatra put the ax in it."

Jimmy wanted to trust Donna's judgment, and he usually

did. But he would rarely admit it; on the contrary, he would make her feel he was rejecting her. As Donna put it: "I was not an educated person, but I didn't lack common sense. I told Jim my feelings about these guys when I first started. At one point I said to him, 'Who am I going out with? You or these guys? These are assholes. They no sooner leave my apartment than they're standing near the elevator talking about me.' But he got the laughs. He reminisced with them. You see, some people will pay a price for that, and he's paid dearly. He got his biggest rocks impressing one of these nobodies. I don't know if it's a sense of approval that he belonged or what. He was the one always picking up the tabs, but he didn't care."

Much as he sacrificed common sense and logic in dealing with wiseguys and their ilk, there were times when Roselli exercised sound judgment as well. According to Donna, one instance was in his dealing with Sinatra over the years. "When John Gotti talked to Jimmy about Sinatra, Gotti said to him, 'Look, if I can do something to help . . .' Jimmy refused because what's it gonna mean? If someone wants to do something, they have to do it with their heart. There were occasions at Jilly's when Sinatra went out of his way to be cute. 'Hi, star,' he said to Jimmy. Jimmy handled it perfectly. Because he knew the man's character. He was waiting for Sinatra to turn around and say, 'Who the fuck asked you to be here?' Or whatever. Jimmy wouldn't put himself in that position. Jimmy was sharp where he wanted to be sharp. But we're all weak in certain areas."

In Donna's estimation, Roselli also took away some important survival lessons from his bruising experiences with wiseguys. "One thing Jimmy always said: '[The wiseguys] taught me so well and then they get upset because I was a great pupil.'" Roselli would observe how different wiseguys operated, and learn from them. He always, for example, carries a bunch of cash in a money clip. "When I first went out with him," said

Jimmy with Sammy Davis, Jr., at the Copacabana, 1965

Jimmy at his sold-out Carnegie Hall performance, September 12, 1966

Jimmy with WNEW radio personality William B. Williams at Carnegie Hall. Sinatra's favorite disc jockey, Williams hosted the influential Make Believe Ballroom *show and was one of Jimmy's earliest supporters*

Jimmy at a performance, age forty, 1966

Jimmy with comic Joe E. Lewis. When Lewis tried to appear at a nightclub not under Mafia control, his throat was slit. It took him years to recover

Jimmy with Jimmy Durante. Durante gave Jimmy his first big break in 1954 when they appeared at the Latin Quarter in Boston

ABOVE: *Jimmy with arranger Ralph Burns, recording* The Italian Album, *1967, a classic collection of Italian love songs.* BELOW: *Jimmy with Frank Sinatra in an undated photo. Jimmy grew up at 514 Monroe Street, Sinatra at 415. When Sinatra heard Roselli's two-octave range, says Jimmy, "I never heard from him no more after that"*

Jimmy, age forty-six, 1971. In a contentious incident in 1970, Jimmy canceled an appearance at a concert for Joe Colombo's Italian-American Anti-Defamation League. Jimmy was boycotted by clubs and radio stations for several years

*Jimmy with his
beloved aunts,
Anne, Frieda,
and Antonetta*

*Jimmy with his daughter, Anne
Roselli Bernstein, in 1990*

*Jimmy with his second wife,
Donna, in 1997*

Jimmy appearing in Westbury, New York, age 71, in November 1997

Donna, "and I was just a young kid, he'd say to me, 'You see this? This is what they call "fuck-you money." They can ask me whatever they want, and this gives me the right to say, "Fuck you. I don't need it." ' He always has the money with a rubber band in the clip. It's sickening, but this is him. I just wish in time he can find an inner peace."

One night a wiseguy from Boston came over to the house, Donna remembered, and he wanted Jimmy to sing at an affair without payment of any kind. Jimmy refused, and stood up, ending the conversation. He told the mobster, "Look, I have no intention of singing for nothing. You can punch, you can do whatever you want."

Another time Jimmy came back to the apartment with a black eye, panicking Donna. "Here I am, a twenty-five-year-old girl, what's happening here? He was always a man's man. He just took the punches." She recalled a conversation with the same guys who'd stolen the money at Roselli's Carnegie Hall concerts. They were again trying to coerce Jimmy into signing a new contract with them. Jimmy told them, "You can shoot but I'm not signing. I'm not making any deal with you; it costs me money." The hood looked at him and said, "You're out of your skull." Jimmy said, "No, I'm not. I only have to die once."

Through the years Donna has come to the conclusion that because Jimmy didn't have a mother or a father, he always had to do everything on his own. "Granted his grandfather did a great job and his aunties did the best job they could—nobody ever really did anything for him. I mean, I thank the Lord he turned out the way he did. And I think it's because of his grandfather ruling with an iron hand the way he did, setting these principles in him. That you can never take away from him."

Donna understands this because she was raised with that

same kind of thinking. "But if I was in pain, I had my mother to say, 'Okay, honey, it's okay.' My parents were there. He didn't have that. So he built this wall around him. He feels what I feel. But he doesn't know how to express it, how to express emotion.

"He's like a walking time bomb sometimes. Each step is a different move. Even when I talk to him sometimes, his mind is twisting it. Half the time he doesn't mean it. It's a defense.

"I was timid in many ways, but being exposed to Jimmy at such a young age, I grew up with him. He was always a challenge, as I had to be for him in order for us to succeed for each other. He wanted me to be that soft woman, yet he wanted me to be strong.

"I said to him, 'You know you have so much love in you, and you don't bring it out. Why?' It's a defense he learned on the streets. That's the only way he was able to survive. But I knew I was his whole life, as he was mine. And I wouldn't have changed it for all the money in the world. I can only sum it up in this way: As my dad used to say, 'There's a lid for every pot.' "

11

FOR PETE'S SAKE

BY 1969, PETE CAVALLO HAD BECOME THE PERSON WHO, after Donna, made the most profound difference in Roselli's life. Jimmy was extraordinarily lucky in both cases, for the late 1960s and early 1970s were to be his darkest years. Boycotted by the wiseguys, shunned by much of the Italian community, Roselli felt extremely isolated. "[The wiseguys] put their hooks on Jimmy," Vito Pedesta related. "The only place Jimmy could sing was the New York metropolitan area and the East Coast. Sinatra had the pull with [the wiseguys]. But Jimmy had friends here [on the East Coast]. Sinatra kept him out of the rest of the country."

In Hoboken, the atmosphere was very strained. "There were those who believed Jimmy," Pete Cavallo recalled, "and those who believed the rumors [about his refusing to sing at the Anti-Defamation League concert]."

A gentle man with a wry sense of humor and surprising perspicacity, Cavallo, an associate of his confided, has often been in debt and "would have been dead a long time ago if it weren't for his personality." His devotion to Roselli has lasted through the stormiest years. Aside from Donna, he is Roselli's only adviser, as well as his canny protector. But Cavallo is mostly an unpaid adviser. These days he exists on his Social Security check and the small sums Jimmy pays him when he works Atlantic City or other venues.

Obese, with dancing eyebrows, twinkling eyes, and a sweet smile, Cavallo has a deep understanding of what makes Roselli tick. Jimmy relaxes perceptibly in his presence. Still street kids, Cavallo and Roselli sneak hot dogs when Donna isn't looking; they are tuned in to each other's needs like brothers. "I know him better than anybody," explains Pete. "I know his moods, his motives. We could be in the dressing room with his fans. He don't have to say anything, he just has to look at me, and I know he's tired or whatever. And I'll say, 'Jimmy, we have an interview, we have to go now.'" And Roselli admits, "I know what he's thinking and he knows what I'm thinking."

"When I met Jimmy in 1968," recalled Pete, "he was still fulfilling his obligations at the Copa with Buckalo [one extended engagement a year], but he wasn't with anybody."

Jimmy was brushed off by the wiseguys, and by 1970 he also discovered that no agency wanted him. William Morris, which had represented him since 1966, refused to continue representing him. And the rejections only increased his suspicions. "He didn't trust *anyone*," emphasized Cavallo. "Himself only. That includes me, his wife, anybody. And today he's basically the same way."

Roselli and Cavallo took a new approach in dealing with the mob. "We decided at that point we're not gonna ruffle any feathers, okay? They did what they had to do," Cavallo explained. "They didn't say, *'You can't sing'* or *'We find you singing,*

we're gonna shoot you.' But they really believed that by doing what they did, they would just send his career down the
toilet."

As Jimmy put it: "They went around bum-rapping me all
over the city."

But Roselli continued to turn out albums: In 1970 his tribute
to Al Jolson, *Let Me Sing and I'm Happy*, was released by UA.
Produced by Roselli and arranged and conducted by George
Siravo, the album contains Roselli versions of all the Jolson
standards, including the title song, "Swanee," "My Mammy,"
"Ma Blushin' Rosie," "Anniversary Song," "Sonny Boy," and
"Back in Your Own Back Yard." Roselli contributed exhila-
rating versions of "All by Myself" (Irving Berlin) and "After
You've Gone" (Creamer and Layton). The wiseguys could not
have been happy with Roselli's photograph on the back cover:
wearing an open shirt and a black sweater with the initials J.R.
in white, his thumbs stuck into his belt, Jimmy, looking tanned,
robust, and gleefully defiant, grins at the camera.

With his back against the wall, Roselli typically did his best
work. His next album was *Come Into My Life* (1970). He produced it himself, and it is one of his best English-language
records. It features "When Your Old Wedding Ring Was
New," the 1912 song he had rediscovered and made his own,
and it would help keep his career afloat in the dark years. The
title song by Phil Badner became one of Roselli's signature
songs, and in "You Are Mine" (Panzutti-Jerome) Roselli hits
some of the highest notes of his recorded career.

A song he recorded that year, "A Million Dreams Ago"
(Jurgens-Howard), is the memory of a love, and sadly in November 1970, Jimmy's Aunt Frieda, who had given so much
of herself to Jimmy as a boy, was diagnosed with leukemia.
Jimmy learned of it in a phone call and left with Pete for

Philadelphia immediately. Roselli's relationship with his aunt had become strained when she married. "Her husband was jealous of me," Roselli said. "They fought like cats and dogs over it. Frieda would say to him, 'You're jealous of this kid.' And he was."

Jimmy and Pete went to the hospital every day. "She was a good woman," Jimmy said. "She was a sweetheart. They had her wrapped like a mummy. You couldn't see her face."

In the evening Pete and Jimmy sat in their hotel room. "Jimmy would sit there with tears in his eyes," Pete said. "She died at the end of the week."

The next year *Jimmy Roselli*, a double album of both English and Italian songs, was released by United Artists. Produced by Leroy Holmes, it had scores of highlights: "Angelina," a lilting song by Sol Parker; the classic "You Made Me Love You" (McCarthy and Monaco); Hank Sanicola's "I'm Coming Home, Los Angeles"; "Welcome to My World" (Winkler and Hatchcock), the Dean Martin hit; "Senza Mamma e Innamorata" (Donadio); and "T' Ne Vaie" ("You're Leaving") by Bovie and Valente. The album cover featured a grid of miniature Rosellis in tux in all the motions of singing—a perfect cover for those who could not get enough of him.

The albums kept coming, but how to get them played was another matter. And where to get work became a critical problem. Pete went from one talent agent to another, pleading with them to take Roselli on, but he was damaged goods. There was another brutal blow: WNEW-AM, New York's popular music radio station, yanked Roselli from the airwaves. He had been featured regularly on the station, which was considered the Sinatra station in New York. WNEW played every major talent of the day, including Duke Ellington, Tony Bennett, Billy

Eckstine, Dinah Washington, Carmen McRae, Billie Holiday, Louis Prima, Lou Rawls, Johnny Hartman, Bobby Darin, and Ray Charles. These were the serious artists of Tin Pan Alley, the interpreters of Berlin, Gershwin, and Rodgers and Hammerstein. For a major recording artist and nightclub performer like Roselli to be excluded from the airwaves was disastrous. "They used to play the hell out of my records. Sinatra must have said this guy is moving too much, or whatever," speculated Roselli. After a pause, he said, "Of course it was Sinatra."

Whether it was Sinatra or not, the reality was that Roselli was suddenly excluded from the most important station in the country for his kind of music. As he told *The Wall Street Journal* in 1991: "To get a record of mine played on that station now, the Lord has to intercede."

Probing further, the *Journal* found some who agreed that Sinatra was the cause of Roselli's exclusion. Al Glasgow, a casino consultant in Atlantic City, was quoted as saying, "Sinatra supposedly had him blackballed." On the other hand, Joseph Coffey, a top investigator at the New York State Organized Crime Task Force, contended that "we believe it was the Gambino family." WNEW's station manager at the time, Gary Brandt, confirmed that Roselli didn't get airtime, but told the *Journal* he "seriously doubted" that the mob ever had anything to do with what the station played.

With Jimmy's career in eclipse, Roselli and Cavallo decided they would try some innovative steps, such as independent concert venues outside the traditional routes dominated by the wiseguys. In 1971 Cavallo and Lefty Jimmy Geritano rented Club 802 in Bensonhurst, Brooklyn (later to become the 2001 Odyssey, where the dance sequences in *Saturday Night Fever* were filmed), for ten Roselli shows. Jimmy performed for two weekends (Friday, Saturday, and Sunday) and was paid $14,000. Cavallo and Lefty Jimmy paid the band. The same year Pete and Jimmy decided on a six-city tour: Boston (Symphony Hall), Buffalo (Kleinahan's, a nightclub, and Theatre Series, Inc., a concert venue), Baltimore (Civic Center), Providence (Concert Hall), Chicago (Orchestra Hall), and Springfield, Massachusetts (Springfield Municipal Auditorium). As Pete explained it: "That way we didn't have to deal with club owners. These were individual concert promoters that didn't have to account to anybody. That's why we took that route. And United Artists helped because Jimmy was recording with them. They assisted in every city with newspaper ads and publicity. Jimmy would sign copies of his albums and sell them at stores. At the same time I would go to the local stations in each city and set up interviews. And I'd go to the Italian organizations like Sons of Italy. It was a whole promotional tour which we did without any interference from the wiseguys.

"We had a backer named Hal Rose, who was in real estate," Cavallo continued, "and we rented the venues in each city. We paid the twenty-four musicians, and Jimmy got $5,000 a show, and all his travel arrangements and mine were covered."

The tour became a test of whether Roselli could circumvent wiseguy control of major venues and attract audiences in spite of the rumors the wiseguys had spread about his disloyalty to the Italian community. The results were mixed: each city had been booked for two concerts, but Roselli was able to fill only one. In the process, the friendship between Roselli and Cavallo strengthened as they tried ever harder to resurrect Jimmy's career. In the dark days of winter, they'd sit in hotel rooms in lonely towns as Roselli unburdened himself by telling his story to the compassionate (and very funny) Cavallo.

Cavallo also won Roselli's trust by going the extra mile that Jimmy demanded in his personal relationships. As Donna knew, Roselli's emotional needs were sometimes demanding in the extreme, and he would never forget the poverty of his earliest years. Bob Gans said that in the 1970s he had once opened Roselli's bedroom closet and found it stuffed to the ceiling with food. "What's this for?" he had asked. Jimmy paused and said, "I used to be hungry."

Pete proved his devotion not only during the tour but also later by expending his own money on projects that Roselli questioned. Cavallo was convinced that "My Way" was really Roselli's story, not Sinatra's. He begged Roselli to sing it, but Roselli demurred, since he rightly felt the song belonged to Sinatra. Cavallo, whose finances were always limited, paid $500 for the musical arrangement of "My Way" that Roselli ultimately sang and recorded, because Pete believed so deeply that it expressed Roselli's take on life. Cavallo has been rewarded ever since, although not financially: "My Way" is the one English song for which Roselli always receives a standing ovation wherever he sings it. And the largely Italian audiences applaud for more than artistic reasons: they know he has earned the hard way the right to sing the song.

Cavallo inspired Roselli's confidence, and it enabled Jimmy to speak freely about painful memories that ordinarily he would not divulge to another man. In *Blood of My Blood*, Richard Gambino described the controlled demeanor of Italian-American men, which he claimed derived from the medieval chivalry that had been preserved in southern Italy: "The posture of Mezzogiorno [southern Italy] men is a revealing anachronism. Body erect, back straight, shoulders back, even when sitting. Their faces are impassive. They are silent until spoken to. . . . They are offering a reminder that for a man, the ever-present obligation is *agire da maschio*, to act in a manly fashion. . . . Severe and demanding qualities of character are needed. . . . The essence of the manly ideal often goes by the name of honor, *onore*."

But Roselli's personality also reflects his own deep-rooted

insecurity. A wellspring of feeling is carefully guarded alternately by silence and by a loud and confrontational brashness.

Even though the tour was free of the wiseguys' control, Roselli and Cavallo still observed a kind of wiseguy etiquette with the top bosses. "Wherever we went on tour," Pete recalled, "when we would go into a town, the first thing, we had to go to the restaurant of the big boss of the town with his girlfriend, his mistress. On the second night we had to go to their houses with their wives. On the third night it was their grandmothers and aunts. And they still wanted Jimmy to do weddings. He did many weddings for the big guys, but even the little guys wanted him. We actually had to run out of town just to say we were out of town."

There was one recurring incident on the tour that explained some essential facts about Jimmy to Pete. "I would call home every day," Pete tells me. "God forbid something happened to my mother. I wanted to be aware of it, and if anything happened, I would have to go home. And Jimmy would catch me on the phone and say, 'Ya call your mother every day? What are you, a mother's boy?' You see what was coming out? It was only frustration, hurt, that he didn't have this. Jimmy loved my mother. I knew where he was coming from: that I had someone there I love who loves me. A lot of people, it would go right over their heads. But I understood."

Jimmy rarely changed his basic repertoire of music on the tour, although that repertoire did contain a wide variety of songs from which he made selections on a given night. On May 15, 1971, for example, Roselli appeared at the Municipal Auditorium in Springfield, Massachusetts, and a local reviewer covered the performance. The basics were in place, and would remain so over the years: Billy Dennison conducted the orchestra of thirty-two men, and the bill was opened by comic

Lou Cary, who would appear with Roselli at Caesars Atlantic City twenty-seven years later. The closing number was "Rock-A-Bye Your Baby with a Dixie Melody," as it still is today. Pete would do the advance work.

At first the audiences were sparse. According to Pete: "In Buffalo, Jimmy was booked for two shows but could only fill up one. So this hurt the man. At Kleinahan's [in Buffalo] I saw him do the greatest show I've ever seen in my life. I saw him come off that stage, tears coming down his eyes, like 'I showed these people.' That show is so vivid in my mind. Now, the stubbornness of Jimmy Roselli: We went back six months later and packed the place. Because everybody who went to this show told somebody. He proved the point. 'Okay, this is who I am.' And he did it. For some reason, when Jimmy was up against it, he would sing from his *balls*. As nuts as he is, he does have that kind of charge—I guess courage, in a sense. When his back is up against the wall, like a rat in the corner, he strikes. There's no one better at that. In all the years I've been in the business, the people I've known and booked, there's none better at that." But Jimmy was not as comfortable with success. Pete urged him to do another tour of the six cities the following year, building on the impact he had made. Jimmy did perform at Kleinahan's again, but refused to do the others.

"Jimmy also turned down San Francisco in 1971," Pete recalled. "Mayor Alioto wanted him to come out there and guaranteed he would sell out the place. He said he'd give Jimmy five thousand dollars. Jimmy said no; he wanted more money. He bucked everybody."

What sealed the relationship between Pete and Jimmy was the fun they had with each other during that tour. Jimmy did a lot of the teasing at Pete's expense, and the subject was usually Pete's weight.

"I was always on a different diet," Pete remembered. "One time I had to eat five fruits in one day. I would come with my new brown paper bag and we would go out on business."

Jimmy remembered differently. "I'd pick him up in Brooklyn. He'd come out with a little paper bag with an orange, an apple, a pear . . . This was it for the day, he said. But by the time we got to Manhattan, the whole thing was gone. The only thing he didn't eat was the bag."

Once they were in a New Haven office talking about a job. "They put these pupu platters out," Pete recalled. "Jimmy's talking with this guy and I figured he wouldn't see me. So I took a spare rib . . . I ate the whole platter. He didn't say a word."

"I seen everything he ate," Jimmy corrected.

"Afterward he says to me seriously," Pete continued, " 'I want you to do me a favor. I want to get on your diet. Can I eat like that?' "

Another time they were in Toronto when Jimmy said to two friends of his, Luke Massero and Nunzio (Clarkie) Pascalle, "Let's take a walk." He pulled the car up right in front of a custard stand. Pete said, "No, I'll wait." Jimmy persisted. " 'Come on, get out of the car.' He got me out of the car and locked it; he won't let me sit in there. So now he and his friends are gone about twenty minutes."

"He couldn't walk more than a block, he was so heavy," explained Jimmy.

"Ten minutes pass," said Pete. "I can't take it. I love custards, okay? So I looked down the block and nobody's coming. I went to the custard guy and I said, 'Give me a big one.' So it's coming out of the machine. Then I see Jimmy and his friends coming down the street. So I said to the guy. 'Just give me what you got.' Now you know when you eat something that's cold? I take a bite and the cold zooms to my head. It was leaking; it was a hot night. I thought, 'What am I going to do?' So I go and throw it under the car. They come back. Clarkie says to Jimmy, 'Rosie, look.' Jimmy looks down and catches me under the car throwing the custard away. He used to catch me on every diet.

"And he never let me sleep!" Pete exclaimed. "He'd watch to make sure. I'd sleep with one eye closed and keep the other eye open. And he'd think I was awake. He'd open all the windows in the car to let the cold air in. I used to beg him: 'Just give me five minutes to close my eyes; I want to rest five minutes.' Five minutes went by and the windows were open again."

At times the two acted like grade school pranksters. Disembarking from a plane, Pete found the distance to the baggage claim too far for his bulky body. So Jimmy deposited him in a baggage cart and wheeled him down the aisle, while Pete called out, "Watch the baby! Watch the baby!"

Indeed, it's difficult to imagine how Roselli would have survived without the many interventions that Pete Cavallo effected in his life, for Jimmy made his share of enemies, and not only among wiseguys.

Even while attempting to remake his life, Roselli was haunted by his past associations. In early 1971, the FBI had released the transcripts of the wiretap evidence it had introduced at the conspiracy trial of Gyp De Carlo. Since Roselli's name appeared several times in the transcripts, he was summoned to appear on January 22, 1971, before a special Nassau County grand jury probing mob infiltration on Long Island. The New York *Daily News* reported that Roselli "was questioned about his alleged connection with reputed mobsters Paul Sciacca and Sonny Franzese. . . ." But Roselli had long ago severed his connection to De Carlo, and for him the questioning represented a painful reminder of a period of coercion, humiliation, and ridicule imposed on him by the mobster, one from which he wrenched free at the risk of De Carlo's murderous wrath. Those were not the kinds of facts the FBI was looking for, and Roselli wasn't about to disclose them anyway. In fact, Roselli disclosed nothing at all.

Martin Scorsese has written in *Scorsese on Scorsese* that "where I come from [Manhattan's Little Italy] the worst thing you could be was an informer." Roselli would never be a rat. He was constitutionally incapable of it. The code of *omertà*, of silence in the face of inquiries by authorities, ran deep in him. It was part of being "L'Uomo di Pazienza" (A Man of Patience)—the highest ideal of manliness, dating back to the old values of southern Italy, where noncooperation with authorities, as Richard Gambino interpreted it, was an expression of defiance against oppressive and exploitative outsiders.

According to Dennis Della Fave, Frank Sinatra made derisive remarks about Roselli in response to news coverage of the Nassau grand jury probe. Della Fave had seen Sinatra onstage at the Garden State Arts Center in the early 1970s when Sinatra himself was being investigated by the New Jersey Commission about his alleged mobster ties. "Frank's onstage and he brings up the subject before he even sings a note," recounted Della Fave. "He says, 'I don't know what the hell they're bothering me for. Why don't they bother those no-talents like Vic Damone, he needs the publicity. Or get Jimmy Roselli. They gotta know that he's mixed up with everybody. . . . ' Rosie would never have done that to anyone. I walked out."

After the upstate tour, Pete Cavallo again sought representation for Roselli. Unfortunately, Jimmy's reputation had preceded him. Pete finally turned to CMA, Creative Management Associates, and its president, Buddy Howell. Howell was interested, for even as the wiseguys maintained their pressure, Pete said, "the blackballing was beginning to wear off as he kept singing. The women always supported him. And a lot of the wiseguys would sneak into places where he sang. Low profile, sat in the back. Because their wives and girlfriends insisted on going."

Howell signed up Roselli, and offered to get him into the prestigious Royal Box of the Americana Hotel. Roselli was frightened that "his people" would desert him, that they would not come to a luxurious hotel in tuxes and gowns. And he was afraid that they had turned against him.

Pete argued with him: "You're wrong. The Italian people, when they have their weddings, they buy a beautiful gown for this one time. This is a great shot for them to show off their gowns again." Wherever Roselli went, he asked everyone what they thought about his singing at the Royal Box: "Tell me something: would my people come to a hotel to see me?" According to Pete, Jimmy would ask the question in such an intimidating way the respondent would know what the right answer was: "No, you're right, Jimmy." Jimmy would then turn to Pete and say, "See?" But occasionally someone would say, "I think Pete is right." Jimmy's response to this was a scornful "Aw, you don't know what you're talking about."

Ultimately Roselli came up with more reasons not to play the Americana. The management offered to pay for an orchestra of twenty-one musicians. Roselli insisted he needed twenty-four. Knowing what Roselli was up to, Pete offered to pay $2,000 a week for the three extra musicians out of his own pocket. Roselli accepted his offer, and it would not be the last time Pete put himself on the line financially because of his belief in Roselli. Recalled Pete, "I said, 'Look, I want to prove a point. You'll knock them dead.'"

Roselli agreed, but the matter was not yet settled. The

Americana press office wanted publicity pictures. "He had only very old pictures from when he was a young kid," Pete remembered. "I said to him, 'We need new pictures. These are from your First Communion. All you need is your godfather next to you.' Jimmy was groaning and moaning. 'I ain't going for no money.' So I paid for the pictures—five hundred dollars.

"You see," Pete related, "I wanted to give him a boost. And I wanted him to let me handle his career and I wanted to prove I could do it. I said, 'Let me show you what to do.' "

Did Jimmy appreciate Pete's generosity? "Well . . ." Pete said. "Yes and no. He just said afterward, 'You were right,' but that's it."

All his conditions met, Roselli opened at the Royal Box of the Americana on November 3, 1971. The three-week engagement was a reprise of his Copa years: lines around the block, ecstatic audiences, standing ovations. It was a personal triumph for Roselli. He was paid $17,500 for a six-day week, putting on eight shows. "The contract also stipulated," said Cavallo, "that after each week's gross had exceeded $35,000 ($17,500 for Roselli and $17,500 for the Americana), we went into percentage: 70-30 in the Americana's favor the first week, 60-40 the second week, and then 50-50. We went to 50-50. Jimmy's net was close to $60,000."

And, as usual, the wiseguys could not stay away. Carmine (the Snake) Persico, facing a long stretch in prison, came to the Americana every night straight from his trial. Persico looked as if he didn't have a care in the world, waving his arms and singing along. "It was one of the biggest nightclub grosses in history, as big as the Copa," Cavallo remarked.

"Roselli was back, bigger and better than ever. That engagement turned his life around. He'd made it on his own."

12

MEAN STREETS

MAKING IT, HOWEVER, DIDN'T CHANGE ROSELLI'S AT-titude; if anything, it hardened it. He continued to chart a stormy course that tossed him back and forth between near-fame and obscurity. Jimmy did not last long at CMA. Right after the Americana engagement, "they called up, all excited," said Pete Cavallo, "they had the Latin Casino in Cherry Hill, New Jersey, for Jimmy. They wanted to give him seventeen musicians but he wanted more. They offered him another job in Chicago with sixteen musicians. He said no and quit them."

Jimmy still carried himself as if he were on the mean streets of his youth. He continued to take with him his father's rejection and his feelings of unworthiness. Concomitantly, his need to prove himself of value spurred him on to make enormous efforts—especially when he was down. His energy level was incredibly high, and he needed little sleep. He thrived on conflict; rage was his engine. And he still made the wiseguys weep.

Donald Alfano, who grew up in Hoboken, recalled watching

the wiseguys at one of Jimmy's performances. "They'd sit there listening to him sing these Italian love songs or songs about Mama, about their parents and how they grew up, that fitted into these guys' lives. Bent-nose guys, *big* guys. They'd sit there, a dozen of them, crying. I'd go backstage afterward and Jimmy would say, 'You see those guys? I had 'em cryin' like babies.' He'd get the biggest kick out of that. He told me a hundred times."

The wiseguys were not willing to cry for just *any* Italian singer. Roselli still admired the wiseguys' strength just as they admired his. Their unspoken mutual admiration was also a source of protection for him. Deep down, the mob must have known he respected them—up to a point. The fact that they could not walk all over him may have made them respect him more even as they tried to throttle his career.

At the same time, Roselli was treated condescendingly by Italian-American show business professionals who also were not averse to exploiting him. Jimmy rightfully took these episodes as personal affronts by people he considered family. Approached by Francis Ford Coppola's mother in 1972 to appear in *The Godfather, Part II*, Jimmy was startled at her offer: "She said, 'You happen to be the best Neapolitan singer in the business. We want you for a scene in the film.' "

The scene was the one in which Vito, played by Robert De Niro, walks into the Italian theater with his friend Genco. Vito and Genco watch Peppino weep onstage as he sings about how he's left his mother in Italy. Then Peppino receives a letter informing him his mother is dead. He cries and sings "Senza Mamma" ("Without a Mother"). Roselli was offered the role of Peppino, in which he would sing both songs.

"I said to Coppola's mother, 'Okay, how much you want to pay me?' 'Pay you?' she says. 'We don't want to pay.' So I say,

'What the fuck do I need with you? You're gonna make two hundred million on it and you want me to sing for nothing?'

"I wouldn't have done it anyway. That first song was written by Coppola's father. They wanted me to do that song and sent it to me. But I never liked it; this fucking song was nothing. It was a piece of shit song. The money is not important if I'm gonna do a piece of shit and I'm gonna come off like a dog. It happened for the best. But—no money. No money! You want the best Neapolitan singer and you don't want to pay for it. I was like an animal. I was insulted. Then I heard Al Martino gave them fifty thousand to play Johnny Fontaine in the picture—*gave them!*"

Roselli's moral code was at the heart of his fury, and sometimes—as in the Coppola case—he was entirely right.

Then in 1972, Roselli was approached by Martin Scorsese, who wanted to use his recording of "Mala Femmena" in *Mean Streets*, Scorsese's film about third-generation Italian-Americans in the streets of the Little Italy of his youth. "Mala Femmena" has an electrifying effect in the film, especially in the almost surreal bar scene in which a bloodied gunshot victim refuses to collapse and, instead, lunges at the shooter and grapples with him even as more bullets are pumped into him. Roselli's passionate voice could not fit the scene better—it is a thrilling accompaniment to the action. Jimmy was offered $5,000 for the recording, and he agreed, a sum he would always bitch about. Until today, he seems unaware of how important such exposure is to a performer.

In 1973, *3 A.M.*, Roselli's finest, most introspective album (particularly side two) of ballads, appeared. It is also the one instance of Roselli performing with just a trio. Carol Lees said of it, "Jimmy's approach here is very hard for a singer to do: very vulnerable and risky, a little like walking out on a highway, without a big backup." Yet Jimmy sounds fully at home. The album cover, in purple and brown tones, features a drawing of Jimmy in a posture of one-to-one intimacy, sitting relaxed on a barstool, shirt neck open, red handkerchief in his lapel, holding a microphone. Three musicians—a pianist, drummer, and bass player—sit behind him.

Produced by Henry Jerome and arranged by George Siravo, *3 A.M.* features Mel Lewis on trumpet and Phil Bodner on woodwinds. This is a different sound from Roselli's more purely instrumental, without sentimentality or melodrama. Simple and unencumbered, it is a risky album for Roselli. It is also his most romantic and honest. The sadness of his marriage may have been the emotional backdrop for this remarkable recording. The intimacy and haunting resonance of the songs is a result of his pulling back and inviting the listener in. You don't feel as if there's a singer onstage singing at you; he's in the room with you. The approach is clean and lovingly respectful of the music.

"This record has an extraordinary intimacy coupled with exceptionally good musicianship," Scott Harlan remarked. "Roselli's got an ear that doesn't stop. His pitch is incredible. He's right in the center of every note, and when he isn't, it's deliberate and has more impact. He knows exactly why he hits the note and when to arrive."

Roselli's version of George and Ira Gershwin's "But Not for Me" is remarkable for being possibly the slowest version of the song ever recorded. Jimmy doesn't play the song sadly, yet it's melancholy and there's a certain grace to it. On *3 A.M.* he sounds more confident and defined, beautifully drawing out the melody of "But Not for Me," gentle and caressing on "Music

Maestro, Please." This is the mature Roselli, who has fully found his style.

Roselli followed *3 A.M.* up with another superlative album in 1974, *The Best of Neapolitan Songs*. With arrangements by Ralph Burns and Peter Moore, this double album includes "Mala Femmena," "Guaglione," "Statte Vicino Amme" ("Stay close to me as the ocean caresses the sand"), "Anema e Core," "Passione," "Dicitencello Vuie" ("Just Say I Love Her"), "Passione Ardente" ("An Ardent Passion"), "Aimmo e Napule . . . Paisa" ("We're from Naples, Countrymen"). Jimmy produced it himself, and it stands as one of the greatest Neapolitan records ever released in this country.

His last album for UA was *Sweet Sounds of Success*, and it features a suave Jimmy Roselli on the album cover, red jacket and red handkerchief in his lapel, ascot, hands in pockets, two glamorous women draped over him. Conducted and arranged by Larry Wilcox and George Siravo, the album's highlights are a beautiful version of the Mack Gordon and Harry Warren song "You'll Never Know," a fine rendition of the old Platters hit "Only You" (Ram and Rand), and a solid "You Always Hurt the One You Love" (Fisher and Roberts).

On May 18, 1974, Jimmy Roselli was the first American-born entertainer to receive the annual "Italian-American Entertainers Award" as voted by the Italian radio audiences of WHBI, WRNW, and WNLK as polled in New York, New Jersey, Connecticut, and Pennsylvania.

The award was presented during his performance at the Westchester County Center. In a review of the show entitled "Jimmy Roselli Shines Out," Lou Cevetillo wrote in the White Plains, New York, *Reporter Dispatch* (May 21, 1974):

If you missed the Jimmy Roselli concert . . . you most likely missed the entertainment highlight of the season. Roselli's performance on that mammoth stage clearly eclipsed any and all of the similar star attractions heard by the county this year. . . . What occurred during [Roselli's] opening number could only happen between an Italian folk hero like Roselli and his devoted public. As if they were paying homage to a visiting bishop or cardinal, or perhaps to the local "don," many of his fans as a sign of deep affection and admiration came forward to the foot of the stage to reach up to touch Roselli's graciously outstretched hand. . . . Roselli's image is anything but presumptuous, from the simple crucifix pinky ring, that is usually a gawdy diamond ring on other entertainers, to his appreciative smiles at his adoring public. There is no room for pretense. The audience always seems to know that he is one of them, and conversely, that they are one of his. . . . The sheer vocal mastery and majesty of Roselli's delivery gave ample proof of his popularity with people who enjoy real singing. . . . What is most incomprehensible is that Roselli is veritably unknown outside of the Italian areas of this country. This is primarily due to his lack of exposure on the air. Something is drastically wrong if this voice continues to be unheard. . . . [He] continually makes each person in his audience feel he is singing just for him.

Roselli continued to rely on his solid relationship with the Italian community. With the advent of the Columbus Day weekend, he was booked for a week into the Westchester Premiere Theater in Tarrytown, New York, and played there to capacity crowds from October 8 to October 14. Then the next spring, March 15, 1975, was proclaimed Jimmy Roselli Day in Suffolk County by Suffolk County Executive Peter Cohalan in a ceremony on radio station WLIM. Similar proclamations were presented to Jimmy by Brookhaven Town Supervisor Henrietta Acampora and Patchogue Village Mayor Norm Lechtrecher.

By that time, however, Roselli reached a point of no return with United Artists. The company had released twenty albums since 1965 and Roselli had never received any residuals, after an initial payment when the contract was signed. Now UA was claiming that Roselli owed *them* $150,000 because they had never made back their recording costs.

Roselli exploded with rage. "I used to keep quiet," he explained, not entirely accurately, "but it's too late now for that. When I was a young boy, I thought, 'Well, let me keep making these records. They were good records and I was happy with them. It was food for me. I wasn't getting any money, but it was a lot of food. I was filling my belly up because I loved what I was doing."

Roselli wanted to sue United Artists, but he sought the advice of another "boy from the neighborhood," a criminal lawyer without show business experience. "Roselli's fatal mistake," Pete Cavallo recalled, "was having a friend working on it, a Popeye lawyer, who was a *criminal* lawyer, for three and a half years. I had pleaded with him to get an entertainment lawyer." Roselli thought he had a bargain with the criminal lawyer, because he wasn't paying him anything. The understanding between them was that the lawyer would institute a lawsuit against UA, take his expenses from the outcome, and then split the settlement 50-50 with Roselli. But the lawyer never made a move. As Pete put it: "Jimmy just didn't want to lay out any money" for an appropriate attorney.

While meeting with an entertainment lawyer on another matter, Cavallo mentioned Roselli's problems with United Artists. The lawyer told him, "If we represent Jimmy, the worst that can happen is that we'll get UA to erase a lawyer's fee and erase the $150,000. And it's likely we'll get Jimmy some real money."

Pete rushed to Jimmy and they made an appointment to see the lawyer together. When they met, the lawyer repeated what he had told Pete, and asked for a two-thousand-dollar retainer. "Oh no. Take it off the top," Jimmy said. The lawyer insisted he needed cash up front for the initial work. Roselli turned to Pete and said, "Pick up the stuff. Let's go." Pete never forgot the expression on the lawyer's face. "He looked at me like I was crazy."

While sitting in the Russian Tea Room afterward over a drink, Pete was stonily silent. "I had a puss on," he remembered. "Jimmy says to me, 'What's the matter with you.'

" 'What's the matter with me?' I said to him. 'I don't know where you're coming from. We finally got a lawyer who will save you lots of money and even make you money. You got an asshole lawyer who did nothing but bullshit for three years. *They're gonna make settlements with you! Don't you understand? What's wrong with you?*' "

Roselli took out his checkbook and handed it to Pete. "Write the check out and take it to them," he said.

Pete looked at him. "Now you want me to go up there with my head between my ass—"

"Oh, come on," Roselli said, "you can do it."

Reluctantly Pete went back. "I had to go through a whole spiel," he recalled. "I said, 'You have to understand, this guy's been through a lot, you know how singers are . . .' "

Three weeks later, Roselli received a check for $42,500 from

UA. Soon after, another check arrived for $17,500. The checks kept coming. All told, Jimmy received about $100,000.

Once again, Cavallo had come to Roselli's rescue without asking a penny for himself, a pattern that has remained constant throughout their relationship. And it appears to be a pattern that Cavallo is unable to break. Whatever differences the two men have had, Cavallo has always been there for Roselli, the most loyal of friends—brother, bodyguard, psychologist, adviser, pal.

The outcome of the struggle with UA constituted one of the biggest coups of Roselli's career—a victory that gave him a financial security denied to most singers. In the wake of the settlement, Roselli decided to take his recording career into his own hands. First he put a call in to Mike Stewart, president of United Artists, and asked for a meeting. At that meeting, he spelled out what he wanted: all the masters of his records, the complete catalogue. "I want anything that has my picture, my voice, my likeness on it," he told Stewart.

He had seen what happened to other performers. "Stewart had the Four Lads for years," Roselli explained. "He was their manager. They made tons of money. When they were all finished, they were broke. UA owned their catalogue. The Four Lads also had a great publishing firm. UA owned that." It was a story repeated over and over again about the fate of singers whose rights were not protected.

With Stewart, Jimmy was his usual shy self: "Let's make a deal here," he said. "Otherwise I'm gonna get ten lawyers and six Jewish accountants, and we're gonna have a lot of fun. You know you've been robbing me. Give me my catalogue. And put a price on it that's not exorbitant."

Roselli walked away with his complete catalogue, the absolute owner of every record he's ever made. Today he is the
president of his record company, M&R Records ("M" stands
for Roselli's original first name, "R" for his last), one whose
value increases steadily. He produces only his own albums for
the label (only one other recording, by comic Lou Cary, was
released by M&R in the 1970s).

Whatever his faults or shortcomings, Roselli in this crucial
instance made the right move at the right time. As with Donna
and Pete, when the choice could determine the most essential
conditions of his life, Roselli—with a little help from his
friends—could be rational, shrewd, and very smart.

But Jimmy's basic conflicts recurred again and again. It was
in the mid-1970s that Roselli found himself on a collision
course with a wiseguy because of a favor he was doing a friend.
A very close personal pal from Hoboken, Marty the Bell, killed
a man he found sleeping with his wife.

"You know, years ago I got in a little trouble," as Marty put
it. "I hit a guy and everything. Jimmy done a benefit for me. I
copped a plea. Anyway, this wiseguy was in my store and he
slammed Jimmy in the face." Not because Jimmy was reluctant
to sing at the benefit, but because he wanted to know who was
going to handle the money so that Marty would actually get
it. "What's the use of doing the show if everybody's going to
jump on the money?" Jimmy asked.

"Anyway," Marty said, "the gangster we're talking about is
no longer around. They found him with five bullets in his head
in the Hudson River—"

"He was a nice fella," Jimmy remarked. "He shoulda gotten
the bullets a lot sooner . . . greedy, greedy bastard."

"Anyhow," Marty continued, "this individual happened to
be in my store that time. He thought Jimmy didn't want to do
the benefit, and was putting the bull on him, you know what

I mean? But now we know why he wanted Jimmy to do the benefit, so there'd be a big turnout and he could take most of the money. They raised—must've been $160,000."

"The guy hits me a shot on the chin in the basement," Jimmy recalled. "Then we go upstairs. He wants to know how my family is. 'What has that got to do with it?' I said, 'You're a sick guy.' "

Marty added, "Jimmy was right. They stole most of the money."

Jimmy was summoned to an investigation of the benefit. Recalled Jimmy, "I says to Marty: 'You kill the guy and I get all the flak!' They broke my chops from morning till night. I walked in there, I had a beautiful pair of slacks on, a beautiful suede jacket. The judge says, 'You gotta come in my courtroom dressed—' I interrupted him: 'Who the hell wants to come in your courtroom?' "

The problem was that Jimmy simply couldn't walk a straight line away from the wiseguys. In the late 1970s, when he needed money, he could be seen selling his records outside a mob capo's restaurant. FBI undercover agent Richard D. Pistone described one scene in his book *Donnie Brasco*:

One time [in 1977] during the Feast of San Gennaro, Lefty and I and Mike Sabella [identified as a capo by Pistone in the book] were sitting in a club across the street from Casa Bella [Sabella's restaurant], which Mike usually closed during the feast because he hated tourists.

Jimmy Roselli, the Italian singer, had his car parked out on the street. He opened the trunk, and it was filled with his records. He started hawking his own records out of his car trunk right there at the feast.

Mike couldn't believe it. He went outside and said to Roselli, "Put the fucking trunk down because you're fucking embarrassing me by trying to sell your fucking records right here on the street!"

Nor could Roselli resist his little altercations with Sinatra. On one occasion at the bar owned by Jilly Rizzo, Sinatra entered and sat down. Roselli was seated on the other side. "Buy the kid down the end a drink," Sinatra told the bartender. Roselli acknowledged the gesture in a friendly way: "Thank you," he said to Sinatra, "I already got a drink in front of me."

When Sinatra went into the hospital on one occasion, Roselli sent flowers. But when Sinatra opened in Atlantic City, Roselli sent a telegram: "In case you need any help, Frank, I'm here."

"I'm sure that Frank didn't take these things as a joke," observed Dennis Della Fave. "Jimmy loves that kind of humor. And whatever he gives out he's gonna take back."

On New Year's Eve in 1981, Jilly Rizzo called Roselli with the message that "Frank wants you to come to the Factory, Jimmy."

"What's that, Jilly?"

"It's a fucking disco."

"Listen," said Jimmy, "tell Frank thank you very much. God couldn't get me out of this bed right now. I had my dinner and a few drinks and that's it."

"What should I tell Frank, Jimmy?" Jilly said nervously.

"Just tell him what I said," Jimmy said. "Don't change a word."

There are few people who wouldn't have jumped at the opportunity, no matter how humiliating Sinatra could have made it.

Jilly's phone calls had a certain poignancy for Jimmy. They

had been friends; Jimmy was Jilly's favorite singer, and Jimmy had even recorded a song about his bar: "Meet Me at Jilly's." But because of Sinatra's hostility, Jilly and Jimmy rarely saw each other in later years. But there wasn't a day he didn't listen to his music, he told Roselli.

Then in early January, Jilly called Roselli again. "Frank says we're all going to Palm Beach and we're all going swimming in the nude in Frank's pool. He wants you to fly out with us."

Jimmy replied, "Tell Frank I don't look good in the nude. Thanks very much, but no thanks."

Jimmy hung up.

Roselli's most quoted (and cruelest) remark about Sinatra was made when Dolly Sinatra's plane disappeared in a crash and was never found. When he heard the news, Jimmy looked up innocently and asked, "Was Frank on the plane?"

There were now ongoing tensions with Roselli's daughter, Anne, who had fallen in love. It was Roselli who introduced Anne to her future husband, Herb Bernstein, in 1977 as a music arranger, composer, and teacher when she wanted to be a singer. "I had met Jimmy in the late 1960s, although I had seen him sing earlier in Brooklyn," Herb recalled. "I was at Lenox Records, producing and arranging. I had a lot of respect for Roselli. He was always a perfectionist and would never tolerate anything less than a first-class presentation. Later, when he didn't have a record contract, he formed a company and paid for the records himself. He never scrimped on the quality. He paid for forty-two musicians and eight singers. Come on, who records like that? Tony Bennett goes in with a trio. And at his shows, if the sound or lights weren't right or the band couldn't cut it, Jimmy would blow his top.

"Then in 1977 I'd had a bunch of hit records and one day Jimmy called me and asked me to come over to his office. I hadn't seen him in years. He wanted to talk to me about Annie.

He wanted me to write some arrangements for her new singing act. He said, 'Come over for dinner and meet her.' She was nineteen years old; I was forty-six.

"Jimmy and I were in the parking lot, and Annie pulled up in her car. She got out and walked over to us. I flipped. 'That's your daughter?' I said. It was instant love."

Anne confided, "I went inside and told my piano player, Hutch Davies, 'You see that man that just came over with my father? I'm going to marry him. My hand to God.' "

"We got together," Herb said, "but somehow we never got to the music . . . Well, Jimmy went crazy. I was much, much older. Annie was separated but still married to her first husband. And I was Jewish. If he were a different kind of guy, I would probably have been dropped off a roof somewhere. Now as I look back, I probably wouldn't have acted any differently if it were me; I'd probably have busted the guy's jaw. I can't fault Jimmy. Here's a girl, your only daughter, a guy twice her age.

"He called me up and said, 'I don't want you seeing my daughter.' It was pretty tense and ugly. The conflict went on for a long time. He was very emotional about it. Now when Jimmy screams, I know he's really got a heart of gold, but it was different then. What probably saved our situation was that soon after, Annie's mother and Jim got divorced and he had Donna. He was distracted. Now Annie was living with her mother and Jimmy was a little bit out of the picture. And he was seeing Donna. I'd known Donna for years, and I think she was a big influence in helping us with Jimmy.

"And once Jimmy finally realized I was sincere and not just using his daughter, things changed. When he got to know me, and I got to know him better, it started to come together more. Today: this is funny, because his audience is sometimes ninety-nine and nine-tenths Italian. He announces onstage at every show that he has a grandson and his name is Michael Roselli Bernstein. They all fall down. It's funny, but it's great."

The kind of independence Roselli demonstrated with the wiseguys and in his dealings with Sinatra was also reflected in his recording decisions. As president of M&R Records, he has continued to make records of the highest quality at his own expense.

His recordings after UA were anything but cottage industry albums. Roselli hired the best arrangers, among them Leroy Holmes, Larry Wilcox, George Siravo, Ralph Burns, and Peter Moore, as well as forty-plus outstanding musicians. He journeyed to London to record with Peter Moore, who produced Bing Crosby's last three albums, and the result was music of enormous technical and artistic merit.

Astonishingly, six albums were independently produced by Roselli in 1978. *Daddy's Little Girl* was produced by Roselli for his own company, Agita Productions, and released by M&R Records. This is a recording thick with sentimentality, its subject fathers and children: Jolson's "Sonny Boy," "Don't Cry, Little Girl, Don't Cry," "My Melancholy Baby," "Daddy, You've Been a Mother to Me," and, of course, "Little Pal." The title track, a song performed by several other singers over the years, is beautifully sung by Roselli, but the highlight of the album is another relative unknown that Roselli unearthed, "You May Not Remember" (written by Ben Oakland and George Jessel). The album is a delight, and as unstylish—with its cover photographs of Anne Roselli as a baby—as you can get.

Love Love Love came next. This was one of Jimmy's first collaborations with conductor and arranger Peter Moore. Roselli began to travel regularly to London to record his albums because costs were lower there and he had a special fondness for England. He had also built up a level of popularity there over the years. Recorded at Chappel Studios in London, the album has considerable power. Standouts include the Al Frisch and Fred Wise song "I Won't Cry Anymore" (where Roselli injects a little Arthur Prysock with his deep concluding note), his version of "My Way" (by Paul Anka, Jacques Revaux, and Claude François), Leonello Casucci and Irving Caesar's "Just a Gigolo," a swinging interpretation of Gershwin's "Our Love Is Here to Stay," one of his emotional concert blockbusters, "Why Did You Leave Me?" by Norman Kaye and Steve Nelson, and covers of recent hits by other singers, "It's Impossible" (Perry Como) and "For Once in My Life" (Tony Bennett). His "Just a Gigolo" is a tour de force, segueing briefly at the end into a few lines from *Pagliacci*. Like the other excellent albums he produced in the 1970s, *Love Love Love* was greeted with a thundering silence.

Jimmy remained undeterred. He produced two Italian albums that year, *Love and Naples*, another collection of the "stardust" of the Neapolitan catalogue, and *Notte Lucente*, songs not from the concert hall but from the street and the music hall.

These were followed by *The More I See You*, which represents Roselli's brief—and misguided—flirtation with modernity. Margaux Hemingway adorns the jacket—as does her autograph "Margaux Loves Jimmy." Arranged and conducted by Peter Moore and produced by Ken Barnes, the album was recorded in London. But this is a derivative recording, and Jimmy seems uncomfortable with it. In trying to be modern, he strays too far from his roots. The best cuts are masterful renditions of "I Fall in Love Too Easily" (Sammy Cahn and Jules Styne), "Say It Isn't So" (Irving Berlin), and "Over the Rainbow" (Harold Arlen and E. Y. Harburg). They highlight the fact that ballads are Jimmy's greatest strength, and his singing on them here is at once more sophisticated and expressive. Jimmy holds his voice back a little, and his restraint has a poignant effect without losing its gritty edge.

With *Saloon Songs, Vol. 3*, Roselli returned to the "saloon song" format after a hiatus of eleven years. The tone is set perfectly by the cover: Roselli singing within the frame of an old-fashioned three-knobbed radio. Unlike his performance on *The More I See You*, Roselli is completely at home with "I'm Nobody's Baby," a 1921 song by Davis, Santly, and Ager, "Somebody Else Is Taking My Place" (Howard, Ellsworth, and Morgan), the Depression classic "It's Only a Shanty in Old Shanty Town" (Young, Siras, and Little), the 1913 chestnut "Oh! You Million Dollar Doll" (Clarke, Leslie, and Abrahams), and "It Had to Be You" (Kahn and Jones).

Jimmy ran M&R from his home in Jersey City with a staff of two. He also ran it in the face of overwhelming indifference. He became the invisible man of show business who kept on singing like the kid on the street corner, in an incredible act of defiant affirmation and belief that his own talent would not die.

In the face of the isolation, discouragement, and poor financial return in which he worked during these years, his creativity, resolve, and tenacity are remarkable. But Jimmy was playing to an empty house. His real audience had become the studio.

13

REBOUND

IN OCTOBER 1982, ROSELLI WAS SERVED WITH DIVORCE papers. It was the last thing in the world he expected, and it plunged him into a state of shock. "He had a lot of anger about the divorce," a friend confided. "He wanted to get out of the marriage without it costing. Things were convenient as they were. He had everything he wanted. He's not the marrying kind to a certain extent. He's too independent to really feel for people in a very caring way, as much as he loves Donna and relies on her."

"This was a total shock to him," said Donna Roselli. "His body broke out; he looked like he had leprosy.

"Angie had always said she'd never give him a divorce. And the first thing he ever told me was that as much as he cared for me, his family came first. And I accepted his life with me under those terms."

Accompanying Jimmy in a van to the Watchung house to pick up his things, Vito Pedesta recalled: "As we walked in,

Angie was looking at me. I couldn't say a word, I was embarrassed. We had been close, all of us. On the way down with the last load, Angie said, 'Jimmy, please don't go. You can have your *gumma* [girlfriend]. But don't leave.' Jimmy didn't even answer. We just put the stuff in the van and took off."

Jimmy's relationship with his daughter had been strained ever since she had moved to Rome in 1976 at the age of eighteen with her first husband, Eddie. Although she'd long been aware that there was "another woman" in Jimmy's life, it was there that she found out about Donna. "My father was there with Donna; he passed her off as a secretary from his record company and gave her a false name," she confided. "They were speaking back and forth to each other in Italian. And my ex-husband spoke fluent Italian and was eavesdropping on them. We were in a restaurant and my father and Donna were both crying. I'm looking at Eddie and I'm saying, 'What's going on, what's this all about?' And he's whispering, 'It's her!' He was the one who blew the lid on the whole thing. At first I didn't want to believe it. Then I did. The whole thing came together."

"Now that the divorce was under way, the tension only increased. "When I was in my early twenties, I became very rebellious," Anne recalled. "My father had been very rigid about curfews, about many things. I was off on the road singing with bands, wild and crazy. I was estranged from my father. My mom had filed for divorce. I went through a period of blaming Donna. But actually it was Donna who got my dad and me back together. She initiated it.

"He was tough when I rebelled," Anne remembered. "He'd yell at me. One time when I think I was drunk, he pulled my hair. In retrospect, he was realistic about my singing. He knew the business. He wanted me to be professional. If I was going to do it, he wanted me to do it right. I think he was as supportive as he could be. Looking back, he did what he thought was right. I think he did the best he could in all ways. He was a very strict Italian father, the quintessential Italian father. And when I look back at it, he was right."

The divorce was finalized in February 1984. Under the financial agreement he reached with Angie, she obtained the Watchung house as well as $2,500 a month the first year (the monthly payment would be reduced by $500 a month three times). Roselli would have to start all over again.

"He went through a bad time psychologically," said a friend. "He was feeling poor. And his friends left him. I never saw that gang around again. I think they were leeches, good-time boys."

There was more to come. Jimmy moved into an apartment in his office, part of a building he owned in Jersey City. Donna moved out of Roselli's apartment in March 1984 after a series of protracted arguments. "Look, I've had it," she told him. "I can't go on with this façade anymore." Jimmy had made no mention of marriage or of any change in their relationship despite the fact that he was now free of his legal ties to Angie. Their arrangement had been going on for so long, she maintained, that she was not even seeking a marriage. "I was just looking for a written agreement as far as security was concerned," she said. "He always said he would take care of me. But I felt that unless it was on paper, you never know what can happen in life. Jimmy said, 'If this is what you want, okay, go ahead and leave.' "

Two weeks went by. Donna did not call him.

Roselli consulted his friends about what he should do. He really didn't know. All the security blankets of his life—his marriage, his arrangement with Donna, the many years of high earnings—had disappeared. Now he was faced with the unknown. And he was not a man who admitted to any fears or vulnerabilities at all. Nor did he admit to his love for Donna.

He expected her to understand his needs and cater to them at all times—even to understand that he loved her deeply and could not allow himself to express it.

On April 4, 1984, a Wednesday morning, at 1 a.m., tipsy, he lurched into Donna's apartment in Lincoln Towers. "You want to get married?" he said.

"What?" Donna replied. "It's one o'clock. What are you doing here?"

"Isn't that what you're looking for? To get married?" he asked her.

"Well, I'll have to think about it."

"You're fucking nuts," he said. "What are you talking about? What do you want from me?"

"Jimmy, I said I have to think about it."

They made love, and he left in the morning. He made a series of phone calls to Donna's mother and sister.

"My sister called me," Donna said, "and asked me, 'Isn't this what you want? After all these years, he's trying to do the right thing by you. What's going on with you?'

"I said quite honestly, 'No, I just want security. That's it. I don't want to get married. I don't know what I want.'

"She and my mother said I was crazy. So naturally they talked me into it. I think I would have come around to it anyway. But I was frightened of it. Knowing the way Jim was, the possessiveness he had. And he was his own man. If he said something, that's what it had to be, right or wrong. And I was my own person. When I wasn't married to him, I would often say to him, 'Look, I'm not fucking married to you.' I was afraid that might change and I didn't know how to handle it. Here I'd been at his beck and call all this time and now all of a sudden I want to be his equal. It doesn't work that way, especially with an Italian guy."

Despite Donna's qualms, Jimmy and Donna were married

two weeks later, on April 18, 1984, at Jersey City's City Hall. Mayor Jerry McCann presided over the ceremony. Both Jimmy and Donna cried when they said "I do." Louis Lavella, the brother of Jimmy's mother, Anna, was best man, and Donna's best friend, Diane Magro, was matron of honor. According to Donna: "I kind of felt it was silly to dress up because I wasn't a young bride with a gown and all that. I just wore a white suit and a red silk blouse."

After the ceremony, a celebration dinner was held at Cacalle's restaurant in Hoboken. Jimmy's two living aunts, Etts and Annie, were there, as well as Jimmy's daughter, Anne, Donna's mother, brothers, and sisters, Al Certo, Jimmy's cousin Anthony, Billy Dennison, Jimmy's musical conductor, and Sol Parker, an old buddy and composer. After the dinner, once the cake was brought out, Billy Dennison and two other musicians began a jam session.

"Jim and I were seated," remembered Donna, "and then Jim got up and sang 'My Funny Valentine' to me. He was crying. I had always stayed in the background all those years, never sitting out front during Jimmy's shows, but staying backstage. But all of a sudden I got up and I stood right next to Jimmy at the piano. I kissed him and I said, 'Oh! I'm allowed to do this now.' Everybody burst out laughing."

Donna recalled that day as the last time Jimmy ever drank too much. "It was the funniest thing, that day really," she said. "Because we got married at noon, and from one to five we had the dinner. Jimmy drank, I think, fourteen martinis and fell right to sleep when we got home. My brothers had to literally pick him up and carry him upstairs to the bedroom. Then he stopped drinking and he never seriously drank again after that."

Donna felt that the bond between them deepened because it was a marriage without children of their own. "Because I didn't have any children, he was my child, my lover, and father image," she said.

But there was a deep sadness and bitterness in Jimmy, and Donna knew it was too late to change him. She would do everything in her power, however, to give him the love and peace he needed. Jimmy said that when he thought about Donna, it was in terms of one of those saloon songs from the Gay Nineties he loves and sings so well: "Oh! You Million Dollar Doll." ("If you were the kind to be sold—you'd be worth your weight in gold . . .") Three years later, praising Donna, he would say, "She's good as gold."

Roselli was beginning to recover from the toll of the divorce, but he was essentially consigned to the margins of show business. But he still commanded a hefty price on those margins, and his appearances at the Westbury Music Fair, the Playboy Casino, and other venues were sold out.

What was new was the stability of his emotional life, a factor which he would not easily admit. The buttressing of the marriage contributed strongly to the comeback he would make in the 1990s. He was no longer flailing about in desperation; he had a home to return to; and his mood would be greatly elevated by the birth of his first grandson, Michael Roselli Bernstein, in 1989.

But in the mid-1980s, Roselli was still searching for ways to climb out of the professional hole he had dug for himself. He began to look for new ways of generating income, and one possibility was Europe. In a reflective interview he did with Winnie Bonelli of the Hudson/Bergen Counties *Dispatch* on October 8, 1985, he summed up Sinatra's reaction to the Dolly Sinatra incident as "Bye, bye, Jimmy." Bonelli wrote that "in more concrete terms it meant a succession of closed career doors." "There's nothing more he can do to me professionally,"

Roselli remarked. "I'm looking forward to entertaining in Europe, especially England and Italy. Interest has been expressed over the years, but I never took them up on it until now." His trips to England would include engagements at the London Palladium. Soon he would be producing records there again.

Jimmy also wanted to get back to headlining on a regular basis in Atlantic City, where he and Sinatra had always been the special favorites of the high rollers. But without an agent, he took the usual convoluted Roselli route.

Jimmy's brother-in-law, Bob (Hot Rod) Labutti, the husband of Jimmy's half sister from Phil Roselli's second marriage, was one of the highest of the high rollers.* "Hot Rod lost millions in Atlantic City," Pete Cavallo said. "I was once at a table where he lost $145,000 in forty-five minutes. So Trump Plaza gave him anything he wanted." One of the gifts Trump gave Hot Rod was a brand-new Mercedes—annually. And he could call in other favors, too. One day he called Jimmy and asked if he'd like to perform at Trump Plaza.

Referring to Hot Rod as a "half cuckoo clock," Jimmy said that Labutti had lost eleven million at craps in Atlantic City. "That's how much you need to be a partner in a casino," related Jimmy. "The guy was legitimate, though. Bred racehorses. He'll start abusing everybody around the table when he loses, like one night when there was all Chinese people around the table. Bad luck, according to Hot Rod. He pays $5,000 in tips at a time. He's deucing everybody."

In 1989 Edith Labutti, Hot Rod's daughter, got Jimmy into Trump Plaza in Atlantic City for $30,000 a week. Roselli drew capacity crowds, and his pay was upped to $40,000. As agreed between them, Jimmy paid Edith a percentage for her help

*A high roller is someone who gambles $20,000 or more. In Roselli's circles, a high roller probably gambles $50,000 to $100,000 or more.

in landing the job. (Jimmy claims he gave her 50 percent of his salary.)

Hot Rod then got in trouble with the Internal Revenue Service, and Trump Plaza distanced itself from him. At the same time, Jimmy's contract with Trump had expired. But because of Roselli's ties to Labutti, Trump did not renew it.

This led to Jimmy's reunion with one of his old William Morris agents, Lee Salomon. With his brother-in-law out of the picture, Jimmy decided it would be best to have a "legitimate" agent to help him make his comeback. Salomon negotiated for Roselli a high-priced contract with Trump. It was not the happiest of reunions—more a marriage of convenience—as Salomon had been the senior part of the team (with Larry Spellman) that had dumped Jimmy earlier. As luck would have it, Salomon was suddenly fired from William Morris after forty years of service, and was forced to become an independent agent himself. When he called Jimmy to tell him he'd been fired, Jimmy replied, "What took them so long?"

Jimmy's new contract hardly pleased Edith. According to Jimmy, Edith felt that because Trump had been so rude to her, Jimmy should share her pain and not deal with the organization anymore. Jimmy told Edith, "I'm sixty-seven years old. How many years I got? I'll be over the hill by the time you resolve this." Soon after, Jimmy received another call from Edith, who said, "You owe me $300,000 for Trump Plaza." This, she maintained, was the interest on the money Jimmy was earning. "I want the fucking money," she explained. Jimmy hung up on her.

"You see, it's still happening," said Pete Cavallo. "The gal [Edith] won't do nothing. But still she wants Jimmy to believe she's with 'some people' and she'll do something—a threat. It won't happen, because Jimmy knows *better* people than Edith knows. If he had to run to somebody. Which he don't want to do, because then he owes them a favor. He wants to stay away from that, not get involved. You ask for one favor, they want fifty favors. He got away from that shit years ago. He's at peace. You wouldn't know it by the way he rants and raves. But he's really at peace with himself."

Perhaps it was his new marriage that inspired Roselli to write in 1989 his first and only song, which supplied the title of the album he produced and released in 1990: *They Used to Call Her Mary, Now They Call Her Ma*. This is a stripper/flapper song, like something out of a time warp. One would assume that it was written around 1912—except that it swings. There's a genuine old-time feeling, an infectious melody set against a rousing Dixieland beat, and an unmistakable sense of fun as Jimmy sings, "They used to call her Mary; Then they took the 'r' away; She wanted to be a flapper; With a beautiful name like May . . ."

As on the *Saloon Songs* albums, Roselli sounds relaxed and joyous. The song reveals nothing about Roselli except his fondness for old music hall melodies. It's not even lifted from his youth, but from an earlier era out of George M. Cohan. And it works. It also raises the mystery of how he came to write it, for it shows a lighthearted sense of humor and revelry that Jimmy rarely displays.

As Jimmy's star rose in Atlantic City, he also gained fans overseas. In 1989, the unexpected success in London of his old hit, "When Your Old Wedding Ring Was New," brought him a much wider audience in England. He had previously recorded five albums in London, and in the fall of 1990 Roselli went there again to record a new album (*What Is a Song*) and to make his debut at the legendary London Palladium. As usual, he did it his way: in this case, with no advertising at all. Roselli played to standing-room-only crowds, and was a smashing success.

The critics were nonplussed—not by his talent but by his obscurity. Writing in *The Stage and Television Today* (July 13, 1989), Eric Braun noted:

> Why, as his two Palladium concerts—the second a sell-out—went like the proverbial bomb, has Jimmy Roselli left it so late to appear in the UK, considering his several visits to record LP's which have sold in millions, all with British-born arranger-conductor Pete Moore . . . for the superb orchestra which accompanied Roselli here? It's a mystery as everything about this belated debut worked so splendidly from the word "Go." . . . From the moment Roselli ambled amiably on, . . . settled on a stool and sailed through what he called his bar-room numbers everything went admirably well, with the orchestration and sound balance a rare treat for these cacophonous times. The choice of material would have won me over even had the singer not had such an effortless flow of honey-smooth melody at his command. Gershwin, Porter, Rodgers receive their full measure, but there's a bonus in such personal favorites as "How Did She Look?" and "Just a Gigolo."

"Let's Hear It for Who?" was the headline of Ruby Millington's review in the London *Evening Standard* (November 20, 1990). "Who is Jimmy Roselli?" asked Millington. "That would have been the question on everyone's lips last night—if anyone had known he was here. Roselli . . . is appearing for three shows at the London Palladium—unadvertised and unannounced, even outside the theatre itself. . . . The applause was rapturous. . . . So who is Jimmy Roselli? Jimmy Roselli, it seems, is a star."

"The audience went for him in a very big way," said Peter Moore, who conducted for him at the Palladium and arranged five of his albums. "He has a great following amongst the street-smart working class in London. The sort of essential street people, the Liverpudlians, and the cockneys from London have a great rapport with him. He has a sound that comes across as being a hundred percent genuine. I think it's one of the best sounds I've ever heard, and I've worked with Crosby and Peggy Lee. Crosby had a great way of delivering songs, very sophisticated and stylish, but he didn't have quite the great feeling for drama and emotion that Jimmy has."

Moore seemed particularly moved by the way Roselli related to people of all classes in London. "He will treat the poorest little carny in a restaurant the same way he treats a big entrepreneur, with the same consideration and good manners," Moore related. "One doesn't see this very often. It endears him to many people. And he has an ability to be very tactful and gentle when he wants to be, but very direct and factual when he wants. A great gift to know who he's talking to and what is the best way to approach that person in order to get his point across. I've seen him be very direct with people, but I've never seen him offend anyone.

"When he's onstage," Moore continued, "he's very aware of the audience and very sympathetic to them; he takes the time and trouble to work to people. I've never seen anyone work better."

Of Roselli and Sinatra, Moore said, "They're both flutes, but quite different. But I'll tell you this: Jimmy as a performer, the sound of his voice, is second to none."

Sinatra will always be known as the Chairman of the Board,

but Roselli's continuing fame in some parts of the United States was again confirmed when he returned to New York from London. Residents of Melbourne, Florida, had collected 2,018 signatures on a petition imploring him to sing there. WMMB-AM, a radio station in Melbourne, had done a promotional campaign asking its listeners which singer they would want to sing at their daughter's wedding. The station, which had been playing Roselli constantly, most especially his recording of "When Your Old Wedding Ring Was New," was bombarded with calls, and Roselli came in first, Sinatra second.

Roselli responded by telling Larry Brewer, the station's disc jockey, that 2,018 signatures were not necessary: just one would do, and on a check that was big enough. It wasn't. Jimmy did do a ninety-minute radio interview with the station, and he made a personal appearance where he signed autographs.

But Roselli couldn't resist catering to the darker side of notoriety when, for instance, he made his much-talked-about appearance on April 22, 1990, at the wedding reception of John Gotti's son at the Helmsley Palace in Manhattan, captivating the crowd with "Little Pal."

Afterward, Gotti gave Jimmy a $5,000 gold watch. Shortly before starting his jail term in 1992, Gotti wanted to do something more to express his gratitude to Roselli. This was the moment he called Jimmy and offered to broker a truce between Roselli and Sinatra. Jimmy refused.

Roselli's personal distaste for Sinatra was based on a moral code he felt Sinatra had violated, though part of it, of course, was due to his own jealousy and resentment: "A guy like Frank, he jumped in bed with anybody. He didn't give a fuck as long as his career went ahead. A friend of mine, a millionaire, one night he said to me, 'I'd like to meet a couple of girls.' I said, 'Listen, I'm a singer, not a pimp. If you want to meet girls, I have nothing to do with that. I *sing*.' But Frank, if he knew anybody, he'd introduce you. I'm sure he was instrumental in Marilyn Monroe meeting Jack Kennedy. That in essence is a pimp . . .

"For every little good thing [Sinatra] does," Jimmy said, "he does that much bad. So if you put it on a scale . . . Look, I don't even want to be in his company. Because I see how he acts. I seen him at Jilly's. He's hitting guys with cream pies, with ice cubes. He throws firecrackers, big bombs, under somebody's chair. He don't even know how to have fun, this guy."

But there were also times when Roselli spoke more sympathetically of Sinatra. Recalling the period in the 1950s when Sinatra's career was in eclipse, he said, "When Frank went down the first time, he was bitter at the whole world. Because everybody scattered like somebody dropped a bomb."

As the news of Sinatra's mental and physical decline began to filter through in the early 1990s—and Jimmy heard it personally from Matty (Action) Jordan and many others—Roselli expressed genuine concern. "Everything leaves you," he commented. "He's an old man. Your youth, your stamina, your strength, your memory." Ten years younger than Sinatra, he was sensitive enough to identify with the aging of his competitor—and public idol. "You know," he said to his office manager, Marie Greene, one day, "if Frank was down and he would call me, I would be there for him."

Jimmy had experienced his own bout with mortality back in December 1990. "That day, he was so agitated," Donna recalled, "pacing back and forth. His coloring had been pale for two weeks. He decided he was going to make veal and peppers that night. He hadn't cooked himself in a long time. So he goes to the bakery, the butcher, he gets his fresh peppers, his fresh mushrooms. He makes all this food, and then he eats like he was going to the chair, and he eats fast.

"He went upstairs," Donna continued. "I found him there

sweating. I said, 'Let me rub you with alcohol.' He started walking up and down. I said, 'Maybe we ought to go to the hospital, because I can't do anything more for you. I've done everything but wipe your ass.' He said, 'Go to sleep, leave me alone, don't bother me.' All night long he's white. Next morning he's green."

Donna called Bitterbeer (Pete Lobabarra), another childhood buddy from Hoboken, who hurried to the house. She then phoned Dr. Macken, and said, "Dan, I have a problem . . ." "Don't waste time," he said. "I'll meet you in the emergency room."

Bitterbeer drove Donna and Jimmy to the emergency room of Columbia Presbyterian Hospital. "Jimmy sat down," Donna said, "and I filled in the papers. We wait a half hour; they're still not taking him. I went over and said, 'I believe my husband is having a massive heart attack. Do you want to move?' Finally they started to act as Dan Macken came in."

Donna was right. The tests disclosed heart damage and abdominal blockage. "Dan told me, 'Jimmy has suffered a massive, massive heart attack. I don't know if he'll make it through the night.' " Macken ordered quadruple bypass surgery for Roselli.

Jimmy was operated on for eighteen hours, and spent ten days in the intensive-care unit. Donna, Anne, Pete, Al Certo, and Al's sister, Joann Viggiano, were at his bedside.

"During his operation," recalled Anne Roselli Bernstein, "I was so petrified he was going to die. He wasn't the least bit frightened. If he was, he didn't show it. 'Whatever will be, will be. I'm sure I'm going to be fine, but if not, you know I love you.' He said all this before going into surgery. 'You know I love you, don't you?' I said, 'Of course I know it, Daddy.' "

"The first time I ever saw him cry was when he was wheeled into the operating room," Joann Viggiano recalls. "When he came out, I had to let him know it was over and everything was all right. So I yelled, 'Roselli! It's JoJo! Everything's over with. You're okay.'

"Later he said to me, 'You know, I heard you, JoJo. I heard you. And I just closed my eyes and I went to sleep.'"

"Essentially he had it without any warning," Dr. Macken said. "Jimmy got to the hospital, and, I tell you, that was a team effort. He was in the intensive-care unit for ten days. Usually people are out in two or three days, max.

"But he's astounding. We've tested him up, down, and cross-ways, more than once, and I want to tell you he's as healthy now as you and me."

Within months, Roselli was determined to fulfill his next engagement at Trump Plaza. He wanted to find out if he would be able to sing again. He also feared that the strain of singing might provoke a fatal heart attack.

"He was very nervous that day," Dr. Macken recalled. During the afternoon rehearsal, when Roselli insisted on doing what he always did, singing his entire repertoire over and over until it was perfect—a four-hour stint—he was shaky at first. In the evening, Dr. Macken, Donna, and Pete were with him backstage. The audience knew of his surgery, and waited expectantly. The orchestra began playing. As always, Roselli incanted, "*Cante, guaglione, cante.*"

Then Jimmy walked out onstage, resplendent in his tuxedo, stretched out his arms, and sang, his great voice resounding through the nightclub. "It was thrilling," Dr. Macken remembered. The members of the audience jumped up, many crying out with joy. Tears ran down the cheeks of Donna, Pete, and Annie.

Fans cheered and wept. Among them, of course, were the wiseguys and their wives, girlfriends, mothers, aunts, and grandmothers.

Jimmy began the concert by hitting a high G note in his opening song, "Aggio Perduto O'Suonno." He concluded with a kiss to the audience, and held his hands high in the air.

Backstage, Donna and Annie embraced and held him.

Pete said, "Jimmy, I thought you would take it easy. I never heard you hit that note before."

"I wanted to see if I could break something," Jimmy replied.

14

THE CONTENDER

IN *RAGING BULL*, BROKEN AND UTTERLY ALONE AND RE-hearsing his seedy nightclub act, Jake LaMotta looks in the mirror and recites the lines from *On the Waterfront* in which Terry Malloy, the character played by Marlon Brando, accuses his brother Charlie of ruining his life by making him throw a fight: "I coulda been a contender. I coulda been somebody . . ." But in the mirror he sees himself. LaMotta acknowledges that he, and no one else, was the engine of his own destruction.

Roselli has never been alone: he has always found defenders and supporters to protect him from himself. But inwardly he has always felt isolated and cast off, the friendless child deserted by his parents.

And like LaMotta, he has often been the agent of his own destruction. In the pivotal moments of his career—his behavior with Sinatra, Joe Colombo, Ed Sullivan, and the Mafia—whatever his conscious motives, he has been remarkably adept at turning on his friends and embracing his enemies.

Fearful of success, he has sought the comfort of the shadows, the margins, the familiar. Jimmy preferred the company of his old pals from the neighborhood, whether wannabe or actual wiseguys, the tacky environment of the Joe Franklin show, the solace of clinging to the small world of his aging, traditional Italian-American following, rather than venturing out into the wider world of show business that professional managers and advisers could have opened up for him. No one but Jimmy Roselli would have fled from the opportunities offered by an Ed Sullivan, a Merv Griffin, and scores of others whom he felt were deceiving or exploiting him—and lived to tell the tale. Fear was the governing mode, but manifested by a rigid, parochial behavior.

He could still be hurt and surprised by the betrayals of his old Hoboken pals, the Monroe Street Buddies. They still counted for him in a way that Ed Sullivan or Merv Griffin never did, and as a result, Jimmy remained vulnerable.

In 1992, Willie (Eighty-eight) Keys, one of the "boys" from Hoboken, had purchased eight tickets for Jimmy's forthcoming Trump Plaza concert in Atlantic City. The tickets were for Willie's parents and sisters, who would be coming from Florida to see the show. Jimmy was touched by the gesture.

But then "Willie Keys comes up to me," said Pete Cavallo, who handled seating and ticket arrangements at the concerts, "and says his family is coming for the concert. 'You gotta do me a favor. I sold the fucking tickets. You gotta help me.' I says to him, 'How many people?' He says eight."

"Fucking balls!" Jimmy shouted. "Fucking scumbag cocksucker's got balls! Eighty-eight would have moved up a hundred lengths with me if he did that for his family. I said to myself: that's class. And then he sells the fucking tickets."

Pete continued: "I said to Willie, 'Let me see what I can do.' So I went to Donna; I didn't go to Jimmy. A day later, Jimmy picks it up. Now he's fucking furious. His eyeballs are coming out. He says to me, 'If I hear you got this fucking guy in, I'll never talk to you again.' I said, 'Jimmy, whatever you want. You don't want him in, we don't get him in.'

"Now it's Sunday night, around two o'clock in the morning. We're sitting around eating. It's just me and Jimmy. And Jimmy's still fuming: 'This son of a bitch bastard, we gotta get rid of him.' Then all of a sudden Jimmy says, 'All right, get Willie in this time, but only because of his sisters and his parents. I don't wanna disappoint them. Get him in.' I said all right. That's Jimmy: the fucking terror comes out first. Then the pussycat.

"So now Jimmy says he's going to bed, he's tired. I'm tired, too, so I start to leave. But Donna says wait a minute, we'll have a cigarette, bullshit and unwind. So I'm sitting there with her. In maybe three minutes, the door swings open. Jimmy comes bouncing out the fucking door like a fucking madman. From the bed, I swear to God, screaming, 'Son of a bitch! That cocksucker! I can't fucking sleep! I'm tossin'. That bastard, what he did.' I said to Jimmy, 'Are you fucking crazy? Ya gotta do a fucking show tomorrow, fuck him.' His eyeballs were bulgin'! He couldn't sleep!" Pete said. "He said to Donna, 'Give me something to fucking sleep!'"

Jimmy picks up the story. "That cocksucker Willie had me so upset," he said. "When we got back home after, I gave Willie another three hundred dollars. But I don't want this motherfucker near me anymore. He's an aggravating motherfucker. The thing is: I know this guy since I'm six years old. The nervy cocksucker! But you know what it is," he said. "The blood is bad. That's bad blood there."

"That's Jimmy's theory," Donna said to me. "I mean, he's got a fuckin' theory—when the blood is bad—"

"When blood is bad, it's bad," Jimmy said. "Fucking blood is the worst!"

Pete chuckled, kicked his legs, and sipped his Diet Coke. His eyebrows jumped. He turned to Donna. "When I went down to my room, I lay on the bed and I busted out laughing, thinking about this maniac coming out of the fucking door."

"You know how long it actually took Jimmy to fall asleep after that?" Donna asked me. "Hours. I had to give him a sleeping pill, then I had to start rubbing him."

Pete's take on Jimmy was, as usual, appreciative and canny, but Pete too was vulnerable with Jimmy. Sometimes their comical bickering took on the characteristics of a long-married jealous couple.

In 1992 Jimmy had a new pal: Nicky, a bookmaker whom he'd known many years before, feuded with, and recently become reconciled with. Pete was not happy with this new state of affairs and talked to me (in front of Jimmy) about a recent incident that showed Jimmy's "complications": "Jimmy says, 'Come on. I'm gonna take you to lunch.' We got in his car. On the way he says, 'Let me call my friend Nicky. We'll get him to come with us.' 'Go ahead, no problem.' He calls up Nicky on his phone in the car. P.S.: I'm sitting in the front with Jimmy. We pull up to Nicky's building. As the guy is coming down, Jimmy says to me, 'Get in the back seat.' To me, who the fuck is this guy that I have to get in the back seat? That's how I felt. I'm being very honest. So I got insulted. Highly insulted. And he knew it! Because I got in the back *steamin'*, fucking steamin'. Jimmy started telling me something, making some kind of jokes with me, and I was giving him a very abrupt yes and no. He knew I was annoyed."

Jimmy disagreed. "No, I didn't know you were annoyed. And actually if I did, I wouldn't give a fuck either. 'Cause if I asked you to sit in the back, this guy was important to me. And you're a friend of mine. You should understand. I didn't tell you to walk home. I said sit in the back. What's the big fucking deal?"

"Who the fuck is this guy that he's so important?" Pete said. "Because he has more money than me? Is that why?"

"No," Jimmy replied. "I didn't say he was more important—"

"You just said that!" Pete continued. "Anyway, I got in the back. That's my privilege to get annoyed. If it was his doctor, I would understand. But he made it like, who is this guy [Pete], like I was a piece of shit. But I *know* Jimmy. I know he didn't really mean it that way."

Jimmy interjected. "I tell my wife sometimes to sit in the back."

"That's not what I was saying," Pete replied. "The way you did it, you made me feel—"

"Well, you should know me by now!" Jimmy shouted.

"I do, that's why I didn't stay mad at you."

"Maybe I used the wrong words," Jimmy said. "This guy [Nicky] goes back to when I was sixteen—"

"Yeah, but you haven't seen him in twenty-five years."

"We had an argument, but—"

"But that ain't the point," Pete said.

"We go way back—"

"I go back—" Pete said.

"Before you. Way before you," Jimmy said.

"Right. But the years that I spent with you, twenty-five years, he wasn't around once."

Jimmy said to me, "Let me tell you something about this guy. Nicky's a beautiful guy—"

"I'm not a bad guy either," Pete said.

"What?" Jimmy asked.

"I'm not a bad guy either."

"We all got faults," Jimmy said.

"I'm just saying—I got lots of faults. I never said that."

"I wasn't putting Pete down," Jimmy said to me. "Maybe he felt hurt the way I did it—"

"I'm entitled to feel that way," Pete said.

"I may have said, 'Let this guy sit in the back, let this guy sit in the front.' "

"Now, I discussed this with my close friend Lefty Jimmy, who's a very sensitive guy. I said, 'What would you have done?' He said, 'I would have got in the back, but I would never have saw him again.' This guy's a very sensitive guy. Forget about it. Very sensitive. But I says to him, 'Jimmy didn't mean it.' See, I know him very well. I know he didn't mean it."

"It may happen again!" Jimmy yelled. "Because that's Jimmy Roselli."

"It may happen again," Pete repeated. "Maybe the second time I—"

"That's possible too," Jimmy said.

"You're telling me a message," Pete said to Jimmy. "That you know I'm annoyed by it, and if you do that again to me, that's your way of getting rid of me."

"If I want to get rid of you," Jimmy yelled, "I'll tell you to take a fucking walk. If I really want to get rid of you. But I don't want to get rid of you. That's a silly fucking thing to say. All the years we're together, you felt annoyed over that bullshit? That's bullshit."

Pete concluded: "That's part of a guy being complicated in his own way. That's him."

There is a perverse, mystifying element that is an essential ingredient of Roselli's personality: maneuvering things in such a way that he has constantly found himself on the ropes, about to be counted out. But Jimmy is a proven master at fighting back with great determination, and finding his balance and solid ground.

And he keeps getting rediscovered because of a singularly haunting voice that reaches out to the listener in a way unique in American popular music. A genius who conducts his career as if from the back of a candy store.

By the early 1990s, Jimmy had found an astute office manager and right hand in Marie Greene. Her link to Roselli was a personal one, and extended beyond her business connection to him. Her father, Joseph Trimarco, had died in 1973. "My father loved him," she said. "He was very sick, but he would want to sit up in the living room. Every night one of us would sit with him. So one night I said, 'Okay, Pops, what are we gonna do tonight?' He said, 'Let's listen to Jimmy Roselli.' 'Okay, Pops.'

"So I put a stack on, so they'd keep playing. Every time the record stopped, my father would get up to change it. I said, 'It's the modern age, Pops, they play by themselves.' And we're both singing to the records. Now it's twenty to eight. He said, 'You know, I think I have to go the bathroom.' He went in and closed the door. He came out, went to the chair, and sat down. Put his head down. And he was gone. If everyone could die like my father did . . . I said to my brothers, 'Let's continue to play the records because he loved Roselli so much. Maybe he will hear a little.' "

The late 1980s and early 1990s saw renewed interest in Roselli. The *Wall Street Journal* article by Timothy K. Smith on July 8, 1991, was one catalyst. He began to receive more airplay and press coverage, his record sales mounted, and his appearances at his new Atlantic City venue, Caesars Palace, drew huge crowds.

At the same time there was a resurgence of interest in the great musical standards by the Gershwins, Rodgers and Hart, Rodgers and Hammerstein, Harry Warren, Sammy Cahn,

Jimmy Van Heusen, DeSylva, Brown and Henderson, Cole Porter, Jule Styne, and Irving Berlin. The songs were often utilized now on movie soundtracks (*Sleepless in Seattle, Swingers,* and the films of Woody Allen), and the singers who interpreted them were once again being heard. Tony Bennett was discovered by the MTV generation, Sinatra seemed to be everywhere until his health sharply deteriorated, and Dean Martin, sadly enough, received the acclaim following his death that he had been denied in the last years of his life. There were new interpreters of the music as well: Michael Feinstein, John Pizzarelli, Jr., Susannah McCorkle, Julie Budd, and Harry Connick, Jr., among them. Nostalgia was part of it; there was a certain "camp" element at play too. But the music's timelessness and universality were more enduring reasons for its renaissance.

Roselli's response to the attention was characteristic: he reacted by trying to sabotage as much of this good fortune as he could. Still, he couldn't quell the surge, and of course, on a deeper level, he didn't want to. Unlike Sinatra, he had given up smoking and drinking many years before, and his relatively abstemious existence (with Donna's careful guardianship of his health) and the success of the bypass surgery provided him with a continuing productivity in his later years.

A year after his brush with death, on a Sunday in 1992, Roselli strutted up and down his living room in red pajamas as Lefty Jimmy, Matty Rega, and Pete Cavallo watched, dancing to back-to-back recordings by Sinatra and himself of the same songs. Sixty-six years old then, this was a man who still felt he could take on all comers.

That same year he produced a new album in London, *What Is a Song,* and it is one of the most adventurous recordings Roselli has ever made. He has never sounded as relaxed, comfortable, and mellow. As always, he tends toward the romantic in his song selection, in terms of the lyrics he chooses and the melodies he sings.

The album features beautiful versions of the kinds of lesser-known songs that Roselli is adept at recapturing from oblivion, such as "Careless" (one of Roselli's greatest recordings, with a superb arrangement by Larry Wilcox), "I Guess I Expected Too Much," and "It's Breaking My Heart to Keep Away from You," as well as son-in-law Herb Bernstein's ambitious attempt at a more modern signature tune for Roselli: "What Is a Song." The performances are riveting. Roselli's voice is deeper, and has a reflective quality that invokes a feeling not so much of age as of wisdom.

When *The Heart and Soul of Jimmy Roselli* appeared in 1994, a three-disc compilation of the English-language Roselli, Jimmy had thirty-five albums in print with M&R.

But Jimmy had a hard time acknowledging his newfound success. In 1992 he turned down an offer to co-star at Madison Square Garden with Connie Francis, and in 1995 offers of an HBO special. Following upon the use of his records in such films as Scorsese's *Mean Streets* and Nancy Savoca's *True Love*, in 1994 Robert De Niro's company, Savoy Productions, approached Jimmy to license his music for Chazz Palminteri's *A Bronx Tale*. This was a superb Mafia film and a perfect showcase for Roselli's voice. De Niro requested that Roselli's office indicate which of his records were made in the time period encapsulated in the film. Roselli was affronted: who did they think they were, asking him to take time from his busy schedule to hunt down the dates?

With his success in Atlantic City, Roselli's stock began to rise significantly. Augie Renna, former vice president of player development at Trump Plaza, called Jimmy a phenomenon. "Normally, when a major star is playing, we call our high rollers to tell them and send a plane for them. But for certain entertainers, and Jimmy's probably the leading example, the high rollers call us. *They call us.* Actually, if our theater was double the size, we'd be comfortable with Roselli. He's charismatic and he has a following that won't die, that increases."

Roselli's Atlantic City audience will come see him at any time and in any weather. "If he was appearing on Mother's Day," Renna explained, "they'd show up and that would be their gift to their mom. There are really only a few entertainers in the industry that have that draw. Right now the only two I can think of are Roselli and Sinatra. And Roselli's got the mix too. When you look at the audience, it's not all Italian."

During this period, Donald Trump's father promised his construction workers a bonus if they finished a building on time. When he asked them what they wanted, they told him, "All we want is to see Jimmy Roselli at Trump Plaza on Columbus Day."

When the senior Trump called the box office, he was told that Roselli had sold out. He called Donald. "Son, you own the place, get me thirty tickets." Donald called the manager and told him, "Get thirty bums off seats down there. I don't care what you promise them, just get me thirty tickets."

The tickets were delivered.

Meanwhile, extensive media coverage brought Roselli to the attention of a new generation of disc jockeys, and he was once again being heard on radio stations around the country. Ron Cannatella, a twenty-five-year-old disc jockey at WADU-FM in New Orleans, was one of those who became a passionate fan and advocate. In Cannatella's case, the seeds had been planted in his youth. His grandfather, a policeman, had taken him down to the Italian section of New Orleans when he was a boy. Cannatella remembers standing in the Central Grocery Store while the counterman was making sandwiches for them.

"My grandfather was holding my hand and a lot of old guys were sitting around talking. In the background you could hear Roselli singing, and they had his picture hanging over the little counter along with Sinatra and the Pope. It's still there now. His music is like the heartbeat of these Italian enclaves. And today, Norjo's Italian deli here sells Roselli records right in there under the counter along with the imported Italian wines and pastas. The Roselli album covers are just as familiar as the famous labels on the pasta. You talk with these guys about Jimmy and it's a common link.

"In Italian-American communities, Roselli is like a god," said Cannatella. "If you mention him, it's 'Oh, Jimmy!' It's almost like a secret kind of a thing. It's not something you can talk about in any circle, because not everybody knows him. But people who really don't know anything about his music or heard of him before usually wind up running out to the record shop trying to buy as many records or CDs as they can after you turn them on to him. The appeal is not only to Italian people. He can do anything. You basically can put your thumb on the kind of material that most singers will do. The things that Roselli has done over the years have all been different, and very unique. It has a timeless appeal, and he's never sold out on his art form."

Anthony di Florio, a young reporter in Philadelphia for the *Italian-American Tribune*, had heard of Jimmy through his family but didn't take much notice until disc jockey Jerry Stevens started playing Roselli's "Wedding Ring" on radio station WPEN in 1993. "The song really caught on like wildfire," said di Florio. "For a long time you hadn't heard anything about him, but there was more buzz now about him. That was the beginning of his comeback."

Jimmy's comeback had also been helped by significant changes at WNEW-AM, the powerful New York station that had played Roselli consistently for years. For reasons never clarified, the station suddenly erased Roselli in the early 1970s, denying him the exposure he desperately needed to build his career. In later years, one of the station's most talented DJs, Jonathan Schwartz, inaugurated the "Saturday Sinatra" format that was later copied by stations across the country.

But gradually the situation had begun to improve for Roselli. When he was a staffer at the station from 1983 to 1991, Len Triola tried to rectify the absence of airplay for Jimmy. "Every time we played Roselli, the phones lit up," said Triola. "I love Sinatra too. He's great and sings from the heart. But Roselli's got the same quality Frank does. When you pass a saloon on Mulberry Street and you hear Roselli singing that great version of the Harry Warren, Mack Gordon song, 'My Heart Tells Me,' you gotta sit down and listen to the enunciation. He's great. His incredible *3 A.M.* album with Mel Davis on trumpet is up there with *Sinatra and Strings* and Tony Bennett's *The Art of Excellence.* You know, it's like there are a lot of great fighters: Ezzard Charles was around when Joe Louis, Marciano, and Walcott were famous. And he wasn't necessarily recognized as great by the people who lived in the era with him. I think Jimmy was a victim of the era."

But the most significant change in Roselli's airplay came about when WNEW-AM went out of business in 1991 and its successor, WQEW, was formed. With the advent of the new station, the doors opened wide for Roselli. The station manager was a former WNEW-AM disc jockey, Stan Martin. Pete Cavallo, once again without being paid by anyone, took it upon himself to have lunch with Martin to talk about the limited radio time for Roselli. Pete gave Roselli tapes to Martin, called him frequently, and convinced him it was time to play Roselli once again on a regular basis.

Martin had no objections. He admired Roselli as a singer

and liked him as a man. He had continued playing Roselli on his own programs when he left WNEW-AM and moved to a Philadelphia station. "Jimmy has a raw, very direct honesty," he said. "His appeal is multifaceted. For one thing, he's got an incredible voice. For another, he's got such sincerity to his sound. There's a tremendous believability to what he sings." In his role as station manager, he would be able to program Roselli not only on his own show but on all the other programs as well—except that of Jonathan Schwartz. Schwartz continued to be unrelenting about playing Roselli. (Pete Cavallo had an encounter with Schwartz when he visited WQEW in 1993. Schwartz, who was broadcasting that day, left his studio for a break, and ran into Cavallo. Pete mentioned his own association with Roselli and asked Schwartz why he never played him. Schwartz laughed scornfully. "Roselli! I don't like his singing. And besides, he *sucks.*")

"I want to play what people want to hear," Stan Martin said. "I'm not doing my job if I don't address what people want. And Jimmy Roselli is somebody that deserves to be played. I want the station to be able to play Nat 'King' Cole, Bobby Short, Peggy Lee, Mabel Mercer, Jimmy Roselli, and Frank Sinatra."

And besides, Stan's mother adored Roselli. "There's that cantorial quality to Jimmy's voice," he explained, "and when my mother heard me play his recording of 'Vesti la Giubba' from *Pagliacci*, that was the one song she singled out to say she really loved: the passion. He really soars when he hits those high notes. The best version I've ever heard of 'My Yiddishe Mama' is his."

In addition to the sharp increase in airplay, Martin (at Pete's urging) did a full day's remote from Atlantic City when Roselli performed there, with contests and free tickets for prizewinners. Roselli, in a word, was back. In 1996 the station had a

Top 156 countdown. Two of Roselli's hits were in the top 30: "When Your Old Wedding Ring Was New" made 16 and "Mala Femmena" was 19.

Martin called Roselli on the air on his birthday, and brought him on his program several times for live interviews. These appearances on Martin's show were occasions for an extraordinary outpouring of warm recollections and loving tributes. A woman named Maria from Carroll Gardens, an Italian neighborhood in Brooklyn, told Jimmy that her grandchildren "call you Uncle Jim. You're part of my family. I had taken a picture of you at Trump Plaza. And I've got it on my mantel. You and I are on my mantel . . . I remember my parents, when they were playing your records. And every time I play them on a Sunday morning, when I'm making my ragù sauce, you bring back such wonderful, wonderful memories. I love you, and I love your songs, and I'll never, ever forget this, that I'm speaking to you. My heart is just pounding, talking to you." Another caller, Mickey Amato, reminded Jimmy that he had visited a blind woman in her home because she was unable to get out, and had sung to her. "And she—I'm telling you, she cried. And I'll never forget you for that."

A third caller told Jimmy that twenty-five years before, her husband had been diagnosed with a terminal illness and her aunt gave them money to go out and do something enjoyable: "We went to the Stanley Theater in Jersey City . . . and you sang 'When Your Old Wedding Ring Was New.' And we held hands, and I cried and I cried. And he thought I was crying because I loved the song. And I did. But I was crying because he was going to die. Now he did pass away, and over the years I have gotten all your records. And I play them, and especially that song. And I think of him and I always think of you." In response to this call, Jimmy, his voice cracking, said, "Thank you very much."

Yet during one of these live interviews, Roselli began by commenting aloud after his opening record: "Jonathan: That's not Sinatra. That's Roselli." After Schwartz had rendered him invisible for so many years, Roselli's bitterness was perhaps excusable. At the conclusion of his interview with Stan Martin, however, Jimmy went overboard, and exhumed the line he usually applied to Sinatra: "Jonathan," he cooed, "I worship the ground that's coming to you."

In truth, Jimmy had fewer enemies around, and some people feel that his reemergence in the 1990s was due to the decline of the Mafia's power. Jerry Capeci, columnist on the mob for the New York *Daily News* and author of several books on the Mafia, said even before the Sammy Gravano case took shape that more and more informers were publicly thumbing their noses at the mob, an indication of a lack of respect, or a lack of fear. "The clout of the mob is on the wane in certain circles," he observed. "There have been many convictions of many gangsters across the country in the last twelve years. The effort of the federal government has had an impact on the relative strength of organized crime. That's one of the reasons more and more people seem to be bucking them."

Joseph Coffey, formerly of the New York State Organized Crime Task Force, claimed in 1996 that "due to law enforcement, we have now pretty much brought the Mafia to its knees. They're not eliminated, though; they'll always be there as long as there's an illicit dollar to be made. But we've really crippled them by taking their leadership out, and their effectiveness has been diminished greatly. The current-day Mafia's so-called leaders have become the people who use their own products: i.e., cocaine. As a result, their discipline has broken down, the old-line respect is gone, and they don't have the power they once had. And that certainly affects all phases of their so-called empire, including show business. So Roselli might have been able to come out from under all this."

Asked about Roselli singing at Gotti, Jr.'s wedding in 1990, Coffey replied, "Let's put it this way. I know a lot of Mafia buffs and Mafia people. They follow certain entertainers: Sinatra, of course, Vic Damone, Jimmy Roselli. So you can't put an onus on him because of that." The mob-buster even seemed to be pulling for Jimmy: "He's a *great* entertainer."

While Coffey's assessment of the Mafia's diminished strength may be accurate, it is also true that, as Robert Buccino asserted, what is left of the Mafia is even more of a scattershot killing machine. Roselli still has to be careful.

Buccino put it this way: "This guy [Roselli], he really got hurt bad [in the past]. If he had turned down Gotti, this is a whole different era. Now they don't set examples, they set them by killing you."

This was a continuation of a feud Roselli had been waging and losing for years. With the media attention he was now receiving, Jimmy, to use his expression, was getting big balls again, and he had resumed his attack on Sinatra whenever he was interviewed by the press. On October 14, 1993, The "Hot Copy" column in the New York *Daily News* reported that Roselli sang "My Way" at his Westbury Music Fair concert. At the time, Jimmy told the reporter, "I figure I sing [the song] better than he does, so I might as well do it. With him, the band does all the wailing and he doesn't sound too spectacular if you ask me . . ." The column went on to reprise the Dolly Sinatra charity benefit story, with Jimmy referring to Dolly's sending "two half-assed bookmakers [to] tell me I *had* to sing at the benefit." Jimmy concluded: "But I don't bother with [Sinatra] anyhow. I don't need him. @!$& [sic] him."

"Seeing Red Over Ol' Blue Eyes" was the headline of another story in the New York *Daily News* on July 31, 1994. The article was published during the week that Roselli and Sinatra were appearing in Atlantic City across the street from each other: Roselli at Trump Plaza, Sinatra at the Sands. This time, Jimmy took on both Sinatra and the wiseguys. "[Sinatra's] not particularly fond of me," Roselli told reporter Phil Roura. "I don't think Frank cares for people with too much talent." "Didn't Sinatra have talent?" Roura asked Roselli. "He did at one time. But not anymore. He should quit. People don't go to hear him sing anymore. They go to see the legend."

Roura wrote that when he asked Roselli about the mob, "to hear [Roselli] tell it, Roselli conquered the capos—and despite what some people say, he never got 'involved.' "

With typical bravado Roselli said, "They tried to own me. But I came into this world with nothing and I was prepared to go out of this world with nothing. . . . It worked out. They can't keep talent down."

As a result of the *Daily News* articles, Pete Cavallo was approached by some "big people" who were furious at Roselli. "We got problems," Pete Cavallo told me. "I can't tell Jimmy about this. They're hot. They're going crazy about those articles in the *Daily News*. 'Any more of this,' the guy said, 'they're gonna come after him.' Very serious. They're really pissed about the Sinatra stuff, and about that phrase 'half-assed book-makers.' "

"Did this come from Sinatra?" I asked Pete.

"No, Sinatra doesn't know what's going on," Pete said. "He's out of it. It's strictly from this guy who's with him. And this guy is also pissed at Jimmy for not appearing at his nightclub. So he's got like a hard-on for Jimmy to start with.

"Anyway," Pete said, thinking aloud, "no more of this knocking Sinatra shit. Jimmy can't say 'half-assed bookmakers.' They said, 'This guy Roselli, if it weren't for Buckalo, he wouldn't have the clothes on his back. Why is he starting trouble now?' At least they told us first. They could have just waited for Jimmy and beat him up or whatever."

In this climate Jimmy turned up the heat again by talking to an interviewer from the *Star*. Referring to WNEW-AM's boycott of him, Roselli told the *Star* in an August 1994 interview, "Sinatra tried, but he didn't stop me. . . . Sinatra 'ran' that station.

"Besides, I'm a better singer," Roselli continued, enjoying the opportunity to twist the knife. "[Sinatra] used to be one of the best around. But now, he can't do it anymore, and I still can. The guy is on his way out."

Pete Cavallo rushed to the *Star* office to try to change the article that was about to appear, fearful it would make the same guys even angrier. But the *Star* refused to make alterations. Instead, Pete decided to "forewarn" the wiseguys. "I'm trying to tone things down, and make it like from here on there won't be a problem. What's done is done. I prepared them: I told them the *Star* was coming out Monday and it was too late to stop it. They said, 'Gosh, the *Star*.' I said they're quoting stuff said twenty years ago, not today. 'You know how they embellish things,' I said. They said, 'Yeah, it's a rag.'

"And I made a good point. 'Look,' I said, 'the *Star* wanted a photo of Jimmy ripping up a picture of Sinatra on the boardwalk.' " Pete's voice rose as it always did when defending Jimmy. "I told them Jimmy said, 'No good.' So they were happy about that. And I said to them, 'What did Sinatra ever do for you? Jimmy did weddings; Sinatra never did.' One guy said, 'Yeah, I don't like Sinatra. I was in his company and he ignored me.' And I said to him, 'How was Jimmy with you?' 'Jimmy was always good that way,' he said."

Fearful of Jimmy's reaction, Pete put off telling him about the jeopardy he was in. When he did, he would soften the blow.

"I could never tell Jimmy how bad the situation was," confided
Pete. "He'd be in fear. And once again, Jimmy don't want to
get involved with these guys anymore. If he went to some guys,
they'd say, 'We'll protect you.' Then he's stuck with them on
his back. That's what he don't want."

As always, Pete was protective of Jimmy and willing to risk
his own life for his friend. "What you have to worry about,"
Pete explained, "[the wiseguys] have these young kids looking
to make an impression, and go after [Jimmy]. So now it's a
ticklish thing. I'm not going to back up from Jimmy. I'm going
to stay with him all the way. If he gets hit, I'm gonna get hit,
ya know what I mean?"

In the weeks that followed, the crisis was defused, thanks to
Pete's efforts. It was only then that he informed Jimmy of what
had happened.

There is probably no singer more locked into his past than
Jimmy Roselli: its din has never lost its hold. Yet good fortune and luck have not entirely eluded him. By 1997 he
would be earning $1.8 million for nine shows at Caesars
Palace in Atlantic City, "when guys like Jerry Vale, Al Martino, and Vic Damone," according to Herb Bernstein, "are
happy to get $15,000 a night." At last Roselli was gaining
at least some of the recognition that had previously been
denied him.

The 42nd Street and Broadway scene was changing too, due
to an ambitious redevelopment plan and a new generation of
theatergoers who enthusiastically embraced musicals. In 1998
the long-dark New Amsterdam Theater reopened on 42nd
Street, and the abandoned New Victory Theater was literally
moved in its entirety a few hundred feet by workmen and res-
urrected.

But at the same time, those who had been an integral part of Roselli's life—up close or at a distance, the obscure and the famous—began to physically deteriorate or pass away. Clarkie, his Hoboken pal from childhood, died in May 1998. Matty (Action) Jordan was confined to a wheelchair in a nursing home. And then Jimmy's lifelong nemesis, Frank Sinatra, died on May 14. It was an unexpectedly traumatic event for Roselli.

"Jimmy was very upset when Sinatra died," Pete Cavallo remarked. "He couldn't sleep that night. Sinatra died on the day before Jimmy's opening night at Caesars Palace. So we were in the dressing room, everybody's hanging around, and I took him outside. I said, 'Jimmy, you going to say something [onstage]?'

" 'Ah,' he says, 'I knew him for fifty-eight years. He never did a fucking thing for me. I don't want to sound like a hypocrite.'

" 'Hey, Jimmy,' I said, 'you do what you feel you gotta do. If you don't feel like it, don't do it.' I didn't pressure him.

"I just planted a seed in the back door. Sure enough, came the time, he did it. When he got onstage, he said, 'You know, we just lost a legend last night: one of the best singers of all time. We lived only five doors from each other. My grandfather and his father were very close. But we weren't, because there was a ten-year age difference. But the man was a giant, and he can never be replaced. And I'd like to dedicate this song to him.' And he sang 'My Way.' "

"They were having a mass for Sinatra at St. Francis on Jefferson Street," Jimmy told me six days later. "And I brought a big, big, big bouquet of roses to the priest. He said he'd put them right next to the Blessed Mother, and he kissed me.

"I was always an admirer of Sinatra's talent. Not of him as a man. He was too flaky for me. But there was no better talent than him. See, I appreciate him because I remember when he started. He couldn't sing to keep his ass warm. He stunk. He was the worst singer that God ever made. But he was determined. He worked at it and he worked at it, and he finally became a ballsy singer. When he sang with Tommy Dorsey, he just sang, he had no balls. But later on, when he sang with Nelson Riddle and Billy May and Johnny Green, Gordon Jenkins, Don Costa, all the great arrangers, he sang with balls. He was probably the greatest talent for that kind of singing. And he was a good actor—better actor than he was a singer.

"There never was much contact between us. He always had ten years on me. When he was twenty I was ten. But then I ran into him here, I ran into him there. He was never friendly. I sat with him one night at the Fountainbleau [in Miami Beach], the night we took a picture. Afterwards we sat down at a table. He said, 'Me, me, I, I, my picture, my picture, me, I'—I got so fucking tired I said let me get up, I had enough of this. I said politely, 'All right, Frank, it's nice talking to ya,' and I excused myself and I went back to my table.

"Hank Sanicola was partners with him in Cal-Neva [Lodge], a gambling joint in Nevada. Frank was supposed to appear there and the place was sold out. Frank decided at the last minute he didn't want to work. He was going to go to Las Vegas. Hank says, 'I'll put Vic Damone in.' Frank says, 'No, you'll close the joint. You won't put nobody in.' That's the real Sinatra."

The only thing that Jimmy has been sure of in life has been the power of money. He needed its protection badly, because life—particularly his early years—had proven to be so treacherous for him. But as that belief persisted, it hardened into a reflection of his deep lack of faith in himself and in others.

As Pete Cavallo said: "You gotta understand, Jimmy never apologizes. You gotta hear it in other ways."

And there are many ways to hear him—by his silences, his shyness, or the deep feeling he expresses in his music. For when he sings, the voice itself changes, emerging with absolute clarity of tone, the antithesis of the rough-guy voice with which he ordinarily brays and shouts.

"The stage is a different world to Jimmy," observed Dr. Dan Macken. "It's the world that is deep inside of him. All of a sudden he becomes a soft, romantic pussycat. The world is out there adoring him, with the stage, the lights, and that big backup of musicians. He feels secure. And he really is walled off by the blackness, the glare of the lights in his eyes. And then he can really let go, bringing out something that nobody ever sees."

Except perhaps Donna Roselli, without whom, Jimmy admitted, "I would have no sanity." "It's the way he was raised, as was I," she explained. "But I broke out of that pattern, because if we stay mad, who do we hurt but ourselves?"

The discrepancy between the public performer and the private man may have an irony lost on Jimmy, though it's apparent to those who know him well. "The talent and the personality are so far away from each other," Carol Lees said. "Frank was more like his singing. He was a tough guy and he sang like a tough guy. He sang like what he was. As masculine as he is, Jimmy sings like a choirboy: the gentleness, the softness, the purity, the no conning, no manipulating. It's so open, so complete. When Jimmy sings, he's almost like a chalice, a religious vessel of some kind."

And, unlike Sinatra, he could never do anything but sing.

In the winter of 1998, as improbable as it seemed for so
long, Roselli was getting another shot at the big time: a movie
about his life was optioned by Disney. At seventy-three, he was
still a contender. This time around, he might be ready for it.
But even if Jimmy makes it to where he's wanted to be all along,
he may not entirely know it. And if he does, he'll have to
struggle hard to hold on to that realization.

NOTES

1. Ben Morreale, interview by the author, tape recording, Los Angeles, September 25, 1996.
2. Angelo Mosso, *Vita moderna degli Italiani* (Milan: Fratelli Treves, 1906), p. 12.
3. Michael La Sorte, *La Merica* (Philadelphia: Temple University Press, 1985), p. 92.
4. Kay Boyle, ed., *The Autobiography of Emanuel Carnevali* (New York: Horizon Press, 1964), p. 167.
5. La Sorte, *La Merica*, p. 80.
6. Amy A. Bernardy, *Italia randagia attraverso gli Stati Uniti* (Turin: Fratelli Bocca, 1913), p. 162.
7. Jacob Riis, *How the Other Half Lives* (Cambridge: Belknap Press of Harvard University Press, 1970), p. 36.
8. Richard Gambino, *Blood of My Blood* (Toronto and New York: Guernica, 1996), p. 286.
9. Pietro Di Donato, *Christ in Concrete* (Indianapolis and New York: Bobbs-Merrill, 1937), pp. 31–32, 182.
10. Christopher Morley, *Seacoast of Bohemia* (New York: Doubleday, 1929), pp. 10, 28–30.
11. As quoted in Jerre Mangione and Ben Morreale, *La Storia* (New York: HarperCollins, 1992), p. 309.

12. Nicholas Gage, *Mafia, U.S.A.* (Chicago: Playboy Press, 1972), p. 233.

13. Todd Gitlin, *The Sixties* (New York: Bantam Books, 1987), pp. 341, 343.

14. Richard Gid Powers, telephone interview by the author, May 18, 1998.

15. Quoted in David Pichaske, *A Generation in Motion* (New York: Schirmer Books, 1979), p. 219.

16. Gambino, *Blood of My Blood*, p. 130.

ACKNOWLEDGMENTS

MY DEEP THANKS TO JIMMY AND DONNA ROSELLI, Carol Lees, Andrew Blauner, John Glusman, Ruth Wolman, Karen Janszen, Anne Roselli, Richard Gid Powers, Robert Buccino, Beverly Camhe, Al Certo, Marie Greene, Stan Martin, the late Philip Capotorto, Mary Capotorto, Anthony di Florio III, Antonetta Spina, Rebecca Kurson, Bob Gans, Ernest J. Naspretto, Erwin Flaxman, John Homans, Ben Morreale, Joe Farda, the late Lee Salomon, Vito Pedesta, Shelly Horn, Walter Legawiec, Jerry Vale, Frank Gauna, Rose Woods, Len Triola, Ron Cannatella, Marie and Donald Alfano, Matthew Rega, Matty (Action) Jordan, Dr. Daniel Macken, Jerry Capeci, the late Irwin Suall, Joseph Coffey, Velma Hill, Frank Toscano, Giovanni Cafiso, Carmine the Peddler, Bitterbeer, Anthony (Skinny Skelly) Petrazelli, Dennis Della Fave, Lou the Fireman, Joann Viggiano, Sol Parker, Peter Moore, Kippy Palumbo, Harriet Wasser, David Isaac, Arturo and Bette Junta, Herb Bernstein, the late Matteo Cannizzaro, George Siravo, A. J. Benza, Lefty Jimmy Geritano, Augie Renna, the late Clarkie (Nunzio Pascalle), Bob Taylor, Mike Prelee, Scott Harlan, Joe Petralia, Aaron Sachs, Joe Ferrante, Joseph Foti, Phil Bodner, Ron Posyton, Meier Deshell, and Walter Merza.

I also approached Jimmy Roselli's first wife, Angeline Guiffra Roselli, for an interview through the Rosellis' daughter, Anne. Anne contacted her mother in my behalf, and told me that her mother declined to be interviewed.